"I shudder to think of the millions and millions of people who have had their dreams squelched and told 'you can't' simply because they lack a college degree. Somewhere out there is someone who will pick up and read this book, realize his or her potential, take a chance, and change the world."

Michael Kostov, Executive Producer
Kostov & Associates TV & Film Productions
(www.kostov.com)

"Having lived three decades of my life in 'the big time' of government and business, only in the last few years have I come to realize the enormous wisdom of this book. The basic truth that success, however measured, is a matter of attitude and work ethic, is, for those of us who have been out there, apparent. Whether high school grad, college grad, or postgraduate, READ THIS BOOK. Its lessons and perspectives will make a difference in your lives. And for those of you who don't have college degrees, read it with the knowledge that you are not excluded from the highest levels of success in life, indeed your future is in your attitude. . . . Just do it!"

Retired Admiral Bill Owens
Former Vice Chairman Joint Chiefs of Staff
President and CEO, Teledesic

"I wish every one of my employees would read this kind of text. John Murphy nails the chapter on setting goals by cutting right to the heart of the matter . . . get off your butt and start doing it! His style is right up my alley! Thank goodness someone has finally had the courage to encourage folks to stick their necks out and take a risk . . . regardless of their educational background!"

Maureen O'Hanlon
Vice President/General Manager
AT&T Broadband

SUCCESS
WITHOUT A
COLLEGE DEGREE

DISSOLVING THE ROADBLOCKS
BETWEEN YOU AND SUCCESS

JOHN T. MURPHY

Achievement Dynamics, Inc.
Publishers of Self-Education and Personal Achievement Works

First printed April 2001

10 9 8 7 6 5 4 3 2

Printed and manufactured in the United States

Cover and interior design by Lightbourne
Edited by Teddy Kempster

First edition entitled *Success Without a College Degree – The Secrets of How to Get Ahead and Show Them All* printed in December, 1997.

ISBN: 0-9662120-1-0
Library of Congress Control Number: 2001116698

JAN 2 3 2003

To my wonderful wife, Sunny,
who pulled me out of an emotional
gutter, dusted me off, and helped
me get back in the game.

To my sons, Connor, Mitchell, and Trevor,
when you get bucked off a horse . . .

PREFACE

This preface is for those who consider themselves "advocates of higher education." You might be a professor, associate professor, teacher, administrative person, counselor, academic advisor, grade school through high school teacher, college student, a parent of a college student, or just a general believer that higher education is essential in this day and age. I'd like to have a little chat with you to explain my objectives, and to win your support.

When the first edition of this book appeared and people saw the title, many of them jumped to the conclusion that I was arguing against a formal education. I hope that you have not already jumped to this same conclusion. I do *not advocate against* higher education at all. Quite the contrary. Nowhere in this book do I say that a formal education is a waste of time or useless. I freely admit that it can be very valuable and helpful to an individual's career. I won't for a moment suggest or imply that anyone *not* pursue a formal education. I readily suggest that anyone who has the time, money, and inclination to pursue a college degree should do so! Such a person would, no doubt, find it beneficial.

However, I am out to help and support those who have chosen not to pursue higher education. Over 75 percent of the U.S. adult population lack a four-year degree. These people, for whatever reason, have *chosen* not to go. Whether they felt they weren't cut out for it, couldn't find a direction, couldn't afford the time or money, were in a situation in their lives at the time that made it not feasible, or just felt that the classroom scene wasn't for them, they chose not to go.

Society's arguments for higher education contain an implied, and sometimes explicit threat to those who don't pursue college. It is commonplace for people to state openly that "without a college education, you're going nowhere." So prevalent is the notion that no one ever challenges it, no one ever questions it.

The consequence of such conventional wisdom is that those who have chosen, for whatever reason, not to pursue higher education, become convinced that there are no chances for them. They believe they have been doomed to a life of limited options. They quell their dreams and never examine, let alone exploit, their own strengths and talents. All too often, they live lives of quiet desperation.

While an individual may lack a college degree, he or she may not lack the ambition and desire to do something significant in life. I seek to be a voice of encouragement to those enterprising individuals at the risk of appearing sacrilegious and a heretic. I want to give those who feel stuck a methodical way to get unstuck.

This book, in my sincerest hopes, will spur readers to set and pursue goals, even if it includes getting a formal education. I encourage them to chase their dreams, to persist in the face of adversity, to be steadfast in overcoming obstacles, and to never, never, **never** give up. My grandest dream is that this book might be a turning point for readers and change their lives in some positive way, even if only that they believe in themselves.

I do not *discourage* knowledge, I encourage it. Knowledge is critical to success. But must it come from an institution? Must all knowledge be certified? Can it not come from independent study and practical experience?

I encourage the pursuit of knowledge along the lines of an individual's own talents, skills, and interests. I encourage discovery of strengths, passions, and dreams of a better, more fulfilling life. How could anyone discourage that?

Too many dreams have become the casualties of the conventional wisdom, "You'll never amount to anything without a college education." Too many lives have ended in pitiful regret for never having chased a dream.

Yes, indeed, knowledge is critical to success. Without knowledge, dreams are but folly. Yet without dreams, knowledge is but trivia.

Please enjoy my book with an open mind!

STARTLING FACTS

There Are Plenty to Keep You Company
- Over 75 percent of the adult U.S. population lack a college degree. That's over 129 million people. You're not alone.
- The percentage of U.S. high school grads who start college is around 66%. Obviously a huge number of dropouts.
- Think that the U.S. is way behind? Think again. Here are figures on the percent of college grads from other industrialized nations.

Country	Percent with Degrees
Canada	32.2%
Australia	26.3%
Japan	23.4%
Denmark	22.1%
United Kingdom (England)	20.4%
Norway	19.4%
France	16.0%
Germany	13.0%
Sweden	11.0%

The Lack of a Degree Does Not Prohibit Wealth
- At least 63 members of the Forbes 400 Wealthiest Americans never graduated from college. Their average net worth: $4.3 billion each!
- Of the people making over $100,000 per year, over 24 percent lack a college degree.
- There are over 3.5 million millionaires in the U.S. (as of 1997). That comes out to one in every 36 people.
- The average growth rate of new millionaires is about 328,000 per year. That's roughly 898 new millionaires a day, or

roughly 37 new millionaires per hour. As of the year 2000, the projected number of U.S. millionaires is approximately 4.4 million; by 2005 it's estimated that millionaires will number over 5.6 million.

Just a Few Wealthy and/or Famous People Without Degrees

Person	Where you know them from	Net Worth
Bill Gates	Microsoft founder	$92 bill.
Paul Allen	Microsoft founder	$40 bill.
Michael Dell	Dell Computer founder	$20 bill.
Larry Ellison	Oracle founder	$13 bill.
Theodore Waitt	Gateway Computers founder	$6.2 bill.
Micky Arison	Carnival Cruise Lines	$5.1 bill.
David Geffen	Music Industry	$2.7 bill.
Jay Van Andel	Amway	$1.9 bill.
Norm Waitt	Gateway Computers founder	$1.5 bill.
Richard M. DeVos	Amway	$1.5 bill.
Steve Jobs	Apple Computer founder	$1.2 bill.
Thomas Monaghan	Domino's Pizza founder	$950 mill.
Jim Jannard	Oakley Sunglasses founder	$850 mill.
Ernest Gallo	Gallo wineries	$800 mill.
Leonard Riggio	Barnes & Noble CEO	$800 mill.
Bob Pittman	MTV founder	$725 mill.
Peter Jennings	ABC News Anchor	n/a
Walter Cronkite	Journalist/News Anchor	n/a
Harry S. Truman	U.S. President	n/a
Debra Fields	Mrs. Fields Cookies chain	n/a
Stephen Spielburg	Movie director	n/a
John Glenn	Astronaut/Senator	n/a
Ralph Lauren	Clothing designer	n/a
Rosie O'Donnell	Actress/Talk show host	n/a
Wolfgang Puck	Restaurateur	n/a
Ted Turner	Turner Networks	n/a
Marilyn vos Savant	"Ask Marilyn" column	n/a
Wayne Huizenga	Blockbuster Video founder	n/a

The Astronomical Odds of the Lottery

- The odds of winning most state-run lotteries are 1 in 7.5 million. The odds of becoming a millionaire (if you try) are 1 in 383 (*slightly better!*).
- If every state had two $1,000,000 lottery winners every week, that would add 100 new "millionaires" to the population per week or 5,200 per year.
- The average growth rate of new, self-made millionaires adds 6,286 per week, or 328,000 per year.
- Hitting the jackpot in most lotteries does not mean that you are a millionaire. Most lotteries pay annual payments over roughly 20 years eventually totaling the jackpot value. A $1 million jackpot would pay roughly $60,000 per year (before taxes). That's not exactly a life of luxury when you consider that of those making over $50K per year, more than 40 percent lack a degree.
- State-run lotteries are actually a form of voluntary tax revenue. Face it, it's a naïve tax.

Opportunities Abound

- Of the 5,478,047 businesses in the U.S., 98 percent of them have fewer than 100 employees! Ninety percent have fewer than 20 employees! That's 4,930,242 businesses that are going to be less picky about whether you have a degree or not.
- Of those firms with fewer than 20 employees, the average annual revenues are over $570,000.
- Of those firms with between 20 and 99 employees, the average annual revenues are over $5.9 million.
- The annual revenues generated by those companies employing fewer than 100 employees total over $5.6 trillion dollars.

AUTHOR'S NOTE

The first thing you should know about me is that I have a college degree in Business Administration. All that I have learned of value has come since college, and I've succeeded despite my college degree. I'm going to share with you how I went about it.

My first job out of college was selling shoes at $4.00 per hour. My next few jobs were not much better, one of which was selling newspaper subscriptions over the phone. It wasn't until I got technical training in electronics in the U.S. Marine Corps that I was able to break into a career that I was satisfied with. Even then, part of my job included sweeping computer room floors and fixing toilets. All that with my fancy degree.

Just like you, I wanted to get out of the rut of jobs that were seemingly going nowhere. I felt certain there was something important inside me, but I didn't quite know what it was. I knew I wanted to achieve something significant in my career, but I didn't know where to start or how to get that lucky break.

I started reading books, lots of books, on everything from "my inner child," to psychology, careers, achievement, success, and making money. I applied the things that I learned, and, yes, I got ahead. During the job in which I made this transition, I started out as a "quality inspector," copying computer disks by swapping them in and out of computers. Frankly, it was a pretty menial task and well beneath what I expected to be doing, now three years after graduating. I began studying the topics mentioned above, and as I applied what I learned, my career began to excel. In less than six years, I went from the "quality control" disk swapper to Director of Sales and Support with a six-figure compensation package, and over half the company reporting to me. This was for an internationally known and reputable software company.

About ten years after I had graduated, I got a survey call from the university from which I graduated. They asked me several questions about how well my degree had helped me in my career. After answering "no" to about two dozen questions, I came to a pretty significant realization. My college degree hadn't really helped me at all. I achieved what I had through outside study and applying what I learned. It hadn't been back-breaking work, either. I rarely worked more than 50 hours in a week. I had fun doing things and actually accomplishing goals.

Granted, my degree probably helped open a door or two in the application process, but what really got me ahead was not learned in college.

All that was of genuine value to my career I learned after college! The same invaluable learning that I did after college, you can do right now, without a college degree.

In those same ten years I noticed many people around me with college degrees also floundering aimlessly, so it wasn't just me. At the same time, I saw others without a college degree excel way ahead of their peers, become directors of the company, and make substantial, positive contributions to the company. How could that be? That ran totally contrary to what I had been told about getting a formal education.

It occurred to me that someone should tell all those without a degree that what really counts in making big strides in a career doesn't come from a diploma. It comes from something inside a person. I was dismayed to find, however, that those without a degree often had this barrier of believing that they would never get ahead. So much of society had been telling them all their lives that without a college education, they would never accomplish much. And they *believed* it!

I decided to put together all that I had studied from the hundreds of books and tapes into one volume. I figured not many people are going to go out and read as much as I had, but they just might read one, one book that applied directly to them. I wanted to remove all the complicated and boring stuff, and distill the most meaningful information into an easy to follow and understandable translation, in terms to which you can easily relate. I wanted to get rid of all the "rah, rah" fluff that left even me feeling skeptical, and give you insights and ways of looking at things that you can swallow without gagging. I wanted to make the information believable and achievable.

I wrote this book to clue you into the fact that success doesn't come from a diploma. It comes from something you have inside of you already. You may not even believe you have the ability to accomplish anything. I'm here to tell you that you can. You *do* have what it takes, but you may have been ignoring it all your life. You may even know right now that there's something important inside you, that you were destined for something great, but you don't quite know what it is or how to draw it out. I'm here to help you do just that.

As for a degree, I'm here to share with you some truths that few have dared to say about the myth you've been led to believe. When you're handed a diploma at the graduation ceremony, there's not always a job waiting for you at the other side of the stage. Life can be a struggle for college grads too. How many times have you met a college grad that's waiting tables, delivering pizzas, or unloading trucks? I've known plenty. A college degree is no guarantee of success. Many college grads go on to live mediocre lives of quiet desperation.

What's important is that I don't want you to feel any longer like you're missing out because you lack a degree. It's time to stop putting yourself down and holding yourself back because of the myth that you need a college degree to make it in life. There are thousands upon thousands of exciting jobs that are available to you. All too often, we think of the fun things we'd really like to do as jobs without a future, or that you can't really make a living at them, or our parents tell us "that's not a real job." But they *are* real jobs, and people make good money doing them, sometimes enormous amounts of money.

Most importantly, I wrote this book to help you get through the same transition that I went through. I debated a long time on whether or not to write this book. Who am I? I have a degree. Who can expect me to relate to those who do not have one?

Then I thought about all the people who are like I was, aimless and miserable. I see them on the streets every day, and I know what they're going through, and it's awful. You can imagine how miserable I felt with low-end job after low-end job, and me, with my fancy degree. I was an aimless mess and I felt hopeless. But what's worse for those without a college degree is they're convinced that because they lack a degree this is their lot in life. But it just doesn't have to be!

If only they could overcome the belief that they're going nowhere without a college degree. If only they could realize that the real education comes from outside study, that the real value they will have to offer is knowing their strengths and talents. They could capitalize on their strengths and talents, focus their energies on pursuing jobs they like, rather than on jobs they can get or must settle for. They could escape the tyranny of believing you're a nobody without college and live rich, rewarding, and satisfying lives.

I considered writing a book encapsulating the most important points which made a huge difference for me. I thought maybe with just one book that people would pick up because it called to them, I could change their belief about the lack of a degree and their negative beliefs about themselves.

That's when I decided to sit down and just do it.

Do you realize that over 75 percent of the US adult population do NOT have a college degree? I always had the impression the majority had a degree with all the talk higher education gets.

Even though so many lack a degree, there are many who do not lack the desire and ambition to accomplish something important in their lives—*people like you!* But these people have been told a thousand times that "you'll never amount to anything without a college degree." This piece of well-intended conventional wisdom becomes a life-long, self-fulfilling curse. So many people believe this myth that they don't even try. They settle for jobs that they hate and manage to get by until Friday.

At the risk of being viewed as sacrilegious and a heretic, I'm standing up to tell you that you can achieve incredible things without a college degree. The number of people who have done so is enormous—the facts are undeniable. A college degree is not required in order to become a success.

You can, in fact, achieve incredible things. History books are filled with *individuals* who have bucked conventional wisdom, who did what their hearts told them and ignored society, individuals who have altered the course of history. You have that same capability.

I'm not going to guarantee that you will become a multi-millionaire, or alter the course of history, but you certainly have the potential.

I hope to have the great honor of helping you to unlock the greatness within you.

Contents

Roadblocks

ROADBLOCK 1

"This road just isn't open . . . to me, anyway."

The Truth About a Degree

The very first roadblock we'll discuss is the belief that the road to success is not open to you unless you've graduated from college.

Is a college degree a prerequisite for success? Absolutely not! There are many roads to success and a college degree is only one of them.

I will not, for a minute, try to talk you out of college, or attempt to convey that college is a waste of time. A college degree can be a very useful thing and can help you in many, many ways. However, the belief that you need a four-year degree in order to be successful is pure, unadulterated myth.

So far this may sound too good to be true: The curse you have carried with you since leaving high school really isn't a curse after all. You may suspect that any moment now I'll try to get you to buy into some marketing scam, or that I'll tell you of some magic formula that will guarantee you success. You may think that I'm some kind of "success guru" who will give you 1,001 things you must do in order to become a success. You may suspect I'll prescribe a path to success with which you'd feel uncomfortable. Such is not the case. I'll be doing none of that.

There are many characteristics that are important to achieving success. You don't have to be born with them, you can learn them, and they don't come from a college diploma. You likely possess strengths and talents that have gone untapped or that you don't even acknowledge because you feel they are not worthwhile. But they do have value and you can make a living employing the strengths and talents you currently have or wish to develop. My aim is to help you expose them, acknowledge them, and capitalize on them.

Howard Gardner, a Harvard psychologist, in his landmark book *Frames of Mind*, discusses seven key areas of intelligence: verbal, mathematical, spatial (artistic), kinesthetic (athletic or "working with your hands"), musical, interpersonal, and intrapsychic (insightfulness). Academic environments emphasize only the areas of verbal and mathematical intelligence. Yet society is comprised of people exercising talents in each of these areas.

> *There are many roads to success;*
> *a college degree is but one of them.*

In this chapter, we'll discuss what a college degree can do for you, what it cannot do for you, and what kinds of exciting careers can be had without one. Let's remove the wool that has been pulled over your eyes for so long!

What a College Degree CAN Do for You

A college degree can be a very good thing. It can help you in many ways. If after reading this book should you decide upon a career path for which a college degree is very useful or even a must, that's wonderful! If you have the time, money, and inclination to pursue a college degree, please do so. You will, no doubt, find it beneficial. My hat is off to anyone who pursues an education with a specific goal in mind.

It Is Mandatory for Certain Professions

There are many professions for which a college degree (sometimes more than one) is a must in order to take government-administered examinations to become licensed. These professionals include doctors, lawyers, psychiatrists, psychologists, licensed counselors, accountants, architects, public school teachers, professors, and so on. More jobs could be added here, but you get the idea. Without a degree in these fields, you either are forbidden by law to practice, or no one will take you seriously.

Counterpoint. No argument here. If you would like to pursue any of these careers, getting a four year degree, and, in some cases, several years thereafter, is a must. I'd hate to have a brain surgeon operating on me who didn't have the best education possible.

It Provides Credentials

A bachelor's degree, master's degree, or doctorate provide credentials. The more prestigious the university the more clout your degree has. It establishes your authority, allowing your opinions to be listened to or to prevail over others. These kinds of credentials are very useful in working your way up the corporate ladder, persuading others, and achieving goals inside an organization. If you want a career where you work your way up the corporate ladder of a

Fortune 1,000 company, having a four-year, if not an MBA (or other advanced degree) will help you a great deal.

Counterpoint. How many companies are in the Fortune 1,000? Consider that 98 percent of the businesses in the U.S. have fewer than 100 people. Ninety percent have fewer than 20 employees. It's much easier to work your way up the corporate ladder when you're on a first name basis and have lunch with the president.

Also consider that over 63 of the Forbes 400 wealthiest people in America lack college degrees and have an average net worth of $4.3 billion each! That's "billion" with a "B"! While a degree is helpful, a lot of guts, and perseverance makes up for the lack of credentials.

It Prepares You for Certain Jobs

A college degree with a specific major can prepare you to perform certain jobs: biologist, chemist, researcher, programmer, engineer, statistician, and so on. The curriculum for these majors will provide a base of knowledge. Without a degree in these fields, chances are an employer will not even consider you.

Counterpoint. While there are many jobs where a degree with a specific major is the minimum starting point for a job, there are many jobs where the skills it takes to perform the job are learned on the job. Majors such as marketing, business, liberal arts, general studies, and so on only provide a foundation of knowledge. Your real skill development begins once you're on the job.

Spend four years in college and only one third to one half of your curriculum is spent on classes specific to your major. The remainder is other studies designed to "round out" your education, or tough courses to literally weed you out. You'll graduate with much conceptual knowledge but no practical experience.

Spend four years on the job, gaining practical experience, developing job specific skills, interpersonal skills, along with focused personal study, and you'll be much better able to perform the job. After four years, you'll have a wealth of practical experience, contacts, industry know-how, as well as focused expertise.

It Suggests Intelligence

It's sad, but there is a common presumption that if you have a degree, you're automatically smart. Conversely, if you lack a degree, there's an automatic presumption that you're not so smart. Having a four-year degree, regardless of what the major is, will automatically register in the minds of many people that you know a lot about something. Whether a degree holder retains anything valuable from the education or not is beside the point. The projection of intelligence will last a lifetime.

Counterpoint. Rarely does the question of whether one has a degree or not arise in everyday conversation. Sure, it will come up when you're applying for a job, or if you're talking to a higher education bigot anxious to toot his or her own horn about credentials. But generally speaking, people don't come out and ask one another about what college they went to or the degree they earned. People will make assessments about your intelligence from how you speak and how you treat others. Act like a blithering idiot and it won't matter where your degree is from. Act like an intelligent, creative, and considerate individual, and few people will care that you don't have a degree.

It Gives a "Leg Up" in the Job Hunt

A degree gives you a leg up in the job application process. It suggests that if you've been able to stick it out for four years in college, you've got potential to perform and stick with a task on the job.

It also suggests that you are teachable, trainable, and capable of critical thinking. When employers are looking for employees, they want the best quality applicants possible. Having a college degree says something about your abilities without your having to say a word.

Counterpoint. It's hard to deny that a college degree will give a leg up in a job application. However, those with degrees will typically be seeking different kinds of jobs than those without and typically won't run into each other. That is, unless, the college grad is having to start at a lower rung on the ladder, or the non-grad is trying to step up a bit higher.

Generally, an employer is looking for an employee who can hit the ground running or be trained as quickly as possible. If you lack a degree but have practical/industry experience that can be immediately applied, you'll more than likely win out over a college grad. After I graduated and pounded the pavement looking for work, I was often told, "Sure, you have a degree, but what can you *do?*" Even with a degree, the lack of experience *in anything* made it very difficult to get a job.

It Can Get You More Money

Many magazine articles tout how college grads will have, on *average*, a much higher lifetime income than those who lack a college degree. This is very likely true and I'm not about to argue the statistics.

Counterpoint. If you want to be average, being average with a degree will pay more. As mentioned in previous pages, a great many who lack a degree earn much more than average. Besides, this book is not about aspiring to be average. The intent of this book is about aspiring to be exceptional, whether in income or job satisfaction. I hope I can safely assume that you're *reading* it with the same intent.

What a College Degree CANNOT Do for You

I will not argue that a college degree can be useful. If you have the time, money, and inclination to pursue a college degree, do so. It can *help* you, but it *guarantees* you nothing. Success does not come from a diploma by itself. Whether or not you have a degree, the things that will make you successful are the same. If you're looking to a degree to make you successful, you're looking in the wrong place.

Success comes from the heart, not from a diploma.

It Cannot Guarantee You Success

Having a college degree is no guarantee of success. What it takes to succeed in the business world comes from a different set of skills than those it takes to succeed in college. David Goleman, in his *New York Times* best-seller, *Emotional Intelligence,* says, "One of psychology's open secrets is the relative inability of grades, IQ, or SAT scores, despite their popular mystique, to predict unerringly who will succeed in life." Goleman goes on to say that educational institutions almost solely emphasize grades, rote memorization of facts, and the taking of exams. These skills don't always translate into what it takes to succeed on the job. People skills, ability to work in teams, leadership, and ability to bounce back after upsets will get a person much further ahead in life.

A degree is not a golden ticket to the chocolate factory. Those who hold a degree are not catered to or treated in ways that are special simply because they have one. On any job, performance matters most, degree or no degree.

Someone with a degree who goofs around, whines, complains, misses deadlines, blames others, and lets projects fail will not advance (unless they're the boss's family). People with degrees get fired and laid off too!

Someone without a degree who surpasses expectations, performs well, gets along with others, gets others to cooperate, and solves problems will escalate to higher and higher responsibilities.

A friend of mine, Tony G., started at the order desk for a flooring products company. Twelve years later, without a college degree, he was made vice president of the company.

It Cannot Provide You with Direction

Far too many people graduate from college with no direction at all. Millions of students go to college because of parental pressures or because of the belief that it will lead to a "good" job. Decisions about courses of study are based on limited information, myths, and indecision. Most entering college are still young and inexperienced. How are they to know what they really like and want to do without the practical exposure to the real world?

If you graduate with a direction, chances are you went in with a direction. If you enter college with no direction but have one upon graduation, chances are that it had more to do with a personal, life-changing event or person than with the curriculum itself. After all, four years is a lot of time in which a life-changing event can occur.

Four years of exposure to the real world, finding out your likes, dislikes, what you do well, what you don't do well, how to deal with people and pressures of the job is more likely to help you find a direction. Even if you've found more dislikes than likes, you're still far ahead of many who have spent four years in academia and have yet to find a direction at all. Besides, four years of on-the-job training means more practical experience that you can offer an employer.

It Cannot Provide You with Ambition and Goals

Many people go to college expecting the education to provide them with job opportunities upon graduation. Because of this false sense of security, many students fail to spend the time clarifying what they want to do and establishing goals. Often many students are busy indulging themselves in the relatively carefree, independent life away from mom and dad.

Upon graduation many students are stunned to find jobs are not waiting for them. Getting a job is actually a struggle! It is then that they must figure out what they want to do. Graduates with no goals or only vague goals are lost and aimless. The evidence to support this is the randomness with which they apply for jobs. Very often it's for *any job* as opposed to a very specific job. They wind up as waiters/waitresses, pizza delivery people, furniture movers, or in many other entry-level positions.

Students will put vague objectives on their resumes, like, "Desiring a fast-paced job with high growth potential." In essence, they're saying, "I want to make it big and become rich and I was hoping you might show me how." Their goals are shortsighted, to find *something* reasonably befitting a college graduate. Their ambition is often to make mom and dad proud.

> *Without a specific direction, everyone, even college grads, will find themselves in lifelong careers into which they've fallen rather than chosen.*

In a study described in the book *Think and Grow Rich* by Napoleon Hill, a graduating class from Harvard was surveyed regarding their goals. The study showed that only 3 percent had clearly defined goals, the others merely vague goals or no specific goals at all. Several years later, the 3 percent who had clearly defined goals had a combined net worth greater than the combined net worth of the rest of the 97 percent!

It Cannot Uncover Strengths and Talents

Once a major is decided, a curriculum focuses on courses pertinent to that major. All students of that major will go through roughly the same curriculum and receive roughly the same education. It won't help one much toward identifying individual strengths and talents.

If you follow a career that doesn't capitalize on your strengths and talents, you will likely do a mediocre job or become terribly bored. Many college grads who have studied for something that doesn't excite them go on to live mediocre lives.

However, having one or more jobs in the real world will give you a base of very personalized, very valuable information. It will tell you, from a practical perspective, what you like, don't like, what you're good at, and what you're not so good at. Whether you loved your job or hated it, your job experience is valuable information to help you chart your path toward success.

Careers that Don't Require a Degree

All too often when we think of a "job," we limit our thinking to "traditional" jobs, Monday through Friday, nine to five, second shift, graveyard, with either a salary or an hourly wage. We think a job must either be in an office or in unionized labor. We find these jobs in the newspaper and apply for them with a resume or by filling out an application. We often look for jobs we think we're qualified for based on our previous experience, rather than what we'd love to do, thereby creating boundaries and limitations based on practicality at the expense of passion.

Who is to say what constitutes a "good job"? Your parents? Your high school teachers? Your friends? Don't limit yourself to anyone else's definition of a "good job." Spend more time pursuing something that ignites your passions. A good rule of thumb to follow is that if there are magazines or books published about a topic, hobby, or interest, there are people making money at it. So why not you? What's holding you back?

Live a life of your own design, not someone else's.

Why can't a "good job" be one that pays the bills *and* enables you to do what you love?

As soon as you get a job you love, you might be lectured, "But that job has no future!" Who is to say what constitutes a "future"? Must a future consist of working at the same job, groveling for a promotion to the next level, and the next level after that?

Could a "future" not be one of ever-developing skills in either a specific area or in a wide variety of areas in a wide variety of jobs? Must it always be for the same company or same line of business?

On top of that, if you have a job that you love, you will likely pour your heart and soul into it. Work will become play, and you'll naturally excel. The more passion you have for the job, the greater "future" and success you create for yourself.

> *The more passion you pour into a job,*
> *the more life you will get out of it.*

Don't get me wrong. I'm not suggesting for a moment that you should fabricate passion for a job you dislike. Try seeking a job that you love, no matter how frivolous and impractical it may seem. And the more your parents disapprove, the better!

Pursuits of Passion

Below I touch on several areas that are outside the "nine-to-five" realm. I call these "pursuits of passion" because that's what they truly are. Yes, there are people making money at these, sometimes enormous amounts of money. Chances are these people were lectured by their parents about getting a "real job" too! Here's another tip: Don't look in the newspaper for jobs, look in the yellow pages under topics that grab your attention.

In the following sections are listed the many exciting jobs that can be had without a college degree. Pick up a pen, pencil, or highlighter, and mark up things that you find interesting. *Mark anything and everything that you think is exciting!* Don't hold back. You will need this information later.

Adventure pursuits

There are many activities people consider mere hobbies. But when there are many people passionately participating in such "hobbies" there is opportunity for you. Here are just some adventurous activities that can become a career.

Skiing, scuba diving, sky diving, water skiing, jet skiing, snowmobiling, mountaineering, hunting, fishing, piloting, hang gliding, plane gliding, surfing, windsurfing, sailing, power boating, canoeing, kayaking, rafting, spelunking (cave climber), off-road vehicle riding/racing, motorcycle racing, auto racing, drag car racing, roller blading/skating/hockey.

Even throw in things like helicopter pilot and commercial aircraft pilot, neither of which require a degree (just lots of training). Also being a travel guide, yacht captain adventure tour guide, whale watching tour guide, race car pit crew, and so on.

Artistic/Creative pursuits

If you have what one would call "artistic talent" in any manner, whether with canvas and paint, pen and pencil, keyboard, wordsmithing, camera, mouse, anything you can make with your hands, weird or beautiful, you can make a very comfortable living, if not become wildly successful. Visit some gift shops in tourist areas (especially in affluent resorts) and you'll see the enormous amounts of money people charge for their artwork and crafts.

Freelance painter or artist, commercial artist, cartoonist, greeting card designer, illustrator, magazine writer, poet, novelist, "how-to" writer, craftsperson, decorator, graphic design artist, typesetter, page layout specialist, desktop publisher, artistic photographer, landscape photographer, wildlife photographer, human interest photographer, event photographer, photo-journalist, celebrity and fashion photographer, food stylist, commercial photographer, leather crafter, web page designer, copy editor, advertising writer, jewelry designer, pottery designer, lighting designer, household decorations designer, fashion designer, clothing designer, hair designer, shoe designer, woodworker, cabinetmaker, furniture maker, sculptor, welder, etc.

Entertainment pursuits

You may think that you have to have some special training to get into these areas. While it helps, it's not a requirement. And, you don't have to have a college degree! All you need is a foot in the door, followed by passion and persistence. Many of the people you see and hear on radio, TV, the theater, movies, or music industry got there because of their passion and persistence. If it's your passion, pursue it!

> Movie actor, television actor, theater actor, stuntman/woman, makeup/wardrobe artist, storyteller, professional speaker, music star, studio musician, studio technician, nightclub musician, orchestra musician, street musician, singer, back-up singer, choral singer, lyricist, composer, comedian (and they say class clowns will go nowhere), comedy writer, entertainment industry writer, gossip columnist, advice columnist, radio DJ, talk show host, advertising voice-over artist, cartoon voice, master of ceremonies, studio techni-cian, lighting technician, camera operator, radio and televi-sion producer, cruise ship entertainment director, hotel/casino entertainment director, choreographer, dancer, dance instructor, director for plays, musicals, TV, radio shows, and even movies.

Computer-related pursuits

If you have an inclination towards computers, this area is hot. It pays well, and a little bit of experience can get your foot in the door to many high tech companies. If you would like to make a lot of money, the sky is the limit in the computer fields. A computer science degree is helpful to get into some pretty high-paying jobs, but not all computer jobs. Once you're in, you can write your own ticket.

Think all those hours playing video games is a total waste? Your mom likely does. But computer gaming is a multi-billion dollar industry. They need gaming experts for support and new game design. Again, your only limitation is your imagination.

> Computer programmer, database designer, graphics design-er, computer animation specialist, game support specialist, game designer, instructor, consultant, help-desk technician, network technician, computer repair, web page designer, web page host, Internet service provider, Internet mogul.

Athletic pursuits

Nearly any sport you can imagine has opportunities for you. You may not be a pro-football talent, but you can sure be involved in the game somehow.

Cyclist, marathon runner, swimmer, volleyball competitor, tennis pro, tennis instructor, golf pro, golf instructor, triathlon competitor, Olympic athlete, coach, trainer, sports medicine and therapist, massage therapist, etc. Even if you're not competing on the court, gym or field, you can certainly be involved in basketball, football, soccer, baseball, cricket, hockey, weight training, sports nutrition, etc.

Intellectual pursuits

Become a specialist in any topic and you can write books and articles, and provide commentary to people in the media. Your intellect, ability to analyze issues, ability to express ideas, and to persuade people to your way of thinking counts more than anything else.

Writer, historian, futurist, science enthusiast, theorist, inventor, marketing specialist, marketing assistant, chess champion, gambler, politician, political analyst, political commentator, campaign coordinator, survey taker/analyst, etc.

Technical pursuits

Some people are natural tinkerers. They love to fix things and do an exceptional job of making nearly anything work. Even something as ordinary as an auto mechanic, with the right passion, will garner an extensive clientele and a great deal of respect.

Aircraft mechanic, boat mechanic, speed boat mechanic, auto mechanic, computer technician, electronic technician, robotics technician, radio and television technician, inventor, radiologist, medical equipment operator or repair technician.

Organizing and coordinating pursuits

There are multitudes of people who cannot organize or coordinate anything at all. They may not have the ability, contacts, resources, knowledge, expertise, time, or patience. This means lots of opportunity for you to do things you love that others might hate, and make money at it.

> Wedding planner, event planner, party planner, professional shopper, competitive shopping analyst, travel consultant, tour guide, adventure tour guide, out-of-town guest concierge/chaperone, personal achievement coach.

Monetary pursuits

If money is your primary concern, there are lots of ways to make it. Although a degree is a must in the Fortune 500 scene to advance up the ladder, the lack of one won't prevent you from rising to the top of a small outfit or your own company. Sales of nearly anything is a skill that will never become obsolete. Once you learn the art of sales, of dealing with people and persuading them to buy, you can literally make fortunes and never be without a job again (until you retire at the age of 45).

> Real estate sales, computer sales, software sales, auto sales, insurance sales, stock and bond sales, mortgage sales, loan sales, boat sales, airplane sales, commercial real estate financing, bank vice president (believe it or not), investor, investment broker, etc.

Other pursuits of passion

There are many pursuits of passion that may pay less, but reward more.

> Restaurateur, gourmet chef, book publisher, movie critic, theater critic, book critic, music critic, computer industry analyst, animal trainer, animal breeder, rancher, farmer, florist, plant nursery owner, landscaper, magician, clown, bodybuilder, personal fitness trainer, aerobics instructor, fitness club/resort owner, Red Cross volunteer, charity worker,

firefighter, police officer, emergency medical technician, search and rescue specialist, private investigator, crisis counselor, shelter operator, martial arts instructor/school owner, antique collector/shop owner, house remodeler, auto collector, butler, concierge, bell captain, curator, confectioner, country club owner, body guard, laser/paint ball gaming operator, house/log cabin builder/developer, professional pool player, collector (*of anything*), psychic, tarot card reader, winery/vineyard owner.

Jobs Surrounding Pursuits of Passion

You can make money, sometimes enormous amounts, in a variety of capacities and roles surrounding a pursuit of passion, none of which require a college education. What they do require is passion!

Here are some examples of capacities and roles one could fulfill involved with a pursuit of passion.

- **Instructor** to teach those new to a pursuit (for example, sky diving instructor)
- **Expert** to provide commentary or advice (for example, sportscaster or golf course design consultant)
- **Writer,** freelance or staff magazine article writer or book author (for example, scuba diving locations)
- **Business owner** selling equipment, supplies, or services related to any topic (for example, windsurfing shop owner)
- **Association/club director** organizing others in the same pursuit
- **Competitor** in the pursuit, whether sport, craft work, or artist
- **Spokesperson** for brands and supplies for the pursuit
- **Designer** to improve equipment or create variations on a theme
- **Manufacturer's rep** selling product lines in the pursuit
- **Event organizer** to organize exhibitions, competitions, or festivals
- **Web page designer/host** to provide expert advice, opinions, and resources for others (this area is very hot)

Doubtless there are more ways that one can create a role around a particular passion. Your only limit is your imagination.

Take anything that you highlighted in the 'pursuits of passion' section, and one by one, match it up to each one of the roles you see above. Does it sound like something you'd be interested in doing? With so many different possibilities, don't let anyone tell you that a particular job has no future!

Think Like a Successful Person

Far too many people let the lack of a degree become a barrier in their lives. They accept the conventional wisdom that without a degree, they will wind up in low paying jobs with no future. They never even attempt to break down what is a purely psychological obstacle. But, remember, the conventional wisdom that tells us that you'll never amount to anything without a four-year degree is purely myth.

Even without a college degree, there are no rules against:
- starting and running a business
- going to work for a company that is aligned with your strengths, talents, and interests
- making a career out of what others consider a hobby
- working for a small company where you can have lunch with the president or owner and convince him or her of the value of your ideas

A college degree can be very helpful in your career, qualify you for certain jobs, give you credentials to make your opinions prevail, prepare you with a base of knowledge for certain jobs, give you a leg up in the application process, and even yield more income (on average).

A college degree, by itself, *cannot* instill in you the qualities that it truly takes to become successful. It cannot define for you what are your strengths, passions, and interests. A college degree cannot incite you to set goals for yourself and cannot make you take the steps necessary to pursue them.

The only thing stopping you from
pursuing your dreams and passions is you.

ROADBLOCK 2

"I hear
the streets
are paved with
gold there!"

Defining Success

This roadblock is having only vague or false impressions about what success really means. Before beginning your journey toward success, it's a good idea to know what to expect and what it will look like when you get there. Without a clear picture, you'll never know what to shoot for. You may think that it's something unachievable, so you won't even try. This is much like not bothering to shop for any cars at all because you believe they all cost as much as a Mercedes Benz. Clearly, there are cars within your budget, just like there are degrees of success easily within your reach.

Far too many people feel success is beyond them, that the only way they'll get there is if luck befalls them. But success is less about luck than it is about planning, preparation, and methodical pursuit of dreams.

You might feel that in order to be successful you must be very, very smart or work very, very hard. This isn't entirely true either. When you do what you love, work becomes play, and you'll naturally excel.

In the previous chapter you saw that success requires more than a diploma. You looked at many exciting jobs and careers that are outside the realm of what one might consider a "traditional" or "good" job. They may seem like hobbies to many, but lots of people make a good living doing them.

Although you've seen examples of people who lack degrees making a great deal of money, that's not entirely what success is all about. Success isn't just about money, money, money. It's not about big houses, fancy cars, and frequent vacations. There is clearly more to life than these things. So, what is it really? Surveys of job satisfaction show that it's not money that makes a job most rewarding, it is recognition for one's efforts and a sense of contribution.

If you believe success is just about having lots of money, you're more likely to put faith in the lottery or other forms of gambling. Lotteries have astronomical odds against hitting the jackpot, and people spend hundreds or thousands of dollars on them while never seeing a payoff. Yet, the odds of becoming a millionaire on your own, if you apply yourself, are incredibly in your favor. It's not out of your reach or out of the question, if that's what you truly desire.

Even if being a millionaire is not a must, getting part way there is easier still.

Believing that success is all about money can also make you vulnerable to cons or get-rich-quick programs. These "scams" promise a "new, secret way" of making money that lets you bypass traditional methods of "hard work." Not only will they rob you of money, but the biggest crime is they will harden your belief that success is beyond your reach.

Success is about discovering your strengths, talents, and passions, then capitalizing on them in your career pursuits. Dream big dreams, set goals, and you will achieve them and succeed.

If you're caught up in the nine-to-five grind, you may not give success a lot of thought. But if you don't know where you're going, any road will take you there. The real tragedy is that if you're in the process of going nowhere in particular, time elapses quickly, years escape, and you're still aimlessly lost believing success will never be yours.

In this chapter we'll discuss some of the common definitions of success, their merits, and shortcomings. I'll then ask you to give some thought as to what success means to you and to put your thoughts on paper. You will, I believe, realize that success is within your reach. You will, I hope, be able to begin heading in the direction of what you define. The years won't escape you; rather, they will become productive years moving toward your goal.

Common Definitions of Success

Let's discuss these common definitions of success so that when you formulate your own definition, you will already have reviewed these.

Money

Money is a fine thing, and having lots of it can help you in many ways.

Money is the common measuring stick of success. What's interesting is that money is only an external measuring stick. When we see someone else with lots of money, we figure they're a success. But the people who have it may not feel themselves a success. Many acquire a great deal of money only to find their lives devoid of happiness. Everyone else thinks they're a success, but internally, an individual might feel a failure.

Just how much money does it take to be successful? Does how we obtain the money have any bearing on whether or not we're truly successful? Does a million dollars gained from selling cocaine have the same meaning as a million dollars earned through a legitimate business? Does a million dollars won in a lottery add the same value to your life as a million dollars earned through applying your strengths and talents?

How much money does it take to feel successful?

In their book, *The Millionaire Next Door*, Thomas J. Stanley and William D. Danko report the results of interviews conducted with people in each of four categories. Those with over one million dollars felt that their budgets were still tight and felt they needed two million or more. Those who had two to four million felt they would really be successful if they had over 10 million. Those with 10 million or more felt the magic number was over 100 million. Those with over 100 million had a few more hobbies and toys they wished they could afford.

I can recall this from my own experience. When I first got a job at $21,000, I thought I had made it big. But then those around me who made $35,000 made me jealous. If only I could make as much, then I'd really be happy. But when I hit $40,000, I thought it was nothing unless I was making $60,000. When I hit $60K, I wanted $100K, and when I broke $100K, I wanted $300K, and so on.

The point is that whatever you have, it never seems to be enough. People seem to have an insatiable appetite for more money, more toys, and bigger everything.

When you begin to make more and more money, you tend to gravitate to those settings where others make a similar amount or more. If you were living in a trailer park and went from making $10,000 a year to making $100,000, you'd sure feel like king of the trailer park if you stayed there. But, more than likely you'd move into a new neighborhood where your neighbors made a similar amount. People often yearn for the next upgrade in living and lifestyle to get ahead of their peers.

Don't think that you'll ever have enough money. Usually, when judging your own success, the money you make is never enough. When you look at those who make more, you feel like they're the ones who are really successful. Realize right now that however much you make, you'll always be yearning for more.

Does money mean happiness?

While money, in most people's minds, equates to success, does it equate to happiness? Consider the plight of many who achieve fame and fortune in the entertainment industry. There are many tales of people who achieve incredible fortunes, only to live lives of desperation, depression, drug abuse, and suicide. They include Marilyn Monroe, Elvis Presley, John Belushi, Kurt Cobain, just to name a few.

If these people had all this money, why didn't they feel successful? Certainly they had constant reminders of how successful they were and how much they were loved by their fans. What went wrong in their lives?

Is it possible to have all that money and not be happy?

Obviously it is. I have met many millionaires who have lots of toys but are genuinely unhappy. One man I know, I'll call him Wilbur, made a fortune in a less than a decade. You might think that would make him happy. However, because making money was Wilbur's primary focus, he was never able to learn to cultivate his personal relationships with friends and family. His wife left him, his children visit him only begrudgingly, his mother argues with him constantly, and few people care to be his close friend. Most people who know Wilbur very well dislike him.

So, money is by no means a guarantee of happiness. It can buy toys, vacations, and experiences. But it cannot buy sound relationships with those close to you.

Windfalls

A windfall of cash, say, from inheriting it or winning a lottery can make you wealthy. However, *you are still you.* You might not have the knowledge of how to save, manage, or spend wisely such a large amount of money. You're also inclined to live with the gnawing feeling of "easy come, easy go" or that you don't really deserve it since you didn't have to work for it.

The by-product of earning a million dollars is the knowledge of how to earn a million dollars. You'd also have the confidence it can be done. Even if you lost all of your money, you would know how to earn another million. On top of that, having survived the loss of all your money, you'd be doubly strengthened knowing that going broke can't kill you. You'd be more confident about what you're doing and less afraid of failure.

Put faith in making your own fortunes, rather than in luck and winning them. Overall, you'll be a stronger, more resilient person.

Get-rich-quick

There are countless schemes out there where others will try to *sell you wealth*. These programs lure people who believe they won't be able to earn much money by traditional methods or by any means that they can see or envision at the present. They describe "new, secret" methods, either never discovered before or hidden in plain sight all along.

My only advice to you, having been taken in by them myself a time or two, is be cautious of anyone wanting to *sell* you a program to make *you* rich.

I'm not saying that all are scams. Some are legitimate businesses and many, many people have prospered employing program methods.

However, my suggestion to you is that you feel good and right about doing it. Don't be dazzled by claims of making fortunes overnight doing something in which you have no experience. Take time to carefully consider what it would be like to be participating in the program, what you're being asked to do and how. Can you realistically see yourself doing it? Would you feel comfortable? Would you feel okay telling your friends about it? The bottom line is, use caution, make sure it fits within your personality, and take a month or more to investigate it before spending hundreds or thousands of dollars.

There are many other ways to build wealth through methodically using your strengths and knowledge (even if you don't know what they are yet). It may take years, but you'll be much happier in the long run.

A few final thoughts on money

Money is a good thing to have. It gives us more choices in the world. It gives us security in knowing that we'll never starve or live in want, especially when we're in our golden years. It gives us the ability to explore our interests, go to interesting and exotic places, and tell stories of our experiences. It gives us bragging rights. Money enables us to express ourselves and what we believe about ourselves, to demonstrate our worth, either through humble and wise frugality, or through opulence, excess, and glitter.

Power

Power is a fine thing too. Wouldn't it be wonderful to have our bidding done with little or no question? Wouldn't it be grand to direct things the way that we want or believe is right, not only our own lives, but the lives of others?

We seek positions as foremen, in management, in the executive ranks, or as the president of the company. Sometimes we start our own businesses so that we can call the shots. Sometimes as parents we direct our children's lives in ways that will make them what we consider good people, and make us proud of what we've produced. Sometimes we pursue positions of power without necessarily pursuing money, as in the case of government and politics. The power of being able to direct things in ways you feel is right is sometimes more enticing than money.

Once in a position of power, some become benevolent leaders and direct things in ways that are of benefit to all, or at least the majority. Others become tyrants. Tyrants on the scale of a small business might bluster about, telling everyone what to do because they know what is best, regardless of what others think, and sometimes threaten or fire those who oppose them. Tyrants on the large scale of a country mandate rules and laws and sometimes execute those who oppose them.

What is power, really? Is it being able to make things go the way you think they should go? Is it really getting someone to do what you tell them? Is it having control over other people's lives?

When examined closely, power is really about getting others to recognize your worth or importance. When in positions of power, people exercise the abilities they have to get this recognition or acknowledgement. Sometimes they gently instigate this recognition by making you say "Sir," "Ma'am," "please," and "thank you."

Sometimes they force the acknowledgement by not cooperating, delaying what you want, or taking actions to deny what you want until you give them such recognition. In some extremes they retaliate against the failure to acknowledge their importance and value. Sometimes the retaliation means losing a job, a business deal, or, at humanity's worst, a life, all for the sake of recognizing of a person's worth.

Forcing others to acknowledge your value hardly seems like something worth pursuing, yet it happens all the time.

However, there are ways to have your own value and worth be recognized without the negative aspects associated with power. If power is using your abilities to get others to acknowledge your value, start with the most important person in the world—yourself! Why must you rely upon others to prop up your self-worth? Use your abilities to develop a strong sense of self-worth and you'll not likely need much acknowledgement from others, whether gently instigated or forced.

If getting acknowledgement from others is still important to you, use your abilities to do good for your fellow human beings. A natural by-product of doing things for others is recognition for the good things you do. This can come in the form of simple gratitude or in winning awards and accolades.

It is up to you how you use your abilities to garner recognition of your importance. One path will benefit others, another path will denigrate others. Concentrate on fostering your own strong sense of worth and you'll be much further ahead.

Fame

Wouldn't it be great to be famous? Some might say no, but others harbor deep desires for fame.

For those who desire it, fame means people giving you lots of attention, praise, and thinking you're special or great. When you're famous, people will often assume you know many things that they do not, that you are wiser than they. You have immense credibility simply by being famous. Others are more open to you, your ideas, and will listen to what you have to say, sometimes even take your advice. You can gain access to people high up in business and government, and people will almost always return your phone calls!

Frankly, being famous can open a heck of a lot more doors than can a simple college degree.

In the mind of a non-famous person, being famous and recognized everywhere you go, signing autographs, etc., might seem appealing, especially if you're used to being invisible. While it would be wonderful to have the world clearly recognize your worth, even put you on a pedestal, there are many trade-offs that you might not foresee. A close friend, who is very famous, insisted that I mention this in my book.

As a famous person you lose your privacy. Wherever you go, people gawk at you, point at you, take pictures of you, whisper or call out to their friends about you, feel it's okay to intrude on you and your space, and interrupt your quiet evening out. You become a spectacle.

People assume you have lots of money and try to take advantage of it by jacking up prices on services. Others come to you with their hand out for their cause or case.

Unless you're intentionally trying to promote a "bad boy" or "bad girl" image, you must be on your best behavior at all times. Anything questionable seen or said about you could be tomorrow's juicy gossip. If you get shoddy service, you can't pop off to the manager the way you could as a private citizen.

You begin to have serious doubts about people's motives. Are people your friends because you're famous and hoping to get recognition by association? Do people tell you *the truth* about your efforts and creations, about how you look, what you wear, or what you have to say? All feedback becomes suspect.

Seeking fame, like wanting power, is looking for others to acknowledge and recognize your value and worth. Start by recognizing your own strengths and worth and you'll be in a stronger position to move in the direction of success.

Winning

There are those who feel success can only be had through winning a competition. To them, winning isn't everything, it is the only thing. Being the best at some activity is all-important. It is the foundation of an entire attitude, typically male, that nothing is worth venturing upon unless there is a competition. It is very likely rooted in our instincts for survival and group domination, which are still alive and well. Although today we need worry little about day-to-day survival and we have laws to protect us from a "thinning of the herd" mentality, this is only a recent phenomenon. In the course of human history, such prosperous and regulated living has existed for only a relatively short period of time. Our instincts have yet to catch up to our intellect.

With a competitive instinct alive and well, some find success only in winning or dominating anything and everything. It may be sports, it may be debates, it may be political races, it may be in business. To the victor go the spoils, accolades, and glory.

While competition is fine for some, for the rest of society, it has less meaning. Most people just want to get along. There is no winning unless there is a loser and many dislike the idea of someone having to lose (especially if it's them). This is not to say that competition is wrong, but it may not be right for everyone.

Doing What You Love

This definition is getting closer to what makes sense. Who could be happier than someone doing exactly what they want to do? After all, what is it that most people want to do once they get a lot of money? Retire! They want to acquire enough money to have the time to do what they *want* to do rather than what they *have* to do.

Ah, if we could only figure out exactly what we love to do, and if we're lucky, find that it pays well enough to make our lives comfortable. Yet many of us put off discovering what we want to do for the sake of getting a job that pays the bills *today*. In doing so, we cheat ourselves out of living a life of happiness from day to day. We hope that someday we'll have enough money to do what we want. If we manage our money wisely we have a greater chance of achieving that financial independence. However, we can toil for years saving for that someday goal only to be struck down by misfortune, illness, accident, or tragedy.

The time to discover and define what you love to do is now. The future is far too uncertain. Later in this book you'll find ideas on how discover what you really like to do and how to make a comfortable living at it.

Suggested Definition

To come up with a good definition of success we must balance all of these elements and ideas. This will give us something to strive for, something that we can recognize when we see it. Let me offer this definition.

> *Success is the complete satisfaction with who you are, what you're doing, and where you're going in life.*

That's quite a bit to chew on, so let's examine it piece by piece.

Who You Are

Many achieve fame and fortune only to find that they are not satisfied with who they are. They can be immersed in money and self-doubt at the same time. Jane Fonda, the famous actress, once said in an interview (and I'm paraphrasing), "I'm afraid that one day I'll wake up and everyone will see that I'm a fraud." Whether or not Jane Fonda feels she's a success, her comment speaks to the idea that people are not always satisfied just because of fame and fortune. It would also support the reasons why there are so many examples of famous people who turn to drugs and suicide.

To realize who you are is to recognize and accept both your strengths and weaknesses. One can never be great at everything. No one ever criticizes a famous athlete for his or her inability to play the piano or sing.

Count and be happy with your strengths, capitalize on them because they are uniquely yours. Seek employment where you utilize them and you'll enjoy the heck out of your job.

Acknowledge your weaknesses and faults, but don't beat yourself up over them.

> *Everyone has faults, from the President of the United States to your parents. It's okay for you to have faults too.*

Not all weaknesses must be corrected, but pick out ones you can correct and work at it. You'll grow as a person and wind up with even more strength than before.

Being completely satisfied with who you are will help you to accept that you're not perfect and be okay with that. It will help free you from feelings of inadequacy that come from being imperfect. By not dwelling on your shortcomings, you can focus and find greater happiness in your strengths.

What You're Doing

Many get down on themselves because they're engaged in work that they feel is beneath them. You may presently have a menial job that does not utilize your talents or does not impress your friends and family.

There are two things you can do to be happy with what you're doing.

One is that you can seek employment where your strengths will be utilized. This may sound easier than it is, but it can be done (more on this later).

The other thing you can do is look at what you're doing as merely a stepping-stone to a greater goal. Look at your present occupation or situation as a means to get you by until you get a handle on what you want to accomplish. Don't look at pushing a broom *today* as meaning you are worthless and will always have a miserable life. Look at what you do today as giving you time to strategize and plan what you'll do next.

Focus on what you want to do 10 years from now, rather than the humbleness of your job today. The further out you look, the less you'll suffer in your present circumstances. Frame your view of what you are presently doing as a means to a greater end.

Where You're Going

Map out your life as you desire it. Knowing what you want to do and having a clear vision of what you want to become is tremendously satisfying in itself.

If you envision where you will go in life based on where you are today, you'll likely be dissatisfied. If you envision where you will go based on your dreams, you'll be much happier every step of the way. You have complete control over what you make of your life, and if you're actively engaged in constructing it, you will be happier today.

Even a humble job can teach you things about yourself that can be turned into strengths—strengths which can be utilized to achieve your goals. Actively examine a humble job for ways to improve yourself. Find out ways to do the job a little better than expectations, find ways to use your creativity and solve some problems on the job. Your little achievements here and there don't have to change the world, but they will build tremendous momentum. Every little bit, no matter how small an accomplishment it might be, adds up to a great deal of confidence which can be turned into real dollars in the future.

When looking at your present situation as a means to a greater end, success changes from a "someday" thing to a "every step I make today" thing.

An example

A person I believe exhibits every aspect of this definition of success is a man who runs a small-town karate school, Sensei Isaias Valdavinos.

He's satisfied with who he is and his talents in martial arts. He's extremely happy with what he's doing. He inspires and helps hundreds of children and adults to achieve something positive in life. He will be fondly remembered and appreciated by them. His positive influence will help many thousands of people for generations to come.

He's satisfied with where he's going. He doesn't make a fortune from his business, but enough to continually expand, little by little, year by year. The more schools he opens the more people on whom he can have a positive life influence.

Money is not the sole objective in success, it is a by-product of success. The objective of success is finding satisfaction within yourself and the belief that you're worth something, to yourself and to others.

A Few More Thoughts on Success

Success is more than just a goal that you achieve. It is the excitement that you feel day to day in pursuit of your dream.

Success is knowing you have strengths, talents, value, and worth, and being able to demonstrate that value and worth every day through the exercise of your strengths and talents.

Success is the excitement of setting goals, big and small, and proving to yourself and others that you have the mastery of your will power, strengths, and talents to accomplish what you set out to do. It could be amassing great fortunes, or becoming the head of an organization, or competing in either intellectual or athletic pursuits and winning a coveted award and recognition from peers. It can be providing an environment for your children in which they grow to be strong, healthy, and happy adults.

Success, and happiness, are all about recognizing your value as a human being. As human beings, we have the unique ability to question our own existence. At our very core, don't we hope that our existence is worthwhile and that we are good? After all, we are brought into this world involuntarily and left to discover this answer ourselves.

Does not the gauntlet of life cause us to continually question, "Am I good?" Do not the many ways in which we are treated by others whom we look to for answers, who know more than we, help us to shape our own answer? Do not the experiences we have over a lifetime make us draw conclusions about our value and worth? And, when the feedback from others and from our experiences over our lifetimes are inconclusive, do we not struggle to find the answer in the many ways that people define success? When the feedback tells us overwhelmingly that we are not good, are we not devastated?

Imagine yourself drifting in total blackness. It's just you and the universe. When you ask the question, "Am I good?" devoid of everything in the real world, the answer is conclusively, "Yes!" Why would it not be? But when you add back in the realities of the world, does the answer change? Why?

Imagine, too, that everyone else in the world is also in drifting in their own, unique voids, just them and their universes. They, too, are asking, "Am I good?"

They are just like you in their pursuit of the answer. They are no better off in their quest than are you. But because of how we were brought into the world, taught to think based on information from others, we continually seek the answer from others. So, we seek the answer to the question, "Am I good?" by means of the many definitions of success discussed in this chapter. We all spend our lifetimes seeking the one answer.

I'd like you to try something for a moment that I hope doesn't come across as sacrilegious or insult your spiritual beliefs. That is not my intent.

Imagine, for a moment, that you are God, just for the sake of this illustration. You've been busy creating all the creatures of the world, a wide variety of beings. Along the way you create human beings with far more intelligence than the rest of the beings.

To your surprise, one of the things they do with this intelligence is begin asking "Am I good?" As they multiply and prosper, each one asks, "Am I good?"

Again, to your surprise, the human beings begin turning to one another to seek the answer. Some of the human beings have children who ask them, "Am I good?" when the parents still have not found the answer for themselves. Some take it upon themselves to answer the others. Some are benevolent and tell the others, "Yes, you are good." Some, being uncertain, are selfish and tell others, "No, you're not as good as I am."

To your further amazement, they begin all sorts of odd behaviors to demonstrate their worth by adorning themselves with jewels, fancy clothes, and possessions. They resort to doing things to one another to prove to the others that they are good, better, or best of all. Sometimes it's petty insults, sometimes it's running faster, sometimes it's conquering one another. The ways in which the human beings seek to prove their worth or superiority grows more and more elaborate and sometimes perverted. All the while, you, as God, created them all as good, worthy beings.

As human beings, we have all been created "good," or at the very least, equal to one another. Through the interactions we have with others in our quest to find the answer, the view of ourselves can become distorted or perverted. All the while, the answer is still the same. "Yes. You are good."

You will truly cross a significant threshold when you no longer look to others and ask, "Am I good?" but alter the words and confidently recognize, "I am good!" Your journey to success will be about exercising and developing your strengths and talents to demonstrate to everyone the wonderful things you can do with your gifts, whether playing guitar or changing the world.

Crafting Your Own Definition

You are at liberty to define success however you like. It is solely up to you, and you may certainly include money, power, fame, winning, and doing what you love in your definition. There are no rules in defining success. However, here are some questions you might consider to help you craft your definition.

What are the aspects of you, the things which you believe are most important about you, that you would like acknowledged, by yourself and by others? They may be strengths that you know you possess but haven't had much opportunity to exercise.

Here are some sample phrases that you might use, but feel free to make up what ever is important to you. Circle or highlight as many as you like.

I have worth. I am smart. I am lovable. I am likable. I am strong. I am confident. I am charismatic. I am good. I am noble. I am fair. I am creative. I am the best at whatever I set out to do. I am a good athlete. I am thoughtful. I am inventive. I am attractive. I am beautiful/handsome. I am happy to be me.

Write down any other important characteristics of you that you would like one and all to recognize.

_____
_____
_____
_____
_____
_____
_____
_____

Let's look at your strengths and talents. Using the characteristics you described above, identify the strength or talent that you can use to demonstrate that characteristic. For example, if you circled "I am creative" the talent you might write is "I paint/draw well." If you circled "I am noble/fair" the strength you might write is "I'm good at getting people to cooperate and agree."

What strengths and talents do you have now or would you like to develop that would demonstrate the most important characteristic of you?

_____

_____

_____

_____

_____

_____

What can you envision doing that would enable you to exercise your strengths and talents to demonstrate the your unique aspects on a regular basis?

_____

_____

_____

_____

_____

_____

At what point will you feel you have achieved success? How will you know when you're a success?

_____

_____

_____

_____

_____

What will you be doing, how will you be utilizing your strengths and talents, what kind of acknowledgement and recognition will you get about yourself, and how regularly?

In your career?

_____

_____

_____

_____

_____

In your family?

_____

_____

_____

_____

_____

In what you think about yourself?

_____

_____

_____

_____

Success Characteristics

Take heart, the qualities of character it takes to become a success are the same whether you have a college degree or not. They are not determined in childhood, nor by the activities in which you did or did not engage in high school, nor are they reserved only for those who have walked the straight and narrow. You can become successful even if you got in trouble in school or with the law, had a bad childhood, had addiction problems, ran away from home, got fired from jobs, or wound up homeless.

The qualities it takes to become a success are within us all, regardless of education level, race, class, or upbringing. They are within you too, no matter what your present condition or situation. They are not something that you earn or deserve based on what you've done in the past, or whether or not you read _The Wall Street Journal._ You can _activate_ these qualities at any time in your life simply by acknowledging them and applying them.

There are hundreds of books on the subject of success, each with their own theme and delivery. Here is a review of the qualities they cite as being responsible for success. Let's examine them briefly now. Later in this book, we'll discover how you can tap them within yourself and apply them.

Direction

Direction is an idea of what you would like to do in your life that will best utilize your strengths and talents.

Goals

Goals help you focus your efforts and energies. Goals are milestones in the direction that you've chosen. Goals help you to solidify your dreams into something attainable, something for which you can plan and strategize. Many describe goals as "dreams with deadlines."

Ambition and drive

Ambition is the desire to be something greater than you already are. Drive is the willingness to take action to make it so. Reading this book is a clear demonstration that you have these qualities.

Optimism

Optimism is crucial to holding onto a belief that you can achieve your dreams. Optimism enables you to interpret events in your favor and enables you to find something to learn in the face of failure. Pessimism, on the other hand, is the death knell for your dreams. Optimism can be cultivated through purposeful interpretation of events in your favor.

Vision and visualization

Vision is the ability to take dreams and give them shape and make them practical. Visualization is the ability to project an image of actually being in successful situations.

Self-acceptance

Acknowledging your strengths and talents is key to knowing you have something to work with. Accepting and allowing for your faults is key to keep from dwelling on them and believing you're not a good person because of them. Self-acceptance helps you to persist because of your strengths despite your faults.

Belief and confidence

Believing you can is half the battle. Believing you can enables you to take the first actions and to build momentum toward your goals. Without the belief that you can, you will never take the first step. Believing you can enables you. Believing you can't disables you. It's that simple.

Persistence

Coupled tightly with the confidence you can, persistence means that you don't give up when things are looking down, you learn from setbacks and failures, and try again. The most successful people in life try just a few more times than those who give up after one or two tries.

Focus

Focus helps you to avoid the distractions that can derail your plans. Focus helps you assess which activities will help you toward your goals and thus avoid or delay activities that take you away from your goals.

Doing what you love

Doing something you love turns work into play. The more you love what you do, the harder you will apply yourself, and more you will excel.

Whether or not you feel you have these qualities, they all exist within you. They may be trapped inside you under the lock and key of believing that you can't succeed. But once unlocked by believing you can, they will all become quite apparent and characteristic of you.

Think Like a Successful Person

Having a personalized and clear definition of success will give you something to shoot for. Understanding that success isn't just about money, power, fame, and winning will help you to dispel these misleading myths and help you focus on what success really means to you. You will realize that it is within your reach, worth pursuing, and achievable.

Success is really about utilizing one's strengths and talents in such a way that it demonstrates and gains the much-desired recognition for one's value and worth. Acknowledging and recognizing one's own value and worth internally is an essential element in the pursuit of gaining recognition externally.

ROADBLOCK 3

"This old jalopy just isn't cut out for a trip like that."

Overcoming the Past

Of all the roadblocks you might encounter, none is as formidable as that which no longer exists—your past. Your past can be a nasty and persistent barrier. It keeps popping up at critical junctions when you're deciding between a challenging road with big reward, and an easy road with little or no reward. Not only that, sometimes it will get caught on your bumper or underneath the carriage, and drag along with you as you drive.

Learn how to conquer your past and not only will you be able to confidently choose challenging roads with big rewards, but every other roadblock in your life will become child's play.

People who have lost limbs run marathons. People who have survived prison camps go on to become world leaders. People who have endured extreme hardships and battled great odds go on to succeed. So what is it that holds you, a reasonably able-bodied person, back?

Very likely it's your past.

Your past defines for you who and what you think you are.

Your past convinces you that you can or cannot do something.

Your past causes you to question and doubt your worth and worthiness.

Your past sets what you believe to be your limitations.

Your past has established the walls of your comfort zone.

Your past inhibits you from trying.

Your past goads you into quitting.

Your past fills your mind with clutter, much like junk in an attic. You may feel this clutter is absolute truth, when in actuality it is a mix of false impressions, biased information, and unfounded doubts. There are genuinely good qualities in you that you can't see for the clutter, just like the antiques and valuable finds in an attic filled with junk. We just have to clear out the attic of your past so you can see the true value that you possess.

The events of your past helped you form an opinion of yourself. Interactions you've had with others over a lifetime have shaped who you are, what you think, how you behave, what you believe, the jobs you choose, the foods you choose to eat, even the clothes you wear.

If you're not completely satisfied with any of the above, you can change. And, because it is your past that convinces you of what you can or cannot accomplish, the biggest roadblock you will encounter will be your past convincing you that what you're doing is "not you," to quit, or worse, to not even try.

The good news is you are at complete liberty to alter the meanings of past events, even redefine for yourself what you can or cannot do. Anthony Robbins says it best: "The past does not equal the future."

The limitations you believe you have are often based on false information and incorrect assumptions. You are actually able to achieve a great deal more than what you might currently believe you can. What you are genuinely capable of, your talents, and abilities, have very likely gone untapped. You have the ability to recreate yourself and redefine the person you would like to be.

Success isn't just about making money. It's really about the sense of worth you derive from utilizing your strengths and talents. To get to the point where you trust that sense of worth, it's important to conquer the reservations and doubts you hold about yourself that stem from events of your past.

You might still be saying, "Sure, success is easy for you because of (this or that). But how can I succeed when I have this in my past?" Your past might include everything from neglect or abandonment, physical abuse, sexual abuse, emotional abuse, to continuous nitpicking, or perfectionism on the part of parents. If one or more of these applies to you, okay, shame on them. Now what?

Everyone has a past—everyone! But many people succeed despite their past! You have a choice. You can use your past as an excuse for achieving little or nothing, continually seeking apologies and sympathy for what cannot be changed, or you can choose to live a successful life despite your past. It is all your choice, but you have to live with the consequences of your choice.

> *You can blame your past or succeed despite it.*
> *But it is you who must live with the consequences.*

For many people the meaning of their past has gone unquestioned. They accept or blame it, but still live with the negative result. It's as if it were against the rules to challenge its meaning.

This chapter is all about challenging your past, challenging the people who helped you form the opinions you have of yourself, and challenging what you feel to be the inescapable truth. The real truth is that you can redefine yourself however you wish.

The Attire of a Lifetime

We wear the events of our past much like a suit of clothing. All too often, once this suit has been donned, it remains with us for life. Rarely do we remove or change it.

We are, of course, all born naked. The nature of the family (or caregivers) into which we're born begins defining the clothes we'll wear for life. The care with which we are dressed has more to do with the quality of our clothes than does the wealth or poverty of the household.

As the years go by, we have new clothes added, item by item, stitch by stitch, piece by piece. The stitches and pieces not only come from parents, but from siblings, other children, the parents of other children, teachers, and neighbors.

Early on, the general nature of our suit of clothes is established. Soon we learn to take on only those new items, stitches, and pieces that coordinate with the nature of our suit of clothes.

If our suit of clothes had been of high quality and well pressed, we will continue to take on only new items, stitches, and pieces that are also high quality and well pressed. If someone hands us a rag, we will reject it.

If our suit of clothes had been of poor quality and filthy rags, we will continue to take on only new items, stitches, and pieces that are also poor quality and filthy rags. If someone hands us a fine new suit, we will reject it.

With a suit of fine clothes, we feel strong, polished, and confident. We feel the suit of clothes represents us well and are ready to take on big challenges and accomplish great things.

With a suit of rags, we feel like paupers, undeserving, and always questioning our worthiness and value. We also believe, unfortunately, that the clothes represent us all too well and define who we are. We fear becoming a spectacle by attempting anything challenging, or being in a situation where a suit of rags would be laughed at.

We take what we can get because we believe we don't deserve

more. We believe the only way we'll ever get to wear a fine suit of clothes is if luck befalls us. We dream of being free of the suit of rags. We often times resent those who wear fine suits because we believe we'll be forever denied them despite how much we covet them.

We keep company with others who wear suits of rags because it at least makes us feel okay. To keep company with those wearing fine suits would make us feel uncomfortable and ache to get back to our friends in their rags.

Sometimes we are disgusted with the suit of rags we've been made to wear, and we shake our ragged fists at our parents, our bosses, or at the world and shriek, "Look at these rags I'm forced to wear! My parents made me wear these rags! Other people made me wear these rags! You make me wear these rags!" Yet, no matter how much we shriek and feel disgusted, we continue to wear the rags.

The truth is, we can take off the clothes we've been given by others and wear whatever we like. Some people do! Some people are born into a house of rags, but, at some point in their lives, realize they can change. From that point forward, they refuse to accept the rags which no longer represent them, and only accept fine clothes which they feel represent them well.

Ragged friends and family may chastise them, "You can't wear a suit! You belong in rags!" Sometimes the person trying to change doubts his or her efforts and returns to rags. Yet a suit of fine clothes is theirs merely for the asking.

What kind of clothes do you find yourself wearing? Are you comfortable with them? Do they represent you well? There are no rules that say you must continue to wear clothes just like what you were given early on. The choice is yours.

> *You have both the ability and freedom to craft yourself into what ever person you wish to be.*

Let's examine the suit of clothes you find yourself wearing and how that came to be. It's time to challenge your past.

The Shaping of "You" by Others

The suit of clothes you find yourself wearing today was created largely by other people. As children, we automatically look up to adults as all-knowing, always right, always good. If we meet with their disapproval, we believe it is because we are wrong and bad.

However, just because someone is an adult or our parent doesn't mean they are automatically right or smart. It isn't until much, much later that we realize that our parents, teachers, and elders are mere human beings with faults of their own. By then, however, the impressions and beliefs they've left us with have become hardened into stone.

There is no certification required to become an adult or parent. Many adults and parents are inept, unqualified, people who've selfishly acted in their own interests, who've been misdirected, and who wear a suit of rags themselves. They adorn their children in suits of rags because they don't know any better.

In *Your Child's Self-Esteem*, Dr. Dorothy Corkhill Briggs gives advice to new parents about how to interact with their children. She illustrates many common child-rearing situations, how people typically respond, and what kind of impact the response can have on a child. She suggests alternative methods of dealing with children that will induce a desired behavior without causing emotional damage.

I read this after my first son was born because I wanted to be a good father. It was an eye opener for me. I saw myself in many of the harmful scenarios, not as the parent, but as the child!

I realized that my parents, older brothers and sisters, other kids in the neighborhood, teachers in school, and other authority figures had dealt with me in ways that had shaped the adult I had come to be. I recalled many situations that were turning points in my life. Generally, each turning point was negative, or fueled the negative self-perception that was evolving within me.

This negative self-perception colored my view of all other events in my life, big and small, and I saw only those things that supported my negative perception. When something went right, I looked for errors and how it wasn't reality. When something went wrong, I saw that as being reality and a true reflection of who I was.

Dr. Briggs further emphasizes, in *Celebrate Your Self*, that who we believe we are is a result of the reflections we get from other people in our lives. How other people interact with us will largely determine how we come to feel as adolescents and adults.

Positive and supportive environments in childhood generally produce confident, secure, well-adjusted adults. Negative and abusive environments in childhood generally produce unconfident, insecure, and neurotic adults. There are always exceptions, of course. Sometimes people will turn out exactly opposite of what one might expect.

What was your childhood like? Can you recall specific people that shaped your self-perception? Can you recall incidents that have had a lasting impression? The incidents don't have to be traumatic, they can be subtle, but the effects can be equally devastating.

Understanding Mistreatment

Parents, siblings, teachers, and other children have all helped to create the suit of clothes you now find yourself wearing. Why would anyone want to give their children rags to wear for the rest of their lives?

Were they all out to get you? No. It was not a conspiracy. You were not singled out because it was "you." You just happened to be in the wrong place at the wrong time. We cannot choose the environments into which we are born.

Is it because you were an evil child? No. Misbehavior in a child is often due to a parent's poor handling of a wide range of situations. You may even have been hyperactive, but that does not make you flawed. How you are handled in response to hyperactivity may have left you *feeling* flawed.

Then why? Why would other people treat you in ways that would harm you and not in ways that would yield a healthy adult?

I'll talk about four main reasons why parents, siblings, authority figures, and other children may have treated you in harmful ways.

They Didn't Know Any Better

Parents often handle children the way their own parents handled them. Their parents may have mistreated them, as did the parents of their parents. In his book, *The Inner Child*, John Bradshaw calls this the "poisonous pedagogy," (or education). Poor methods of dealing with children are handed down from generation to generation, each generation rearing another generation of injured children.

"That's just the way it is," most people figure. "I got spanked, even beaten, when I did wrong, and I turned out okay."

"Tough love," some call it.

Imagine, if you will, a television repair shop. But this one is slightly different. In this TV repair shop, the TVs fix one another. The first TV up for repair is made to work by the new shop owner who gives it a slap on the side, a shake back and forth, then side to side, jiggles the antenna, twists the knobs in front and back, turning it off and on several times. He's never repaired a TV before and his methods are amateurish, but eventually it works. The picture is sometimes quirky, and the colors get weird periodically, but overall it works.

Now imagine the next TV coming in is to be repaired by the first TV. The first applies all the repair techniques it learned from the shop owner to the second TV. Eventually, it works too, but it has its own set of quirks. The next TV is repaired by the second in similar ways and so on.

A TV is a complicated thing, but mysteriously, they all get working via amateurish methods, none have been properly fixed, there's much unseen damage from the repair methods, and none are very well adjusted.

This is a great deal like how generation upon generation of people raise children. Few of us have been raised by well-trained parents in supportive homes. Most of us are raised by unprofessional parents who have no training in child rearing other than what they've learned from their parents. Many of us have been raised using the same amateurish methods as in the odd TV repair shop above. On top of that, we are also indirectly reared by the amateur parents of other children with whom we've interacted while growing up.

A human being is a complicated thing, but mysteriously, we all get working via amateurish methods. Few have been properly reared, there's much unseen damage from the rearing methods, and few are very well adjusted.

The result is that we have skewed perceptions of ourselves when we become adults. We were taught to wear a suit of rags, so we believe that a suit of rags is all we deserve.

They Didn't Realize Their Impact on Us

Very few people (as a percentage of the population) have degrees in psychology. Fewer still understand or even consider the impact words and actions have on others, especially on children.

Imagine driving a motorboat across a lake for the first time in your life. In addition, you have blinders on so you see only what's in front of you. As you speed along, passing by other boaters and swimmers, you don't realize that you're leaving a wake behind you that affects others in the water. If you go barreling along, you create a tremendous wake that rocks the boat of others, even washes over swimmers entirely. When someone else comes barreling along and creates a tremendous wake in front of you and rocks your boat, you curse at them, shake your fist, and get mad as heck. All the while, you've been guilty of the same thing. Some people spend all their lives cursing at others who leave wakes, while at the same time, leaving enormous wakes of their own.

This is much like how we interact with others. We don't often realize the effects unless we're the victims. We go cruising along, seeing only what's in front of us, seldom aware of the impact we have on others. Sometimes it's a big impact. We physically or verbally lash out at someone and alter his or her life forever. Sometimes we say something with no harm intended, but it's misinterpreted, having a similar life-altering impact. And chances are that the people who have had a negative life-altering impact on us were not aware of this impact. It may have been traumatic verbal, physical, or sexual abuse, or it may have been innocent criticisms. Chances are the perpetrators don't even remember it, but we are stuck with a lasting impression of ourselves in their wake.

They Had a Troubled Soul

People suffer from emotional problems at any age, parent or not. Some are able to come to terms with their problems, others are not. Some go to their graves riddled with self-doubt and tremendous regret.

Envision that people are much like conduits or pipes through which negative treatment passes like water. Pour some bad treatment in one end and it's going to come out the other end on the downhill side. People often treat others the way they themselves have been treated. Sometimes the treatment they pass on is a result of how they've been treated that day. Sometimes it's the result of how they've been treated over a lifetime. In doing this, they recoup a bit of the self-worth they feel they've lost. If they try to hold the bad treatment in and not pass it along, one day the pressure becomes too great and they explode.

And, just like water, the treatment will seek the path of least resistance. Negative treatment gets passed along from someone who is stronger, either physically or of will, to someone who is smaller or weaker. The negative treatment is, in turn, passed along again to someone who is weaker still.

If a boy gets bullied at school, he's likely to bully younger siblings or smaller children in the neighborhood. If a girl is ridiculed by parents at home, she's likely to ridicule others at school. This behavior is widespread in adults. When adults are troubled at work, they tend to take it out on the kids or kick the dog.

Take some time to think about this. If you were treated badly, chances are the perpetrator was treated badly by someone else. Ask yourself what that person might have been going through. It may have been an incident that day, or a series of incidents over a lifetime, or both, but there's generally a reason. The important thing to realize is that being mistreated had little to do with you.

> *Hurtful words come from a troubled soul.*

This will be an important phrase to memorize and keep with you for the rest of your life. Whenever someone mistreats you, for any reason, whether in a loud display of anger or with sly backstabbing, the perpetrator has something troubling him or her. You simply have the misfortune of being a convenient target. You were the path of least resistance.

Typically, the more misgivings people have about themselves the stronger their response to any negative treatment they receive. If someone believes him or herself to be a terrible and worthless person, they explode at you when you make a mistake. When a teenager feels being tough is the only worth he has, merely being looked at the wrong way can cause a violent reaction. If a person is extremely frustrated by living a "rat race" life, he or she may pull out a gun on the freeway and take shots at the next person who cuts them off in traffic.

Hurtful words come from a troubled soul.
The louder the shout, the more the self-doubt.

They Wanted to Enhance Their Own Self-Image

Another reason people may have mistreated you in the past is in an effort to enhance their own self-image. Sometimes the outward motives seem noble, sometimes nasty, but they pull off this self-enhancing behavior at your expense.

When motives seem noble . . .

It is common for parents to attempt to enhance their own self-image at the expense of a child's freedom of choice or the child's self-esteem.

Many times parents will attempt to produce children of whom *they* can be proud. While saying it is for the child's sake, covertly it is for their own sake. The children become instruments through which the parents can feel good about themselves.

They bring us up to be respectable in the community. They tell us how to behave so as not to risk embarrassment, such as by using foul language (which the majority of adults use anyway). They teach us to stay out of trouble, be respectful of neighbors, and so on.

Parental self-esteem is also elevated if they can produce a lawyer, a doctor, or whatever society holds in high status. They spend lots of money on expensive universities and private colleges to put on display "the education I gave my kids."

Often parents live vicariously through their children by making them be the things they wish they could have been.

A father might push his son hard to practice at sports, to become the best, to become the champion the father wishes he could have been, or to uphold a reputation he, himself, established in his youth.

A mother who feels trapped in a marriage because of financial dependence may push her daughter relentlessly to excel in school so as not to suffer the same fate.

Parents like these often disregard what the children genuinely desire. Any sign of reluctance or indifference to the goal handed down by the parent comes to represent laziness and irresponsibility. In effect they threaten, "you'll never amount to anything unless you do what I'm telling you." If the child does not follow the prescribed path, they become the black sheep. The child who follows the prescribed path becomes the "good" son or daughter who gets great respect and praise within the family. Children who live their lives for their parents' approval will live a life of the parents' design, not their own.

There are no rules that say you must live up to the expectations of others. You are not obligated to live a life that will make someone else happy.

> *Live a life of your own design, not someone else's.*

When motives are self-serving . . .

Another way in which people attempt to enhance their own self-image is by putting others down. They do this through:

- brute force or intimidation
- criticizing, belittling, and making others feel stupid
- chastising and making others feel like outsiders
- controlling the situation by manipulating others
- emotional blackmail, making others feel guilty or rotten

> *People often make you feel bad to make themselves feel good.*

You may have been subjected to this behavior for reasons that had nothing to do with you. Or, you may have some physical characteristic that made you an easy target for someone like this to exploit for their own self-interest. If you have the misfortune of being made to feel small, stupid, or rotten, realize what the person is doing and why. If you accept their treatment, you have helped them accomplish their own selfish goals. They have won at your expense. Such people often forget about the incident, while the victim remembers it for the rest of his or her life. If you let it, the perpetrator wins at your expense *indefinitely.*

Sometimes our peers put us down. They want to be the "coolest" or the most popular, whether children or adults. Putting you down may have helped them achieve their goal by making them look witty, cool, or smart.

Sometimes authority figures put you down. They have their own ideas about what's right and wrong, and you may not have complied with their expectations. They make judgements about you to support their own opinions of what is right. Authority figures may be teachers, principals, police, or bosses. However, just because they're in a position of authority does not make them right or smart. They're simply in a position to use their authority to make their opinions prevail or to persuade others to believe as they do.

However, parents, peers, and authority figures are in no position to render judgements of you and your worth. Everyone on Earth has his or her flaws. Of all the people that I have ever met, *I cannot recall a single one who was an officially certified judge of character.* There is not a person alive who is truly qualified to render a judgement of your worth—except yourself.

> *People who judge you are seeking to elevate themselves at your expense.*

Don't let this happen.

Consider that all inputs you have received to this point in your life have been biased by what someone else believes is right. Yet no one is qualified to do so. You can discard all of their judgements about you and ways in which they treated you as inadmissible evidence, and therefore, irrelevant. To continue to give their biased and faulty opinions any credence, from this day forward, is working against your favor and completely unnecessary.

> *The negative feelings we have of ourselves are shaped by the unqualified and unsubstantiated opinions of others.*

Everyone's a Surgeon

Imagine that everyone who's important to you is a cosmetic surgeon. Imagine also that the surgery is relatively painless and that these people could do it right in the kitchen when you sit down for dinner or come to visit. So painless is it that you barely notice it while they're chatting with you. Because it's been going on all your life, you don't realize that you can refuse their services.

Each person you encounter has his or her own ideas about how your face should look so he or she gives your face a nip here, tuck there, etc., whatever they feel like doing at the moment. If they goof, oh well, it's not their face. They're not obligated to make repairs or even apologize.

Some manipulate your face with the very best of intentions, to make your face as beautiful as can be. Some do it just to amuse themselves and don't care about the results. Others do it with malicious intent, to make you look more horrible than they feel.

Imagine how your face would look with all these different people shaping it. Imagine looking in the mirror after all the well intended, indifferent, or malicious "artwork" people had done to your face.

Sound monstrous? It's *more* than monstrous because *it's true!* But it's not your face that these people have shaped, *it's your life!* No one ever said that the people important to you were any good at shaping your life, they just did it! And if they goofed, oh well, it's not their life. *It's yours!*

Your Core Belief

The result of all of this treatment over a lifetime is that we come to have a core belief about ourselves. We believe we have one or more major flaws—we see them in ourselves, whether or not anyone else can see them. We may believe that we are unlovable, unlikable, unable to make friends, unable to achieve, to win, to stay with a program, unintelligent, unattractive, or just unimportant in the world.

We may hide this belief and engage in activities that help us cover them up. Or, at the other extreme, we may tell our faults to everyone we meet in a cry for attention, acceptance, or help.

Whether or not we share our core belief about ourselves with others, we never forget it, and it is always very close to the surface. It haunts us like an unwanted ghost, always there, always bothering us, following us throughout our lives. We may go for days without thinking about it, but emotionally charged situations bring it right to the surface.

The closer that words and actions come to our core belief, the more painful it is. Even casual encounters, where someone accidentally focuses attention on our core belief, can make us feel embarrassed that someone has exposed our greatest flaw, and we feel small and worthless because of it.

Some react to this by laughing on the outside while hurting on the inside. Some become embarrassed and withdrawn. Some retaliate and throw insults back, with or without the façade of a "joke." Some react violently, seek revenge, or even kill.

Whatever your core belief, you can usually trace it to a specific reason. Chances are it had to do with how another person or persons interacted with you (or failed to interact with you). It is important to understand that the core belief you have of yourself comes from unreliable, self-interested, biased sources that are unqualified to render judgements of you. It was established on shaky evidence. Whatever it is you believe about yourself, your limitations, your faults, or your failings is up for question, and likely incorrect.

Recall that in the previous chapter I asked you to envision yourself floating in total blackness, just you and the universe. When devoid of everything else in the world, ask, "Am I good?" Again, setting aside everything else in the world, the answer is, "yes." You are good. You are a good and worthy creation, as good as any other.

The important question now becomes, "Why would you be anything less than a good creation?" You will quickly see that any explanation you might be able to come up with comes from the interactions you've had with other, unqualified, biased, self-serving people in your life.

Envision that these other people who have helped to shape you are also floating in their own voids and wondering about their own worth. They all walk around with that question in their hearts, "Am I good?" They are no better off than you. They are not qualified to render judgement of you, let alone make you feel that you are not a good and worthy creation.

You can choose to let the interactions with these people influence your life, or you can choose to discredit whatever influence they had on you. Are troubled people very credible when it comes to judging your worth? You can begin to change your core belief about yourself.

Don't let troubled people ruin your life.

Stop Nurturing Your Core Belief

Although the seeds of our core beliefs were planted long ago, we unknowingly continue to nurture them for the rest of our lives—that is, unless we take deliberate action to stop.

This core belief is like the suit of rags we come to find we're wearing. We've believed all along that this is all we deserved, or we can shake our ragged fists at the world and shriek, "Look at this suit of rags I'm forced to wear," so others feel pity for us. But we're still wearing the suit of rags.

We fret over the injustices of the past and spend too much time puzzling over why someone would hurt us so. We attempt to right the wrongs by telling everyone we know about it and the unfairness of it all. We secretly scheme about how we would seek revenge if we could.

While we dream of revenge and victory over those who have hurt us, *they continue to vanquish us!* Very likely they don't recall the event(s) nor are they interested in continuing to vanquish us. But we let them just the same by continually dwelling on the past. They continue to hurt us for years on end because we don't let go.

In her book *Fire Your Shrink!,* Dr. Michele Weiner-Davis explains how dwelling upon the reasons why you are the way you are is wasted time. She recalls her many patients who worked with her for years to understand how past events made them unhappy. After several years of therapy with little or no improvement in the condition of her patients, she made a tremendous discovery.

While it helps to understand what has made you the way you are, to dwell on it incessantly is expending energy on the wrong thing. You will never become happier by dwelling on past events that made you unhappy. Rather, she suggests taking action on something positive. You'll improve your life, build strength, and accomplish things of which you'll be proud. You'll be much happier, she suggests, *doing* rather than *dwelling.*

How do you shed the emotional baggage of your past?

Just let go! *Holding onto it continues to hurt you and does you no good!*

You may be reluctant to do so. You may believe that there are wrongs in your past that should be righted, injustices that need to be made just, or people with whom you should get even. Understand *that the past cannot be changed.* By letting go, you free yourself from the shackles you have continued to impose upon yourself. Revenge is not sweet, but freedom is!

> *Forgive those who have hurt you, not for their sake, but for your own.*

Define Who You Wish to Be

If you could recreate your life from scratch, how would you do it? It's not something we often think of. We can't possibly erase the past and how we got to where we are. But you can do something effective. You can redefine yourself from this point forward.

This exercise helps you to frame your goals and your self within the context of a story. After all, your life is truly a story that you are writing, either deliberately or passively, every day.

Until this time you may have been passively writing, allowing other characters to dictate how the story flows, how the main character (that's you) responds, and so on. But here you are in the midst of your own story.

This is where the fun begins. From now on, you get to write your story *however you wish!*

It's time to take control over your story and determine the outcome. It's time to stop being passive, allowing other people or circumstances to write your story. You decide how your story will end.

> *Your life is a story. Write it deliberately, not passively.*

Create Your Character

In this exercise, you get to create the main character of your story however you like. If you're not completely satisfied with who you are, create a character that is exactly who and what you wish to be. Act like the character you create and you will become that character.

Many actors who play the same role for years often become, at least in part, the characters they play. Their minds become so accustomed to thinking like the character, how the character would behave and respond, that it becomes natural even when they're not playing the part.

A close friend of mine had lived a tormented life as a child. In her mid-teens, she amazingly came up with this approach on her own. She created a character, defined how the character would behave, dress, walk, talk, everything, even adopting the name of her character. When a troubling situation arose, she would ask herself how her character would respond, and she'd have the right answer. Needless to say, she went on to become very successful, an inspiration to and well liked by thousands upon thousands in her community (and, yes, all without a college degree).

> *Discard what others have created of you*
> *and craft a "you" that you genuinely like.*

Now, describe the main character of your story. It's not important that this character be free from faults. Even in the best novels, the main characters have faults, thereby making them human. Also, be sure to discard the "shoulds" and "can'ts" that have been imposed on you over a lifetime. This is your chance to create a character with complete freedom from the demands and expectations of other people.

Think about your main character's story, that is, what's the brief background, the way the character came to be, etc. You don't have to write it down now as it would likely be very extensive. But think about it. Describe the background as you might read it in a novel.

Just for fun, it might help to come up with a name befitting your character.

What is your main character's name (again, just for fun)?

_____

What does your main character look like?

_____

_____

_____

What does your main character do for a living?

_____

How does your main character view life?

_____

_____

What pleasures does your main character derive from life?

_____

_____

_____

_____

How do other people regard your main character?

_____

_____

What is the critical goal that your main character is to accomplish in his/her lifetime?

_____

_____

_____

What is the most important or interesting aspect of your main character, something a reader of your story should really know? This aspect of your main character will help him/her prevail when things look darkest.

_____

_____

What is the primary challenge to your main character in achieving the goal?

_____

_____

_____

What other challenges does your main character face in pursuit of the goal?

_____

_____

_____

_____

Develop Likeable Characteristics

Everyone wants to like the main character of a story. Doubtless, you want to like the main character of *your* story. When faced with troubles in your daily life, ask yourself how your very likeable main character would respond. Envision yourself at a typewriter or computer, crafting and planning how the main character acts, responds, and behaves.

In this exercise, circle or highlight the statements you want to be true of the main character in your story. Cross out or put a line through the statements you don't want to be true of your main character. Leave the undesirable statements legible so that you can still see them.

Remember to identify traits that will make you like and cheer for the main character of your story!

"My main character muddles about every day, wasting his life."

> "My main character is self-directed and actively works towards a goal."

"My main character easily gets depressed and mopes around feeling sorry for herself."

> "My main character actively fights off negative moods and defeated feelings."

"My main character whines and complains a lot."

> "My main character focuses energy on those things he can change."

"My main character's feelings get easily hurt or she reads insult into many situations."

> "My main character shows strength, picks her battles, not allowing pettiness to interfere with the pursuit of her goal."

"My main character seeks approval from others, acts needy, and fishes for compliments."

> "My main character accepts who he is, is self-confident, and free from needing to be propped up."

"My main character derives her sense of worth from the opinions of others, such as a spouse or parents."

> "My main character takes control and defines her own sense of self-worth."

"My main character derives his sense of worth from posses-sions or a job title."

"My main character derives a sense of worth from knowing his own strengths and positive qualities."

"My main character continually beats herself up with or reminds others of her negative qualities."

"My main character allows for negative qualities and does-n't let them overshadow her positive strengths."

"My main character must establish his value with others by telling everyone about things he has done, or about how smart he is."

"My main character feels no need to prove anything to any-one else as he is above letting the petty judgements of oth-ers affect him."

"When my main character is hurt or insulted in some way by an antagonist, she expends a good deal of energy to think about getting even."

"When my main character is hurt or insulted in some way by an antagonist, she lets it slide off her back, and saves her energy for moving forward on her own pursuits."

"My main character lets both big and small obstacles cause her to quit."

"My main character knows that obstacles are inevitable and faces them boldly, overcomes them, and never quits."

"My main character is convinced that past failures means he is a failure as a person."

"My main character knows the number of successes is pro-portional to the number of attempts, and that failures are merely a part of attempting to succeed."

Continue this exercise on a separate piece of paper. If you have a computer and can type easily, take the time to write up a full description of your character. Write as much descriptive detail as you like. Craft a character that you genuinely like and want to cheer for. Have fun with it. The more you embellish, the more fun you will have.

Read what you've written from time to time to remind yourself of what it is you want to be.

> *Think and act like the character you create*
> *and that is who you will become.*

Think Like a Successful Person

The past is what has shaped you as a person. The past is what defines what you *believe* to be your limitations and what you can accomplish. However, those who have shaped you were unqualified, biased, and self-serving.

The impressions you have of yourself, your limitations, and your inabilities are founded upon false information. You very likely have far fewer limitations and far more abilities than you had suspected.

Many people who are successful deliberately choose to reject what others try to define of them and choose to define themselves. You can make that choice too. Take control and free yourself from the self-imposed shackles of your past.

You may not be able to change the events of the past, but you have the ability to stop them from controlling your present.

Create a character exactly like the person you desire to be. Think and act like the character and that is exactly who you will become.

ROADBLOCK 4

"I just know I'll run into a ditch. I always run into a ditch."

Retrofitting Thought Processes

It's easy to let yourself believe that the abilities you have (or lack), your limitations, and chances in life have already been set in stone based on your experiences so far. If you don't change the way in which you think, they might as well be set in stone.

It's now time to learn how your mind works to create your belief system, to learn to control your thinking so that it helps you, rather than harms you. You'll learn how to stop beating yourself up a thousand times over negative incidents in your past. You'll change this chapter's title into "I may have run into a ditch before, but now I know what to look out for so I'll never do it again."

Seldom are we taught about how our thought processes operate. So, we think in haphazard ways, and thus allow our own random ways of thinking to harm us indefinitely. Those who learn to control their thinking master their lives, and those who don't suffer at their own hands (so to speak).

However, you can gain control over the way you think. It may seem hard at first, just like any other discipline, but it can be learned.

It has been estimated that people have some 65,000 thoughts per day. For many the vast majority of these thoughts are negative and self-critical. It's a free-for-all of negative thought and there's been no restrictions, no control. It's time to change all that.

Battleships and airplanes periodically go through a process called "retrofitting" in which old technology is replaced with the latest equipment. This allows both the military and commercial airlines to adapt and stay current. In effect, retrofitting results in a "new craft" even though the body of the craft is several years, sometimes decades old.

In a similar way, you are able to retrofit yourself by replacing old ways of undisciplined, detrimental thinking with new ways of thinking which are beneficial to you. In effect, you can become a "new person" even though your body is several years, sometimes decades old.

In this chapter we're going to discuss new ways of thinking that are quite simple and can help you dramatically towards your goal of achieving success in your life. You'll learn how to take something that you already do every day, alter it slightly, and become a stronger person.

Begin thinking like a successful person and you'll begin behaving like a successful person. If how you've been thinking until now hasn't paid off, it's time to open your mind to new ways of thinking.

How the Brain Works

What follows is not intended to be a doctoral thesis in psychology or physiology, just a simple representation of your thought processes that you can grasp and learn to control.

The brain is the least understood organ of the human anatomy, mostly in that it's difficult to see it operating. Many gains have been made in recent decades in our understanding of the human brain, but it still remains a mystery. For example, some estimate that we use only 3 percent of the brain's potential, others estimate 10 percent. How anyone determines the full potential is beyond me. The truth is, even the experts are still uncertain, guessing, and they frequently contradict one another.

How much of our brain's potential we use is irrelevant. What we've managed to accomplish with what we do use is incredible. What should be most significant to you is that your brain is nearly identical to that of all humans on the planet. You possess the same organ which has accomplished every other great thing that mankind has ever achieved. You have the very same gift, the most powerful force in the world, second only to nature, resting between your ears! The only thing that separates you from those who have achieved great things is what goes on inside your brain, that is, how and what you think.

Daniel Goleman in *Emotional Intelligence* gives a great, if extensive and technical, description of how your mind operates. Here is a brief adaptation of his explanation. Once you begin to understand the thinking process, you'll be better equipped to learn discipline and control of your thought processes.

Your Conscious Mind

Your conscious mind is what is enabling you to read this book right now. It is the active, thinking, reasoning part of your brain. It thinks in words and pictures, and interprets the meaning of all the inputs you receive.

It's estimated that your conscious mind thinks at roughly 600 to 1,000 words per minute. What's unfortunate about this fact is when we have a negative belief about ourselves, the conscious mind will express negative thoughts hundreds or thousands of times a day. When it receives new inputs and interprets them in a negative fashion, it will continually repeat the new negative thoughts.

You need only have a negative experience once, but your conscious mind will replay that negative incident thousands and thousands of times for the rest of your life. Little incidents that had a negative impact on you can haunt you for life. They may have taken only a second or two to occur, but they live forever in our minds and color our lives from that moment forward—if you let them.

What's most important is how your conscious mind gives meaning to the inputs it receives.

Your Subconscious Mind

Your subconscious mind never rests. It is what keeps your heart going, your lungs breathing, and your digestive system working. It also hears, sees, touches, tastes, and smells everything, and it's all recorded forever. It is a vast store of all your life experiences, information, and thoughts. The subconscious mind has many functions that you utilize every day. The two aspects of the subconscious mind I'll illustrate here are the recall mechanism and the automatic pilot.

The recall mechanism

If your conscious mind hears an old song, your subconscious mind will retrieve the lyrics for you. If you go to visit your parents, your subconscious will recall how you're supposed to behave around them (almost against your will). Visit your childhood environment and your subconscious will recall the feelings and memories from that time. Smell familiar perfumes, foods, or anything from times past, and your subconscious will recall the memories associated with that sense. Hear familiar sounds, such as a particular telephone ring, alarm clock buzzer, or other distinctive sounds, and you'll be reminded of everything around the original sounds.

The recall mechanism, in effect, retraces the neural pathways until it finds the location of the same or similar information in your memory. It then dredges back all the other memories, sights, and sounds that happen to be in the same area.

What's critically important to understand at this point is that not only does your subconscious mind dredge up memories, but also the meanings and emotions stored with those memories. The ability to recall memories and emotions based on a single stimulus is both a blessing and a curse. Sometimes the meanings and emotions are good, sometimes not so good. The smell of snow in the air may bring back childhood memories of play, sledding, and snow forts with siblings and friends. Hearing an old song may remind you of feelings of romance or good times with friends in high school, and make you long for the "good old days."

This ability can remind us of negative incidents as well. Sounds, sights, smells, and situations can each trigger the automatic recall of times of crisis, fear, alarm, or great sorrow. However, it's not always the recall of dramatic incidents that hurt us most. We tend to put up barriers and block certain painful memories. It's the subtly negative memories that come through without opposition, time after time, year after year that affect us most.

It is not the memory that affects us so, it's the meaning and emotion stored with the memory.

The automatic pilot

The subconscious mind is great at taking over the automatic, routine activities, but is terrible at spotting and interpreting new inputs. For example, our subconscious mind drives our cars for us and we give the task very little conscious thought. But if we left the task entirely up to our subconscious minds, we'd be in a wreck for sure. Our conscious mind must intercept new inputs, such as someone in traffic slamming on the brakes, cutting us off, or approaching a stop sign. After the conscious mind has experienced these situations and determined the appropriate response many times, they too are incorporated into our automated pilot system.

What's important to understand here is that often times the automatic pilot will automatically assign a meaning to an input without your consciously having to think about it. For example, the image of a stop sign is automatically interpreted to mean "stop" (or at least slow down for a quick glance).

The Reticular Activating System

Your reticular activating system is located at the stem of your brain. It is densely packed with brain cells. In fact, it is estimated that 70 percent of your brain's 200 billion cells are contained in just the stem alone.

The role that the reticular activating system plays is to filter out all stimuli except that which is important to you. It's estimated that your brain receives over one million inputs per second from your five senses. With this flood of information, the reticular activating system screens it all out and only draws the important inputs to your conscious mind's attention.

To take in and process the input from all five senses would result in sensory overload. If you were merely to pay attention to the constant contact of clothing on your body you'd go crazy. How do you suppose you're able to tune out all the surrounding noises on a Sunday afternoon so you can read a book or watch a movie?

Have you ever bought a new car that suddenly appeals to you? The next thing you know, you're seeing that kind of car everywhere. They were there all along, but you just paid no attention to them or did not notice how common they were.

Have you ever slept through a thunderstorm? Yet, when your tiny little digital watch alarm goes off, you immediately wake up.

Your reticular activating system has been operating all these years, but you just took it for granted. You may have never stopped to think about it or even realize that it had a name.

It doesn't just tune out or focus on visual or audible inputs, but on thoughts and ideas as well. If you've had negative feelings about yourself or the world, your reticular activating system has been working against you. It screens out all the positive things and draws your attention to the negative things that support your feelings and views.

However, as you start to focus on new, more positive things, your reticular activating system will begin to work *for* you. Once you establish that you're on the lookout for certain opportunities, all of a sudden you'll start seeing them everywhere. Chances are they were there all along, but you tuned them out before. All you need do is establish something as important to you. Your reticular activating system will zero in on any and all things related to your goals.

The Construction of a Belief System

Here's how the three components of the mind work together to build your belief system. First, a quick review.

Your conscious mind processes inputs and interprets meanings.

Your subconscious mind stores and retrieves memories, as well as meanings and emotions associated with memories. The subconscious mind also takes care of certain routine tasks automatically without the conscious mind having to do much work.

Your reticular activating system filters out all inputs that are unimportant to you.

Throughout your life you continually accumulate new inputs. Your conscious mind processes them, then assigns a meaning (and sometimes an emotion) to each input.

The subconscious mind stores away the input, meaning, and emotions together.

As new inputs pass through the reticular activating system, the subconscious mind retrieves similar events, along with meanings and any associated emotions.

As the conscious mind processes the new input, it compares it with what the subconscious mind has dredged up. The conscious mind will either create a new meaning for the new input, or determine that the new input is so much like the old memory, it must mean the same thing.

Once the meaning of the new input has been determined, it stores the input, the meaning, and any associated emotions away.

Unless the new input has a clearly identified new meaning and emotion at the time of occurrence, it is very likely that it will get stored away with the meanings and emotions of similar memories. The retrieved meaning and emotions are reinforced, further strengthening your beliefs.

When the apparent meaning of the new input contradicts what the subconscious mind has dredged up, the conscious mind has to do some more work. Sometimes the conscious mind figures the new meaning is wrong or untrue and stores the new input that way.

If the apparent meaning of the new input contradicts past experience a great deal, the conscious mind must work extra hard to interrogate it. It may take the easy way out and simply label the apparent meaning of the new input as blatantly wrong or untrue. Or, it may work harder to dissect the new input, find evidence that supports past experience, and label the new input as false because of that one piece of evidence. Sometimes, the conscious mind is presented with new evidence which further supports the apparent meaning of the new input. Even though it may contradict meanings of similar events of the past, the new meaning is assigned anyway.

A common example of this your belief in God, ghosts, or aliens. When you believe one way, little bits of evidence will not likely sway your belief. However, if you have something overwhelming occur, you may be forced to change your beliefs.

The courtroom of your mind

Whew! That was a lot to chew on. So let's use an illustration to help you better understand, as well as to help you remember this stuff for the rest of your life. Let's assign each of the functions described a personality. As I describe them, try to picture each one as vividly as possible to cement them into your memory.

Imagine a courtroom scene (without a jury), and the important people in it. There's a judge, a bailiff, a law librarian, and a clerk.

The conscious mind is the judge with a stern disposition, black flowing robe, gavel (and, like a real judge, is wearing no pants under that robe). The judge gathers information, weighs the evidence, and makes a ruling about the meanings of cases (events and inputs).

The subconscious mind is the law librarian with cat-eye glasses on a chain, sweater over the shoulders, hair in a bun. The librarian stores and retrieves information. The librarian, however, is mute. The librarian never says a word about the truth or validity of the information or meanings. The librarian just stores and retrieves cases and finding (memories and meanings).

The reticular activating system is the bailiff who guards the door, lets in and announces the cases. The bailiff is big, strong, and doesn't allow any fooling around. The only things that get into the courtroom are the important cases when it's their time.

The automatic pilot aspect of the subconscious mind is the

courtroom clerk. The clerk is great at following instructions and handling routine cases, but calls up the judge when a tough case comes along.

The scene opens with the bailiff letting into the courtroom a case (an event or input). The judge takes a brief look at the case, tells the law librarian, "Go get me anything like this case." The law librarian scurries off to the law library (the catacombs of your mind), eventually bringing back similar cases, as well as the rulings on those cases. The judge looks at the old cases, then at the new one. If the new case is similar enough to the old cases, it makes a ruling similar to those of the past. Case closed.

"Librarian, store this case, its ruling, and all that historical information away," the judge directs. The librarian diligently scurries off.

The bailiff lets in the next and the courtroom goes through the same process. The process is repeated, minute after minute, day after day. It becomes routine and tiresome for the judge, so the judge gets the courtroom clerk to stand in while the judge takes a break. The clerk does a great job of handling the routine caseload let in by the bailiff. But if there's anything new or significant, by all means, the judge is brought back into the courtroom to weigh the evidence of the new case.

On a particularly hard case where there's no similar historical information, the judge must work hard to determine the ruling.

If a particular case comes in where the input is said to mean one thing, but the historical information is the opposite, the judge must work extra hard to hash out the evidence.

Sometimes the judge gets lazy. When there are a lot of historical cases similar to a new case, the judge doesn't bother to hash it out, and just gives the new case a similar ruling. Such sloppiness means that if the ruling is negative, the library of related cases associated with that negative ruling keeps growing and growing. Some negative rulings have so many cases associated with them that they become galvanized beliefs. Any new case can quickly be improperly ruled and condemned due to the sloppy system.

Another example

It is easy to see how seemingly small, insignificant events from our past can become hard and fast beliefs about ourselves that we steadfastly hold onto. Let's say that you joined the choir in fourth grade. At that time the music teacher listened to all the students individually to determine the vocal range of each student. The music teacher came to you and asked you to sing "Twinkle Twinkle Little Star." However, let's say the music teacher was scary, made you nervous, and you choked! Your voice came out ragged and squeaky.

The music teacher declared, "Why, you can't sing at all! Your voice is terrible! I tell you what, dear, you just mouth the words." Terribly embarrassed, you comply all the way through each practice until the recital is over.

From that innocent little mistake, you take the word of this authoritative figure, believe that you cannot sing and that your voice is terrible. The next time someone tells you to sing, say at a birthday party, rather than risk embarrassment, you simply mouth the words. Due to a combination of nervousness, fear of embarrassment, and the lack of practice, you never give your singing voice any chance whatsoever. You grow into an adult believing that you cannot sing at all, and you're terribly embarrassed to even think of singing. Even if someone happens to catch you singing and tells you that you have a good voice, you're likely to think they were just being nice to you! You'd become embarrassed all over again and wonder why someone would tell you such a silly thing.

This is, in fact, how you come to believe other limitations about yourself. The seed event may have been traumatic, or it may have been an innocent comment. But gone unchecked, it becomes part of your belief system and a genuine limitation—or does it?

Rewriting Your Past

It is possible to rewrite your past. I don't mean to change the events of the past—that's impossible. However, you can rewrite the meanings associated with the events of the past. It's a simple process, and vast amounts of your past can be re-written in short order.

Interpreting Events

Deepak Chopra describes in *The Higher Self* how there are two worlds that exist for us. There is the world that exists whether you and I are here or not, all the people, history, countries, wars, inventions, family, etc. This is the world around us over which we have no influence. The other world that exists for us is all in how we *interpret* the world around us. In this world we have complete control. We can look at how something exists and give it meaning.

Events have no meaning except the meaning you give them.

A single event can have multiple interpretations and each one of them is true to the person interpreting the event.

A rainy day can have different meanings and interpretations depending on if you're from Chicago, the North Pole, Seattle, or the Mojave Desert. No matter what interpretation you give to a rainy day, it will be true!

A swimming pool may mean fun or fear depending on whether you can swim or not. There is no right or wrong way to interpret the meaning of a swimming pool. Either way, the interpretation is true!

There is no right or wrong interpretation of any event. Interpretations are neither true nor false. Interpreting an event any one way versus any other is equally valid.

The only thing that makes an interpretation of an event *seem* true or false is the meanings you've given similar events in your past (emphasis on the "you've given").

The same can be said for those very same events in your past upon which you're basing interpretations of present events. And what determined the meanings you've given to events of the past were meanings of similar events from further in your past. The foundation of these meanings were often handed to you by parents, siblings, other children, neighbors, authority figures and so on. If the meanings they gave to events were false, biased, self-serving, misinformation, or flat out lies, then what does it say about the basis for your interpretations of present events?

Very often the belief that we have about ourselves, whether positive or negative, seems very solid, as if set in stone and unshakably true. However, the beliefs that you have of yourself, especially the negative beliefs, may very well be a vast web of falsehoods based on falsehoods! This web has been woven entirely by the situations, environments, and other people in your life. Had you been born in an entirely different set of circumstances, with different parents, siblings, surroundings, done different things during your growth, you would, almost without question, be a different person. The web of beliefs would have been woven in a completely differently way. If the web of beliefs were different, the interpretation you give any present day event would be different.

To test this, take a moment to envision what it would be like to have been brought up under completely different circumstances. If you were brought up poor, envision a family of wealth. If your parents were not so good, envision very caring, nurturing parents. If you grew up on the East Coast, envision living on the West Coast. If you had few friends, envision lots of friends. If you were in a big family, envision being an only child. If you were an only child, envision a big family. If your siblings were not particularly nice, envision cooperative, nurturing siblings. If you traveled around a lot as a military child, envision growing up in one place where you knew everyone all your life.

Had your circumstances been entirely different, what kind of person do you suppose you would be? Would you have a different set of beliefs about yourself? With a different foundation to your belief system, would you interpret events differently? What if you had grown up in a radically different culture in a foreign land? Would your interpretations be just as true? It's no wonder no two people see things exactly the same way!

The key here is to realize that if your circumstances have woven your current web of beliefs about yourself, and, given different circumstance you'd believe differently, then what you believe about yourself is not set in stone! You are not helpless to change who you are and what you believe of yourself!

More importantly, the way in which you interpret events is completely up to you! Interpreting events one way simply because they agree with your own set of circumstantial beliefs *does not make them any more true!*

There is no right or wrong interpretation of events. You can interpret an event anyway that you choose and it will be just as true as any other.

If the source of the meanings given your past events is flawed, then the meanings may be flawed as well.

The limitations you think you have are based entirely on circumstantial interpretations.

The abilities you think you lack are based entirely on circumstantial interpretations.

Everything about you is open to reinterpretation!

Interpretations in your favor and against

As discussed above, interpreting an event any one way versus any other is equally true. It may seem false because of the contradiction with meanings associated with similar, historical events. However, the meanings given past events may be faulty.

The key is to learn to interpret events, not in accordance with historical information, but *in your favor*.

If you choose to interpret an event in your favor, it is true. If you interpret an event against your favor, it is equally true. So why not choose to interpret an event in your favor?

When you interpret anything, ask yourself two very important questions.

Whom does my interpretation benefit?

Whom does my interpretation hurt?

When you interpret events in your favor, you benefit yourself and become stronger. When you interpret events against your favor, you hurt yourself and become weaker.

Remember the judge, librarian, and so on? Well, you can persuade the judge to make the rulings in your favor. You're not asking the judge to do something wrong, mind you, since a ruling any one way is just as valid as ruling another. The judge may be reluctant. The judge is used to always ruling in accordance with similar cases and rulings of the past. But lean on the judge a bit more. Convince the judge that the rulings of the past were flawed, and that it would be unconscionable to turn a blind eye and continue to rule in the same way out of practice. So persuade the judge to make rulings in your favor for the benefit of all. Doing so is not unprincipled, wrong, or indecent.

This may sound like a frivolous exercise. However, interpreting events in your favor will *yield immediate benefits* and instill in you considerable power. And, with repeated use, it will eventually make your dreams become reality.

> *Interpret events, not in accordance with events of the past, but always in your favor.*

Again, your mind automatically interprets events so as to be consistent with meanings of similar, historical events. This does not mean that it's the truth.

You can dictate the meaning an event has! Rather than merely wishing and hoping an event has a meaning favorable to you, demand and dictate a meaning that is favorable to you. Such a meaning will be as equally accurate as a meaning that is unfavorable to you.

Here's an example. Let's say that your boss calls you an idiot.

Envision yourself interpreting this factual event against your favor. You believe he's correct and agree that you are an idiot. You mope around recalling all the times when you've done something stupid. You openly admit to others that you're an idiot. Everyone else begins to agree then treat you like an idiot.

How does it feel? Stinks, doesn't it? Whom does it help and whom does it hurt?

Now, envision yourself interpreting this factual event *in* your favor. You believe your boss is incorrect. You're not an idiot. He's a jerk! You get angry and huff around recalling all the times when you were smart, even brilliant, and he was a jerk. Hurtful words come from a troubled soul, you remember. You've convinced yourself and everyone else that you're not an idiot and no one dares treat you like one. If they do, watch out!

How do you feel? Pretty good, huh? Whom does it help and whom does it hurt?

You can apply this same principle to absolutely every situation.

It may take some practice at first. You may feel like you're defying the truth. Your mind has been interpreting events in a certain pattern for so long, that to interpret an event any differently may seem like a lie. Your mind is naturally inclined to keep consistent with how you have always viewed the world.

To begin changing into a stronger person, it's imperative that you interpret events in the way a strong, directed person would. If you want to be a successful person, you have to think like a successful person.

Don't hope that the event has a meaning favorable to you!

Don't wish that a favorable meaning you give an event is *really* true.

Demand that the meaning you give an event be true. It is true! It's as true as an unfavorable meaning.

Don't wait for others to agree with the meaning you give an

event. The interpretation others have of an event will be *biased* and is no better than your own. *They're not gods!* They view the world through glasses colored by their own, imperfect self-images.

Dictate the meaning you want to give each and every event. By doing so, you'll derive incredible power, both at that instant, and over time. This power adds up, and you become more powerful each time you use it. *You will have control over your world!*

Practice sessions in interpretation

Scenario 1: You get fired from a job you didn't particularly like.

Interpreting against your favor: *"I'm a failure! I can't even keep this lousy job!"*

In your favor: *"I'm glad to be done with that lousy job. This will force me to go out and get something I really like."*

What emotions and thoughts are likely to follow each of these interpretations? Which would give you more power?

Scenario 2: You get fired from a job you like.

Against your favor: *"I just can't win! Even when I get a job I really like, I can't hold it. I must be an idiot. I don't think I'll ever be able to get a job as good as that one again."*

In your favor: *"Wow! I didn't see that coming! What could have caused this? Was it something I did? If so, I won't make that mistake anymore. Was it corporate politics? Was it just downsizing? What can I learn from this situation that will help me avoid it in the future? What strengths can I take from this job to help me get an even better job?"*

Scenario 3: One of your parents calls you an embarrassment and a disappointment.

Against your favor: *"I am a loser. I can never seem to do anything right. I've even let my parents down."*

In your favor: *"I'm not a loser. It's too bad for you that I chose to become what I want instead of what you want. I'm not on this earth to live up to your expectations."*

Does either interpretation seem any more true and correct than the other? It's crucial that you interpret events in your favor. Doing so will make you stronger and propel you toward your goals.

Interpreting them against you will make you weaker, discourage you, and steer you away from your goals.

Building a library of strength

Here's where you can truly begin to rewrite your past, and not just one event at a time, but in huge hoards. You can rewrite volumes just as easily as you interpret current events.

As described before, a case comes into the courtroom. The judge sends the librarian to retrieve similar events, and the librarian comes back with a bunch of cases and rulings, that is, memories, meanings, and emotions. Since we've persuaded the judge to make rulings in our favor, the judge can not only make a ruling in our favor on the current case, but also overturn or rewrite the rulings of the past events.

Remember the swimming pool? A pool can mean fun or fear depending on whether or not you can swim. Let's say that you fear pools because you never learned to swim. You approach a pool at a friend's house or at a party, and instantly you begin to tense up. Your mind recalls all the other times you've been close to a pool and in fear, even how others tried to coax you in but you refused. This time, however, someone promises you $10,000 to get into the pool. Ten grand is pretty persuasive, so you hesitantly agree to get in the shallow end. Just then, a professional swimming instructor gets in, teaches you to dog paddle, float, do the side stroke, and so on.

Pretty soon you're a regular fish having a good old time. After hours of frolic and a nasty sunburn, you get out, all excited, and tell your friends, "That was fun! And all these years I've been afraid of pools. I guess I won't be from now on!" All of your memories get rewritten with a new meaning and emotion. Pools are no longer interpreted as danger and fear, but fun and excitement.

A good time to practice rewriting your past is when you've got some quiet time to yourself. When you're lying down to go to sleep, commuting, in the shower, waiting for the bus, recall the times when you've felt hurt by others. Change the feelings of inferiority or shame that you may have experienced during those incidents and rewrite them. Change the meaning of the situations. They were caused by troubled people and not because something was wrong with you. Then store those memories back with the new meanings.

Visualization

Visualization, simply put, is directed daydreaming. Daydreaming by itself is the aimless drifting of your mind over fanciful things. Directed daydreaming, however, takes a bit more discipline, but not much. It can help you actually achieve your goals.

When I was introduced to visualization, it seemed ridiculous to me, or at least some aspects. I was told, if you want wealth, envision wealth. If you want a fancy car, envision a fancy car. If you want something, envision it and it will all come true. It sounded too magical, and I was skeptical, to say the least.

Then I started reading more and more about visualization as a mental rehearsal for upcoming events. I learned about clinical tests that showed how visualization helped athletes practice their sport. It has proved useful for competitive athletes, and it can be for the rest of us as well.

You see, the subconscious mind does not differentiate between reality and fantasy. If I suggest that you envision a neon yellow elephant, your conscious mind will envision it, and your subconscious mind will store it away. Two days from now, if you saw a reference to a neon yellow elephant, you'd likely recall that you'd imagined that before (what's also interesting is that you would likely recall where you were and what you were doing, thinking, and feeling when you first heard it). The subconscious mind just files things away, and dredges them up when needed.

What visualization allows you to do is envision a desirable sort of setting, complete with sights, smells, sounds, tastes, the way things feel, as well as the meanings and emotions, then store that all away. By doing so, you're implanting experiences that you didn't even have, as well as the meanings and emotions of what ever you desire.

So let's take a look at how and why visualization works and why you might care to practice this very entertaining pastime.

Visualization Helps Redefine the Past

You've just seen how you are able to rewrite the meanings associated with certain memories of your past. As your subconscious mind brings memories up for review, you can assign new meanings, store them away, and forget about them for a while. The next time an input stimulates your subconscious mind to dredge up those memories again, you will have the rewritten meanings retrieved as well. Your conscious mind will have an easier time deciding the meaning of an input in your favor.

When you've got these memories up for review, there's no guarantee that you need only to say, "I'll just change the meaning. There, that's done." That's too simple, particularly if the memory is an especially hurtful one. Play with it, have fun, really mess with the characters in your memory. Do whatever you can to discredit the people involved. Do whatever you can to discredit the original meaning you had assigned to the memory. Insult the people in the memory, mock them, humiliate them, do what ever you'd like.

Why not? It's your memory.

Recall, if you can, a humiliating moment in your life where someone else intentionally embarrassed you, not just by accident, but with malice. Take a moment to actually do this. Good!

Now, you've got all the perpetrators involved in the memory. First, decide that they were jerks, fools, and buffoons. There must have been something terribly wrong with them to treat another human being like that. You just happened to be a convenient target at that particular moment, or you were the favorite to pick on. Hurtful words come from a troubled soul, and so do hurtful deeds. Agreed?

While you've got all these idiots assembled, strip their clothes off and watch them run around trying to cover up in embarrassment. Put balloon hats on their heads and big pink clown shoes on their feet. Make them squawk and flap their arms and cry pathetically. Make them act like the biggest fools in the world. What's important for the rewritten memory is that you come out on top. Done that? Good.

Now, tuck that memory away. The memory of them behaving like fools has effectively been stored along with the original, painful memory. The intent of the comical scene is to diminish the negative affect of the original memory.

Be sure to replay this comical scene as many times as you can remember to do so. Chances are you've played the hurtful scene in your mind a thousand times. There are many neural pathways to that memory that can be prompted by hundreds of different inputs. Replay the comical scene each time you can to make sure that it is very closely tied to the hurtful memory. Whenever another input triggers the painful memory, you'll retrieve the comical scene along with it.

You are not limited to making the scenes comical. If you feel someone should have been put in jail, envision them being shackled and flogged for their crimes, or what ever punishment you would like. It's your memory, so do with it what you will.

The most important thing is that you alter the meaning of whatever memories have shaped you in any negative way. Be sure to come out on top and victorious. Be as imaginative, creative, or extreme as you like to emphatically alter that meaning.

Visualization Prepares You for Goals

Visualization helps you rehearse. You can rehearse things you will say, ways that you will behave, and prepare for things that might come up. When the actual event occurs, you will be much more prepared, and the situation will be more inclined to go your way than if you hadn't rehearsed.

Let's say that the President of the United States stops by your house for lunch, unannounced, in a surprise photo opportunity to "relate to the people." You stumble and fumble about, trying to prepare lunch, completely uncertain of what to make, how to act, and how to deal with the situation. It's the first time you've ever experienced such an event and you're totally off kilter. Your mind has to spontaneously and frantically deal with all sorts of new inputs. It is completely unprepared and likely to make many mistakes.

However, if you were contacted months in advance by the secret service and told of the upcoming event, you could mentally rehearse the situation for months. You'd figure out how to prepare, consciously review all the possible inputs, imagine responses, and deal with potential problems.

Because of the certainty of the event, you will imagine everything with incredible detail.

"What will I do? How should I act?" You'd get together with the secret service to find out as much detail as you can about the sequence of events, times of arrival, what's to be done first, second, and so on all the way to the President's departure.

"What will I say?" You'd rehearse some witty conversations, pick topics to talk about, and review current events so you will come across as an informed and conscientious citizen. You'd find out what the President likes and dig up information on that. You'd find out what the President doesn't like and avoid those topics.

"What will I wear?" You'd try on several outfits, consider how they'd look on TV, and then adjust accordingly. You'd envision what kind of hair style you should have and get one.

"What will my house look like?" You'd consider how you would like it to look, then paint, prune shrubs, clean the yard, and so on so that it looks like an average American's home.

"What should I serve for lunch?" You'd try some of your favorite dishes, ask friends for their favorite recipes, and then try out each one until you got it perfected.

"Will my crazy neighbors embarrass me?" You'd probably tell them all what to do and not do, and in no uncertain terms!

By the time the President gets to your house, you will have rehearsed the event in your mind thousands and thousands of times in extremely vivid detail. You will have prepared everything so that it matches what you have envisioned. Provided nothing unexpected crops up, the actual experience will likely turn out very much like you envisioned. You will have envisioned every sensory detail, planned it out, and made it a reality.

Similarly, you can prepare for something other than the President's visit, like your own success. You can envision a point in your future, start with a simple picture of your goal, then determine all the details and how you wish them to be.

What will you be doing in your future? If you don't already know, at least start with a picture of having a goal, then spend time filling in the details. Plan on taking time to explore and discover what you like and don't like, what you can do to utilize your strengths, and where your weaknesses will not work against you.

How much money will you be making? Pick a number you like and don't be shy. The preparations you do will likely get you to whatever monetary point you set, so aim high.

What will you look like and what will you wear? What will others in your life be like and how will they treat you?

Imagine the settings and all the details. Smell the smells, hear the sounds, taste the tastes. Talk with the people, conduct yourself as someone in your position would. Even think of what you will think in that situation.

Don't let undesirable factors creep into your vision. If they do, plan on how you would react or how to prevent them from happening in the first place. *Try things out* to find out how they really are and adjust your plans accordingly.

Because of the certainty of achieving your goal, plan everything with incredible detail.

"But I don't know that my goal is a certainty," you might be saying.

Was there absolute certainty of the President's visit in the scenario above? Just because someone from the secret service said it would be so doesn't guarantee it will happen. Just because reporters come by to interview you and discover your background doesn't guarantee it will happen. There are just as many variables that could halt the President's visit as there are in preventing you from achieving your goals, even more so. An international incident might occur canceling the plans. War could break out, there could be a threat of assassination during the visit, another world figure could die and the President would have to attend the funeral. There are an infinite number of possibilities that could disrupt the President's visit, *but you'd prepare for it just the same!* The idea of the President visiting you and listening to what you had to say would be so thrilling that you'd work like never before to get ready, even without the guarantee.

Just the same, there is no guarantee that you will achieve your goals. But if you can envision the thrill of achieving your goals and prepare for them as if they were to actually become true, when the time comes, you'll be ready. Mentally rehearse how you'd act, what you'd say, what you would look like, what the surroundings would be, and what you'll be doing with such incredible detail, that it's almost guaranteed to happen.

In fact, every bit of preparation work you do will help to ensure that your goals become reality. In the President's visit scenario, anything you did would not increase the chances that the President would actually visit. But everything you do toward your goal will increase the chances that you'll actually achieve them.

Add to this the importance of visualizing things coming out *in your favor.* Don't make the mistake of rehearsing negative outcomes. When you're mentally rehearsing negative actions in your mind, your body may carry out exactly what was rehearsed. Play positive outcomes in your mind whenever possible to make sure your mind and body are well practiced at behaving in ways favorable to you.

Visualize a Path

The early books I read describing visualization failed to mention how to get from here to there. They didn't discuss how you must construct a logical and achievable path from where you are now to your goal.

As you begin to set goals, it's important that you don't just wish for a million dollars, you must plan and visualize a path toward that million dollars. This is actually quite easy to do as well as being fun.

Take your current situation and your goal, then visualize a logical and achievable path between the two points.

Here are some examples. Let's say that your goal is to become a millionaire. I'll describe two entry-level positions and how one could logically get from there to a million dollars.

Video rental clerk

- Tell the boss you'd eventually like to become an assistant manager. This automatically sets you apart as someone to count on.
- Ask for more hours. Volunteer to take other shifts when the slackers call in sick. Doing so demonstrates enthusiasm, which is priceless to any boss.
- Ask to learn important elements of the business, such as opening and closing the store, backing up computers, etc. Doing so ensures your job stability, makes you become the "go-to" person, and gives you experience with important tasks.
- Look for problems to solve. Identify them to your boss only after you've come up with a good solution. Keep track of all problems that you solve and what it means to the business, such as saving money, making more money, or more efficiency. These will be selling points for a promotion or getting a new job at another video store.

- Get a promotion, either at the same store or at another. Go for assistant manager, or manager. Use the experience and problems you've solved as your selling points.
- Study books on working with employees, customer service, basic accounting, etc. Volunteer for every business-related task, such as doing the books, leasing retail space or equipment, negotiating with repair people or contractors doing repairs.
- Develop relationships with anyone related to your business: video vendors, candy vendors, equipment vendors, bankers, and the owner of the store or franchise.
- Study any kind of industry trade journal that you can get your hands on. Knowing upcoming issues and discussing them with those in charge at your store will suggest that you are one of them.
- Put together a business plan of your own. Since you know the problems, practices, people associated with the business, and likely some areas where you can differentiate your own store, you'll have a unique selling proposition to pitch.
- Go into business for yourself. Use your unique selling proposition to attract customers away from the huge chains.
- As you start turning a profit, expand, expand, expand.

Receptionist

- Start by being absolutely pleasant and friendly with everyone who calls. Try to get to know them by name and voice. As you get to know callers to the business, begin asking about personal issues, such as family, hobbies, and things they do. Keep a notebook for this. Send cards for any special occasions. On a receptionist's pay, they will think you're a saint.
- Being on good terms with the people who call your business is the best internal advertising you can do. Immediately after talking with you, they talk to everyone in the business, including the president (depending on the size of the outfit). Every caller will tell their contact how great they think you are. Your reputation will precede you throughout the company, and people will gladly help you open doors in what ever department you wish.

- Let's say you're interested in marketing, putting together ad ideas, improving sales, going to trade shows, etc. Buy books on marketing, read them, bring them to work, leave them on your desk. Tell people who call in for anyone in marketing, "Oh, I'm hoping to get into marketing some day. I'm reading a book by so-and-so on such-and-such aspect of marketing." Word will get out that's your goal.
- Arrange meetings with anyone in marketing, even the VP. Discuss issues, ideas, and solutions you see to problems.
- Seek out any kind of job within the marketing department. Take even grunt work or tasks nobody else wants. Become the "go-to" person.
- Since you were receptionist, you know everyone in the organization (depending on the size), and very likely have contacts in other departments. This is invaluable information. One of the biggest problems any company has is the right hand not knowing what the left hand is doing. Keep in touch with others and what they're doing.
- Try your best to help your superiors look good with information; it's incredibly valuable.
- Create your own positions. Spend some time crafting a position you'd like to help solve a specific problem. Try to get the word "manager" in the title somewhere.
- Volunteer to participate in any committee you can. Doing so gives you more breadth of skills, exposure, contacts, and responsibility. Speak up in meetings with good points. Support others in their points.
- Study marketing techniques, disciplines, approaches, and the competition. Simply knowing what the competition is doing makes you priceless.
- After you've developed a good deal of experience in marketing, either go to work for a marketing firm, or consult to others in your business.
- Start your own marketing firm that caters to a specific niche.

In both of these examples, it's easy to see a logical and realistic progression from one position to the next. They don't seem all that monumental, do they? You don't necessarily have to work 80 hours a week, either. Spend some time studying areas of interest to you or that will help you solve specific problems.

The crucial component is to have a goal and a plan to get there. Continually visualize making these steps, and alter them when circumstances arise.

Think Like a Successful Person

Your future is not imprisoned by your past. You can change the entire direction of your future simply by desiring it and following up with action.

Capitalize on how your mind already works. Make your thought processes work for you to reconstruct the past and build a library of strength.

All events in your life can be interpreted in any number of ways. Learn to interpret events in your favor, rather than against your favor. Interpreting events in your favor helps you and hurts no one. Interpreting events against your favor hurts you and helps no one.

Utilize visualization to reconstruct your past. Recall hurtful situations and turn them to your favor. Use exaggeration to emphasize the new meanings you wish to assign to past events.

Utilize visualization to rehearse and prepare for favorable outcomes of upcoming events. When the event actually occurs, you'll be better prepared and the outcome will likely be in your favor.

Utilize visualization to paint a pathway to your own success. Plan all the steps between you and your goal.

ROADBLOCK 5

"Just
what really is
under my
hood?"

Untapped Potential

People underutilize their abilities because they are unaware of the true power that they possess. They act as though they're driving broken-down junkers when they're really in the driver's seat of the finest luxury, off-road vehicle (pick your favorite make and model), able to drive at high speeds, in all terrain, and in any kind of weather. They're driving at a self-imposed 20mph speed limit when they can really go 160mph with just a little bit of tuning. This chapter is a few pages out of the "owner's manual" on the power of being a human being.

I've already asked you to examine events of your past, and to challenge the validity of any negative impressions you've come to have about yourself, your limitations, and your abilities. In chapter 3, I suggested that you create a character for a story. You might have felt that it was just a fun little exercise in pure fantasy because you feel you could never live up to the perfections of the character you created.

So many people come to believe that they can do nothing when assessing their own personal historical information. They believe that their potential is limited to what little they have accomplished so far.

You too may feel that you just don't have the "special something" that would enable you to achieve. This couldn't be further from the truth.

Envision a stack of new batteries sitting on a shelf. You know they possess power, even though you don't see electrical sparks, or see them demonstrating their power, say, by lighting a flashlight. How do you know they have this untapped power? Because you've seen other batteries just like them light up flashlights, power toys, and radios.

You are much like that stack of new batteries on the shelf. You may not be currently demonstrating your power, but you possess it just the same. How do I know you have this untapped power? Because we have all seen others just like you achieve incredible things. Genetically speaking, you are 99.9% identical to every other human being on this planet. If they can achieve great things, so can you.

As a human being you have incredible powers that separate you from all other creatures in the world. The time to pursue your dreams and achieve great things has never been better in the history of humankind, nor have the opportunities and resources ever been more plentiful and readily available.

In this chapter we're going to look at just how much potential you have, what opportunities and resources are available to you, and what is potentially holding you back.

The Commonality You Possess

You possess the very same organs, no more, and fewer only due to surgery, as all other human beings. Your internal organs are nearly identical, except for relative size. In his State of The Union Address in January 2000, President Clinton related how a geneticist who visited him at the White House told him that, genetically speaking, we are 99.9% the same.

Your external appearance is different, and everyone is a unique individual. But apart from external differences, you are nearly identical, internally at least, to every other human being. That means you are nearly identical to all those who have achieved great things, built fortunes, empires, and monuments. Internally you are nearly identical to those who moved mountains or moved the masses.

Between your ears rests the most powerful force on the planet, second only to nature—your brain. If you were to take your brain, put it on a card table with that of Abraham Lincoln, Albert Einstein, a tribesman from a remote jungle, and Bill Gates, richest man in the world, shuffle them around like shells in a shell game, you would not be able to tell the difference. Your brain is identical, except for relative size, to the brain of every other person alive and in history. It is identical to those who have achieved great things and those who achieve little or nothing at all.

So, if we're 99.9% identical to all other humans, those who have achieved and those who haven't, what is the difference? How come they achieve and you have yet to?

The only difference between those who achieve great things and those who achieve little or nothing is what they think.

The Incredible Powers of Human Beings

When you take time to think about the differences between human beings and all other creatures in this world, you realize that the differences are vast. We are god-like in comparison. While we watch nature shows about how fast cheetahs can run in amazement, we take for granted that humans have invented machines that enable all of us to drive far faster. While we are in awe of blue whales that are so large and can swim so deep, we don't think much about the incredible submarines mankind has created. We are amused at how chimpanzees and gorillas have been able to learn sign language and communicate with us. Yet, we don't spend much time thinking about the thousands of languages in which humans communicate. Some people are even able to communicate in several simultaneously.

Consider that by the time humans reach roughly two years of age, they far surpass the intelligence of the next most intelligent species.

We have been able to adapt and live in every climate under nearly any conditions. Many other creatures would die if moved from one environment to another.

Where we have shortcomings, we invent machines to help us do what does not come naturally, such as fly, dive to the ocean depths, see at night, breathe under water, or go to the moon. We can create life, engineer life, extend life, and end life on a massive scale. We can shape the earth, alter the course of rivers, hold back oceans, and move mountains. We have created a world in which we need to exert very little effort to survive. All other creatures must either struggle to survive day-to-day or live off our surpluses and kindness.

Human beings are truly masters of the planet. Whether you consider humans a blessing or blight, we are truly magnificent. You are too.

So let's take a look at some of the characteristics of human beings as they pertain to your mission of success.

Ability to Turn Thoughts into Reality

As far as we can tell, animals survive by instinct and some internal drive that makes them build nests, migrate, roam the earth, and swim the oceans. They possess some kind of internal clock that tells them when to hibernate, when to mate, when to run and hide, or when to fight and dominate one another.

Humans beings, however, live by an entirely different set of rules. Humans can think about something and then make it a reality.

Because you and I are born into a man-made world we often take it for granted. Yet, consider the fact that everything you see, except those things of nature, were made by humans and once only mere thoughts.

Think for a moment about the book you're reading. It started out as a thought. So too did the paper upon which the words are printed. So too did the ink, the printing press, the graphics, and all the tools used in producing this book. Every man-made thing you touch and see was first a thought.

Envision for a moment all the people who created all the things around you. Think about the how much thought, will power, and effort it took to turn those thoughts into a reality. Look around your room and think of all the men and women who made the things you see. Go to a shopping mall, and all the people responsible for creating all that you see would overcrowd the parking lot.

It is not as if we must make a special effort to turn thought into reality either. Even you exercise this god-like power every day! If you've ever bought a television, stereo, car, even food, you've exercised this power. First you think about it, envision yourself having it, then you go out and buy it. It becomes reality. Ever make a sandwich? Same process. While these are very simple examples, our thoughts shape our lives in exactly the same ways.

People have a tendency to move in the direction of their most dominant thoughts, thereby turning what they think about into reality. This is a natural ability and every one of us exercises it every day, whether or not we're aware of it, whether or not we try. It is automatic.

On the positive side, if we think about achieving great things, we envision what it will be like. We screen out the negatives, and accept or believe those things that will bring us closer to what we envision. Our thoughts and visions become reality.

On the negative side, if we think about disaster and misery for ourselves, we envision our gloomy fates. We screen out the positives and accept or believe those things that will bring us closer to what we envision. Our thoughts and visions become reality.

It is important to choose carefully what you think, as it is almost certain to become reality.

Social Elevation

A question seldom asked is "Why?" Why do we strive to get ahead, make more money, buy more toys and fancy clothes? Why do we build skyscrapers, castles, and palaces? Why do people invent things, solve problems, make laws, and expend the effort necessary to turn thoughts into reality? Why go to any effort above and beyond mere survival, storing of food, and procreation?

What is it that motivates humans to engage in all these activities?

> *Humans have the unique ability to elevate themselves within a social order through perception, rather than through brute strength or beauty.*

Nearly all other creatures dominate one another through physical size, strength, or beauty. They find mates and pass along their superior genes to increase the likelihood of survival for the species (however, only *we* seem to be aware of that).

Why did humans first pick up and cherish the shiny stone we now call gold? Certainly there were many rocks that were equally attractive, especially in the raw state. Why did mankind find special value in gold? Certainly, it does not tarnish, but it's too soft to be of practical value as a tool or weapon.

Humans were able create the *perception* that gold has more value than other stones and metals. Humans were able to create the perception that those who possessed the gold were special or more important within their social order, despite their physical size, strength, or beauty.

Why do some people strive to make money, buy big houses, fancy cars, expensive clothes, and jewelry? Why is everyone not satisfied to live exactly like everyone else, with the same houses, cars, clothes, and so on? To elevate themselves within their social order.

As we've seen, people carry around in their hearts the question,

"Am I good?" People have the ability to use their strengths and talents to demonstrate their own answer and to seek acknowledgement of their value from others. "Yes, I am good because I can amass lots of money." Not only that, some strive to demonstrate and seek acknowledgement that *they are better than others* in their social order, and sometimes the best in the world.

This is a big reason why a lot of money is never enough. There is always someone who seems to have more, and we desire to elevate ourselves above them as well.

I'm not suggesting that we all strive to be "top dogs." Not all of us seek to out-do everyone else, nor do we all exhibit this behavior in the same way. We do it in many ways, not just with wealth and possessions.

We sing songs, write music, and express ourselves through art to show the world that we have artistic value and are special within society.

We learn complex concepts, study abstract topics, work on mathematical formulas, ponder mysteries, and solve problems with inventions to show that our intelligence is of great value and makes us special within society.

We run, swim, and bike in races, build our muscles, dance difficult movements, score points, tackle, hit, and punch harder to show that physical ability is of great value, and therefore special within society.

We build monuments, palaces, skyscrapers, and highways to show that industriousness and ability to create is of great value and makes us special within society. The bigger the creation, the more important we feel.

We write and speak persuasive, compelling words, and write laws and policies to show that we are perceptive, logical, and that we know what is right or wrong, and therefore special within society.

We speak to one another for more than simple communication to stimulate action. We say things because we believe we have something important to say and are therefore important for saying them. We may say things that are funny, clever, observant, insightful, or witty to improve the perception others have of us. We also resort to backbiting, nitpicking, and tearing down the perception held for others to make us appear comparatively better.

Nearly every advance that humans have made and problem humans have solved, has had at its heart the idea that we can elevate ourselves within our social order.

You have strengths and talents that you can utilize to merely answer the question of your worth, or to seek acknowledgement of your value from others. How high you advance within the social order or just how much recognition you desire is up to you.

Ability to Solve Problems

Another significant characteristic of humans that separates us from all other creatures is our ability to solve problems. Sure, squirrels are very clever problem solvers, and cats entertain us by turning door latches to let themselves out. But humans solve problems that make life easier and more efficient. Our ability to solve problems is incredible and makes us even more god-like.

We create inventions to make up for our shortcomings, so we can fly or travel swiftly. We create inventions to save labor and achieve more with less effort. We have sent humans to the moon.

Problem solving is at the very root of our economy and civilization. People pay to have problems solved, whether the problems are for food and shelter, to make lives easier, to help people elevate themselves in their own social order, or to simply help people differentiate themselves with styles and fashion. Chances are that whatever you choose in the pursuit of your dreams will somehow be solving a problem for someone.

You have a natural and undeniable gift for solving problems merely by being born a human. The goals you establish and life you design for yourself are merely problems waiting to be solved. It us up to you to utilize your problem-solving gift to achieve your goals.

Ability to Shape Your Destiny

Humans have the unique ability to shape their own destinies. All other animals live by instinct and do not willingly take on challenges beyond their normal capacities and environments. Humans, however, can and often do change what they presently do simply because of their thoughts. Humans routinely surpass their normal environments and expectations to find and try new things, to "push the envelope" of their abilities.

Why?

To become special and therefore elevated within a social order.

I'm not suggesting that all humans do this, but they can, and many do.

Take another look at all the things around you in your man-made world. It has been said that humans use only 3 percent of their brain's capacity. Isn't it truly amazing all the things that humans have accomplished operating at 3 percent capacity. Think of what might be if we increased that to just 5 or 10 percent.

With all the evidence of magnificence and accomplishments of humankind around us, it is a great irony that we can be fooled into believing that we have no control over our own destinies. Yet, we do this all the time. We figure it must be fate that determines the course of our lives. We readily believe that good and bad things happen only by the whim of good or bad luck or pure coincidence.

One thing many successful people have in common is that they believe they got to where they have by deliberate choices they've made during the course of their lives. It appears that the commonality among those who achieve little or nothing is their tendency to blame external factors for their inability to accomplish anything. The reality is that we all arrive at our present location by the choices we make. If we believe that it is fate that has brought us to our present situation, then it is our choice to believe it is so.

The truth is that your destiny is entirely under your control. As you think, so shall you be. It is as simple as that.

The Opportunity of the Present

There has never been a better time in history to be alive than today. Life is easier than it has ever been, and more options and opportunities exist for you than ever before. There has been no time in human history that has been more conducive for an individual such as yourself to follow your dreams and seek your fortunes.

Since you're interested in getting ahead, it's important to realize just how strongly the cards are stacked in your favor. It's also important to recognize and overcome what it is that leads us to believe we have little or no opportunities.

The Physically Easiest of Times

Consider the advances realized in just the last few generations. Less than 100 years ago, things were very different and life was generally more challenging. Getting ahead was something you did after all these other challenges were successfully faced and conquered.

Food

Life is increasingly convenient when it comes to obtaining food. We don't have to hunt for or grow our food. It is brought to us at a supermarket, convenience store, or delivered to us in 30 minutes or less. We have food in such abundance that we struggle to eat less or the right foods instead of the abundant junk food.

Shelter

Long ago, it was easy to be overwhelmed by poverty and there were few who could or would be able to support the poor. They were struggling to survive too, and there were few, if any, government social organizations that could help. Poverty and suffering meant you could easily die of starvation.

Today, even the poverty-stricken are taken care of with homes, shelter, food, and clothing. Many people who are considered poor have cars, televisions, microwaves, and tremendous opportunities to pull themselves out of poverty. Life in America is vastly more comfortable than it was just 50 or 100 years ago.

Health

Medical breakthroughs help us to live longer, healthier lives. At the turn of last century, it used to be that nearly every family would have a child or know a family with a child who died from disease. If you broke a bone, got shot, stabbed, or got seriously injured falling from a horse you had no place to turn to be mended.

These days in America, children rarely die from disease, broken bones are routine and of little consequence, drowning victims can be revived, heart attack victims can be saved and given another chance at life, diseases are often cured.

If you became paralyzed 100 years ago your life might as well have been over. Today, physically handicapped people do amazing things, such as become world famous astrophysicists like Stephen Hawking, or emotionally move a nation, as in the case of Christopher Reeves.

At the turn of the century the average life expectancy was in the low 50s. Today it is well over 70 and many more people are living well past 100 years of age.

Long ago physical catastrophes would have jeopardized your ability to survive. Today they are comparatively easy to overcome, and one can still live a fulfilling life with a major physical impairment.

Transportation

Whether it's for a purpose or simply to amuse ourselves, we can go anywhere and do just about anything. Only a hundred years ago, traveling across America was a difficult and dangerous proposition. Today, with very little money, we can drive across it in days. We can fly across it in hours. Millions of Americans fly to Europe or anywhere in the world each year just to have a look around, the kind of adventure once reserved for only the very wealthy.

Entertainment

Life is increasingly interesting and our imaginations are exposed to vast amounts of inputs and ideas. Reading, storytelling, and sitting by the family radio are no longer our only forms of entertainment. We have incredibly fascinating stories acted out for us with dazzling special effects and surround sound. Hearing music is no longer a rarity; we have an endless variety of music available to us cheaply and in crystal clear, CD quality.

Work

It used to be that a large percentage of the population worked in agriculture, animal husbandry, and heavy labor. The labor was back-breaking and days were very long. Now machines do the heavy lifting, shoveling, breaking, digging, planting, harvesting, building, and moving. Machine operators can do ten, one hundred, or thousands of times the work of a laborer by simply pushing and pulling levers. Many people today drive to work or telecommute, type a little, chat a little with co-workers, talk on the phone to customers or suppliers, sit in meetings for a few hours, and their day is done. They have to join a health club to work up a sweat and elevate their heart rates.

Leisure time

People have an abundance of time on their hands and tons of ways to spend it entertaining themselves. We watch television an average of 25 hours a week, some not at all, some nearly constantly. We have video games and the Internet to occupy our minds and hands. We have an endless array of videos that we can rent and watch all weekend, and sports to watch 24 hours a day on cable TV. We're now being offered hundreds of channels on satellite TV to endlessly surf for something remotely interesting.

Opportunity

There are unlimited opportunities and an abundance of time to pursue them. With all of our basic needs for survival addressed we can focus our attention on crafting our futures, setting goals, exploring interests, and achieving our dreams. There are countless stories of overnight successes, of companies that start up in a garage or spare room to later become multi-billion dollar companies in a few short years. Unfortunately, the vast majority of people fail to recognize or pursue these abundant opportunities.

Resources, communication, and information

We're amazingly well informed. We have vast amounts of information readily available to us nearly instantaneously. Although it is portrayed that we are learning less than our ancestors, we have an infinitely greater pool of knowledge. We can communicate around the world in seconds, learn about lives and cultures we may never visit, and see places we may never go. All this technology may not have solved world hunger nor eliminated disasters but we become aware of them in the comfort of our living rooms and can send our help.

There are several government organizations and bureaus designed specifically to help industrious individuals accomplish their goals.

Many companies will gladly send you information on areas of your interest. If you need to ask specific questions, want to become more familiar with a specific field, hear insights from those in the industry, bounce your ideas off someone who knows, simply call them—*from* anywhere *to* anywhere. It may take more than one or two calls to get what you want, but you needn't trek across the wilderness to discover such information.

The Internet makes information gathering and communication easier still. Nearly anything you might care to know is available, from around the world. No longer do you need to go through hoops and hurdles to ask your questions. Most companies make it fairly easy to contact anyone inside the organization.

There is also a wealth of information in books on nearly any topic you can think of. If you have a particular interest that you'd like to explore as a career, chances are there are one or more books that will tell you a great deal about it. Can't find it in the library? Bookstores and Internet bookstores can track most anything down and ship it right to your door.

What ever it is that you want to learn along the lines of your interests and passions, there are plenty of ways that you can easily find out about it.

The Psychologically Most Challenging of Times

As compared to our ancestors, the average American lives the life of luxury that was once reserved for nobility. Yet we find ourselves dissatisfied and unhappy. Why?

We have enormous amounts of time on our hands and an endless variety of things to do to fill that time. We have so much time that we spend it worrying about a parade of problems that will never cease and aimlessly pondering what to do with our lives.

When people reminisce about how "simple" life used to be, they must be talking about how few choices people had to make. In times past what one did was largely try to survive. The choices available were dictated by what could get you through the day or week, by what would provide a reliable income, or by your values of family or local community. There were fewer choices and therefore choices were simpler to make.

Today, there are endless amounts of choices, options, and possibilities, and this is where the problem lies. There are so many choices, so many influences, and so many confusing messages that it's hard for a person to decide.

Our minds, ideas, and values have been expanded. We see how other people on television and movies live, whether fictitious or not. Advertisers bombard us with highly influential and effective commercials that tell us, "you'll be better, more attractive, and cool if you buy our products." We become programmed to respond with a particular thought or phrase when we hear the right stimulus, like, "You asked for it, you got it. . . . Toyota!" or "Just Do It!" These phrases stay with us for life.

Television shows depict what's cool, who's hot, who's not. We adopt hairstyles, clothing styles, ways of speaking and acting from our favorite characters. Television and movies shape our opinions about what's good and what's evil in very dramatic and compelling ways.

What's "cool" changes from season to season, month to month, and channel to channel. We're in endless pursuit of what's "cool." Just when we think we've got a handle on "cool" someone changes it, and we're in pursuit again. We're so wrapped up in being "cool" today that we don't give any thought to the future.

Our culture has expanded from the confines and restrictions of the nuclear family and local community to the breadth of the entire country. Our horizons are broad and influences many. So endless and varied are the choices that it's difficult to make a choice. It's much like the channel surfer, watching for a moment, dwelling a bit longer on things that look interesting, then moving along to see what else might be on, never finding something that's quite right. So busy are we value and identity surfing, that we never take the time to focus on what to do with our lives, who we are, and what we want to be

These are difficult psychological times, indeed.

Your Part in the Big Picture

I'll never forget an interview I read with one of the founders of Id Software, makers of Doom, Quake, and other computer games. When asked, "Do you fear Microsoft getting into the computer gaming industry?" the interviewee responded, "No. Not really. A behemoth organization like that moves too slow to come up with anything really innovative. What terrifies us, however, is a couple of guys coding their hearts out in the basement or garage that come up with the next truly brilliant leap in technology."

That interview illustrates a very beautiful, beautiful truth. Each major advance in human history has come about from *an individual* rising up out of obscurity. That could very easily be you.

You have something in your heart. You've got something brilliant locked up inside you. You may know exactly what it is, or you may have yet to discover it. It may be buried beneath piles and piles of negative attitudes and beliefs that others have dumped on you over a course of your life. But it's there, waiting to serve you, waiting to serve humanity.

This book didn't wind up in your hands by accident. You could very well be the keeper of the next great advance in civilization. If so, you owe it to yourself and the world to dig it up and let it out.

> *Each major advance in human history has come from an individual rising up out of obscurity. The next one could be you!*

Think Like a Successful Person

Most people don't take the time to assess and appreciate their own potential. They've been convinced by society or by themselves that they can't accomplish anything, so they don't even try, or try but give up too quickly.

All human beings, including you, have incredible capabilities to turn thoughts into reality, to utilize strengths and talents, and to shape their own destinies.

Never has there been a better time in history than the present to pursue your dreams and make them a reality. Everything about your world has become infinitely easier than it was for your ancestors, who faced enormous challenges just to survive.

The real challenge becomes honing in on exactly what it is you would like to make of your life. There are so many confusing messages about what's of value, what will gain recognition, and what is "cool" that it can be difficult to make a choice. Some are so busy value and identity surfing, in endless pursuit of "cool," they don't spend the time to figure out how to craft their lives.

However, taking the time now to identify your strengths, talents, and what's important to you puts you way ahead of the curve. Simply by doing so, you automatically engage the internal mechanisms that will get you moving down the road to success.

ROADBLOCK 6

"But my
tires are half
flat and I need a
paint job . . ."

Strengths and Weaknesses

The next barrier to success I'll discuss is created when we focus too much attention on weaknesses, often discounting our strengths completely. By learning to refocus your attention on the strengths and talents you genuinely possess, you'll be able to capitalize on them and use them to your advantage.

By now you've learned that much of what you have come to believe about yourself is up for challenge, re-evaluation, and reinterpretation. You've also learned that you have an incredible amount of potential simply by being a human being. You've learned that success and happiness in life are derived from exercising your strengths and talents.

You may be thinking, "But I have no strengths! I don't know of anything that I do well. What can I do?"

Fear not. Everyone has strengths. Everyone!

A few nasty little obstacles may have gotten in the way of you clearly identifying your strengths. These obstacles are neither good nor bad, right nor wrong, just nor unjust. They just exist. The important thing is to recognize them so that they will no longer cloud your view.

This chapter is about helping you to uncover your strengths, and about minimizing or eliminating your faults. In knowing your strengths you will know where to focus your energies, capitalize your efforts, and enjoy your journey toward success.

What's Been Hiding Your Strengths?

Recall if you will Howard Gardner's seven key areas of intelligence—mathematical, verbal, spatial (artistic), kinesthetic (athletic or "working with your hands"), musical, interpersonal, and intrapsychic (insightfulness).

In academic society, math and verbal skills are highly regarded, while the others are downplayed or not even acknowledged. What's most ironic is that society is comprised of people exercising their strengths in all of these key areas of intelligence. However, during the formative stages of your career, math and verbal skills seem to carry all the value, while strengths in other areas don't seem to count. This is much like saying the index finger and thumb are the only important fingers in learning to play a piano, and all the others don't play any notes of real value.

Does interpersonal skills training appear in any high school or college curriculum? Yet proficiency in interpersonal skills will help the broadest audience achieve success in their careers.

Do the powers of insight or perception appear anywhere on a job requirement? But without them one would be hopelessly gullible and be continually taken advantage of. The people who excel at skills of insight and perception are known as savvy and highly regarded.

Everyone possesses strengths in one or more of these areas. But if your strengths are not one of the "holy" strengths, don't feel like they have no value. It's easy to become convinced by society that they have no worth. Your strengths really do count.

Your strengths count, even if they don't show up on the SAT.

Unfortunately, people tend to focus on their faults rather than on their strengths. For some reason many of us enjoy the game "bash myself." We can rattle off our own faults as fast as the a, b, c's. At times *we even point out our own faults* to be certain others won't miss them.

Even when we know our strengths, we have a tendency to discount them because of a few faults. This is much like a baseball star saying, "I'm just no good because I can't sing worth a damn! You should hear me mangle the national anthem."

The truth is that everyone has faults. Everyone! From your parents to the president of your company, to the President of the United States. But everyone who succeeds does so *despite* his or her faults. They don't look at their faults and disqualify themselves because of them. Don't disqualify yourself because you have faults.

Guide your life, not by your limitations and faults,
but by your strengths and passions.

Identify Your Faults

This will be a very important exercise for you, so don't take it lightly.

What we're going to do is identify your faults and do our very best to minimize them or eliminate them. They've likely been consuming you long enough. They've likely been smothering or negating your strengths. This should not be allowed to go on any longer.

Imagine your faults as a nagging enemy who makes your life miserable. Every time you try to exhibit your strengths, your enemy steps in to remind you that you're no good despite your strengths. If such a person existed, you would likely do your best to ignore, minimize, escape, or otherwise remove them from your life. So why not your faults?

You might be thinking, "But how can I do that? My faults are just who I am. They're inescapable!"

Not so!

We're going to examine your faults closely and do what we can to purge them completely, or at the very least, stop them from overshadowing your strengths.

The first step is to get them all on the table. Make a list of your faults, negative qualities, and weaknesses. Write as much as you can. Write all the things that come into your mind. Write out everything that you'd like to purge. If you run out of room, by all means, write them out on a separate piece of paper. Include everything you'd like to rid your life of.

Inventory of faults, negative qualities, and weaknesses

_____

_____

_____

_____

_____

_____

_____

_____

_____

_____

_____

_____

_____

_____

_____

_____

_____

_____

_____

_____

_____

_____

_____

_____

_____

_____

_____

_____

_____

_____

_____

_____

_____

_____

_____

Examine Your List of Faults

We're going to take a very critical look at your faults. Chances are you've let them have free reign over your life without question. If this is so, you've also likely not given your strengths the weight and value that they really deserve. It's time to change all that. We're going to turn the tables and rip apart those things you believe are your faults.

What Are Faults?

What are faults, anyway? They sure do make a person feel lousy for having them. Faults are really nothing more than opinions and judgements handed to you by others. They are opinions and judgements about your behavior, about physical aspects of you, about things you say, and ways in which you interact with people.

Faults are opinions, nothing more.

"That's not so!" you may jump to the defense of your well-nurtured faults. "One of my faults is that I'm lazy. How is that an opinion?"

Well, chances are that you don't feel energetic or enthusiastic about things you don't like to do. Me too! But find something that you like to do, and you're likely all over it. Kids might be lazy about cleaning their rooms, but put them in front of a computer game and they go at it with a vengeance. Kids may not do well in school and feel stupid for not doing well on tests, but give them a computer game *without* instruction, and they'll have the thing figured out in a couple of hours, including character behaviors, rules, and how to win.

There is no rule that says people have to be universally interested in the same things. There is no rule that says people have to universally put high value on cleaning their rooms.

Opinions are subjective interpretations, which means they will be different for everybody. People interpret *events* based on their own historical experiences, do they not? People also interpret *behaviors* of others (and even themselves), based on the same kind of historical experiences. As we have already seen, a belief system is really a frail web of circumstantial interpretations developed over the course of a lifetime. If the circumstances were different for a given person, they would very likely have a different set of beliefs, even if only slightly.

People make judgements and form opinions about you and your behaviors based on their own unique set of beliefs. This does not mean that any judgement or opinion is fact! People make negative judgements of you if and when you do not live up to their expectations of what is right and good. These expectations may be about your behaviors, whether a single incident or over a lifetime. These expectations may be about how you look or any number of physical features you possess. There is no limit to what people might expect of others.

Again, these judgements and opinions are not factual, nor are they right. An interpretation of an event, behavior, or physical trait is neither right nor wrong.

Just because a person is a parent, elder, sibling, or in a position of authority *does not make them right!* It merely means they are more easily able to make their opinion prevail over yours when influencing others to form an opinion.

People make interpretations *of everything* skewed by their own frail web of circumstantial beliefs. The people rendering judgements about you are not gods! They are mere human beings, just like you, fraught with their own faults.

The truth is that we all have our beliefs about what is right and what is wrong, what is important and what is unimportant, what is of value and what is worthless. We continually make judgements and affix labels indicating whether something meets our expectations of what is right and good or not.

For example, a conservative business person might spot someone with many tattoos, body piercings and spiked hair (maybe a programmer working in the data center), make a negative judgement, and label that person an odd-ball. The programmer may spot the conservative business person in a suit, tie, and wingtip shoes and make a negative judgement and label the business person as an uptight, conformist jerk. Neither is right or wrong!

Judgements about you are entirely subjective. The faults you believe you have, are also entirely subjective. These opinions, judgements, and faults may have come from one person, or many, but they are still subjective opinions and not factual.

"But I'm too fat, too skinny, too ugly, too tall, too short, too light, too dark! I have a big nose, funny lips, droopy eyes, big ears, bad complexion, crooked teeth, funny hair, no hair, no legs, no arms. I'm paralyzed, deaf, mute, blind, a poor athlete, and I can't sing worth a damn!"

So what?

Regardless of how it comes about, each society develops its own set of physical traits that it values highly. These traits are not universal among all societies, so they too are subjective. To say that only those qualities that match up to societal values are important and those that deviate unimportant is ridiculous. This is much like saying that only the index finger and thumb are important in playing the piano, and that the other fingers do not play notes of any value.

Just because you have physical traits that do not match those held in high regard by society does not mean that you are flawed. Chances are that there are *thousands*, if not *millions* of people who have exactly the same physical trait that makes you believe you are flawed. Interestingly, even those who seem to be the models of the physical attributes we hold so highly very likely feel flawed themselves!

"How could that be?" you might ask. "They're models!"

Very often seemingly perfect people do the same thing you do. They look in the mirror every day and pick themselves apart too.

In summary, the faults you feel you have are entirely opinions, and therefore, of limited meaning. Only you can give them importance. Whether your faults are behaviors or physical traits, other people are not gods and in no position to judge you. You don't have to accept their judgements.

Such evidence should be inadmissible in your court.

Minimizing and Eliminating Your Faults

Put a big "O" on each fault.

The first thing I'd like you to do is go back through the list of faults you compiled and put a big "O" over anything that is subjective in nature (which is likely the vast majority of your list).

We'll give the "O" two meanings.

One meaning is that it is an opinion, a judgement, an interpretation from someone else about some aspect of you. Chances are the judgement was rendered because you did not meet someone else's expectation of what is right and good. The judgement is subjective in nature, not fact, and based on another person's circumstantial beliefs. Had the person rendering such judgement of you had a different set of circumstances, he or she may not have rendered the same judgement nor held the same opinion.

The other meaning for the "0" is that it has zero value to you. Judgements handed to you by others are typically done for another person's benefit and not yours. Even if it is you who made such a judgement, it is a judgement or interpretation *against your favor.* It is still of zero value to you. It is hurting you, not helping you. You only need to give value to those things that are of help to you.

If you've discounted your strengths all your life, there should be no reason for you to hold back on discounting your faults! Discount the value of these negative judgements mercilessly. Go back and put an "0" on all opinion-based faults. *Do this now!*

Living up to expectations . . .

Is it really your purpose in life to live up to the expectations of others?

When a person put an expectation on you to make them happy, they are not internally happy. There's nothing you could do to alleviate that internal unhappiness. You could follow their life instructions to the letter, yet they would still likely find something to be unhappy about. How many times have we heard the lament, "I could never make my parents happy. I just couldn't do anything right in their eyes."

Rather than becoming enslaved to someone else's internal unhappiness, concentrate on working on your own happiness.

Maybe your guilt alarm is going off right about now. However, ask yourself this. If the person to whom you feel obligated was not in your life, would you make the same decisions? If not, then why make your decisions based on feelings of guilt?

"If you really loved me, you wouldn't make such decisions," you might hear them say.

Counter with, "If you really loved me, you'd let me make my own decisions and be happy for me. Wouldn't you rather I come to you because I genuinely cared, rather than out of guilt?"

Be true to yourself and everyone will be better off in the long run.

Take a stand!

Fight back, if necessary. People who openly make judgements of you or try to sway others with their opinions are doing so for their own benefit, not yours. They are looking to make you conform to what they believe is right and good. If it is not what you believe is right and good, if you do not hold the same values, take a stand and say so.

If someone tells you that you're a slob, lazy, inconsiderate, ungrateful, selfish, arrogant, or whatever they care to say, come back with something in your own defense.

You might retort, "If I placed as much value on X as you did, then I suppose I would feel my behavior is a problem. But your values and my values do not have to agree. And I am in no way wrong for disagreeing with what you feel is important."

Your values are just as important and valid as is theirs. Who is in a position to say otherwise?

A word of caution, however. There is such a thing as prudence. Depending on the importance of the stand you take, it may be easier on you in the long run if you respect what another person feels is important. I'd hate to suggest that you go around angering other people and then suffer from their retaliation in some way. Pick your battles carefully and stand up for those things that are genuinely important to you.

Put physical traits in perspective

You will eventually come to realize what matters in your life is not how you physically compare to others, whether on TV or in your neighborhood. With luck, we become old and wrinkled anyway. We lose whatever temporary benefit we had from good looks in youth.

What will matter most will be the nature of the interactions you have with others. Do others make you feel good about yourself, and do you make others feel good about themselves? We've all encountered someone who made us feel great, whether a parent, grandparent, teacher, or another. When another person makes you feel good, you don't really care what they look like. And nor will they care what you look like when you make them feel good. You may have also encountered someone who is extremely attractive but tends to walk all over people and treat them like dirt. In such cases, their good looks do not save them from feelings of anger for such poor treatment.

Consider also that what we see and compare ourselves to on TV is not a depiction of reality, but of fantasy. Producers of TV shows, soap operas, for example, choose beautiful people as that is what viewers wish their lives were like. Advertisers choose beautiful people when they want you to believe that using their products will make you beautiful as well. This is not reality, so don't even compare yourself to what you see on TV or in magazines.

You do count, regardless of your physical traits.

Fix it or accept it

Remember that everyone has faults, from your parents, to the president of your company, to the President of the United States. This is just part of being a human being. We cannot possibly live up to the expectations of everyone we may ever come in contact with. So pick your battles and work on those faults where it will be helpful to you.

You can't please everyone. Accept the fact that you will always have faults in someone's eyes. Don't beat yourself up for not living up to the expectations of other people. More importantly, don't let opinions and judgements from other people overshadow your strengths.

Identify Your Strengths

Exercising and developing your strengths will lead you to happiness, fulfillment, and potentially a great fortune. It is crucial that you have a handle on not only what strengths you currently possess, but also those strengths you'd like to develop.

Working in a job that utilizes your strengths will turn work into play and you will naturally excel. Whether or not you make a great deal of money will matter less as you will enjoy life every day. Waiting to amass a fortune for retirement to finally get to do the things you love is silly. You could get hit by a proverbial bus and never have fully enjoyed your life. The time to do things that you love is now.

You may already know what your strengths are and exactly what you want to do. Great! You may choose to bypass this section or you may choose to do it to affirm things you already know, or to discover some opportunities that you hadn't even thought of.

On the following lines, write all your positive qualities that you can think of. If you can't fit them all, great, get another piece of paper. If you think of something a couple days from now, add it. Ask friends and family what they feel some of your positive qualities are. They may shock you with things you hadn't realized about yourself.

You might recall earlier in the chapter that your negative qualities are purely opinions, interpretations, and judgements. The very same is true for your positive qualities. Worry not! I had you put an "O" on the negative qualities as they have no value to you. The positive qualities have tremendous value to you, and may even lead you great fortunes.

Inventory of positive qualities

_____

_____

_____

_____

_____

_____

_____

_____

_____

_____

_____

_____

_____

_____

_____

_____

_____

_____

_____

_____

_____

_____

_____

_____

_____

_____

_____

_____

_____

_____

_____

Things that Excite You

What do you love to do? What gets you excited? What do you do to have fun?

Don't just focus on one thing. Include hobbies, interests, and recreation. Don't limit it to what you have already experienced. What things can you imagine would get you excited? Don't think in terms of "jobs." Just write activities that get your motor going. Write down as many as you can, no matter what value you think it has.

Having fun is engaging in an activity that makes you feel good about yourself. Doing this exercise will help you identify activities, environments, and situations that make you feel good, whether you're actually participating, say in a game, or attending, say a meeting. Write any and all things that get you excited and are fun to you.

Activities that are exciting and fun

_____
_____
_____
_____
_____
_____
_____
_____
_____
_____
_____
_____
_____
_____
_____
_____
_____
_____
_____
_____
_____

Review the Jobs You've Had

Review all the jobs you had since and including those in high school. Start with the most recent and work your way backward. You don't have to be detailed or neat about it. *Only you* need to understand it.

For each job, write the general responsibly involved. Then write what you liked about it, what you didn't like about it, what you did well, and what you did poorly. Don't feel obligated to fill in each of the blanks. We have all had jobs that we absolutely hated and found nothing good about.

Most recent job was / is:

_____

_____

_____

_____

_____

What I liked:

_____

_____

_____

_____

What I didn't like:

_____

_____

_____

What I did well:

_____

_____

_____

What I didn't do well:

_____

_____

_____

The job before that was:

_____
_____
_____

General responsibilities:

_____
_____
_____
_____
_____

What I liked:

_____
_____
_____
_____

What I didn't like:

_____
_____
_____
_____

What I did well:

_____
_____
_____

What I didn't do well:

_____
_____
_____
_____

The job before that was:

_____

_____

_____

General responsibilities:

_____

_____

_____

_____

_____

_____

What I liked:

_____

_____

_____

_____

_____

What I didn't like:

_____

_____

_____

_____

_____

What I did well:

_____

_____

_____

What I didn't do well:

_____

_____

_____

_____

The job before that was:

_____
_____
_____

General responsibilities:

_____
_____
_____
_____
_____
_____

What I liked:

_____
_____
_____
_____
_____

What I didn't like:

_____
_____
_____
_____
_____

What I did well:

_____
_____
_____
_____

What I didn't do well:

_____
_____
_____
_____

The job before that was:

_____

_____

_____

General responsibilities:

_____

_____

_____

_____

_____

_____

What I liked:

_____

_____

_____

_____

What I didn't like:

_____

_____

_____

_____

What I did well:

_____

_____

_____

_____

What I didn't do well:

_____

_____

_____

_____

Review the Experiences You've Had

Now recall at least three very positive experiences that you've had where you did something. Don't include parties, or family get-togethers where you were a passive participant. Include anything where you had an active role in some way. These experiences can include work, but only special incidents or occasions at work.

For example, an experience might be, "I represented our company in a toy-collection drive for foster kids." How did you feel? "I felt great, giving, and caring." Why? "Because I felt I was able to help kids who are in a difficult situation. I felt like I was of value to others."

Experience 1 was:

_____

How did you feel?

_____

Why?

_____

_____

Experience 2 was:

_____

How did you feel?

_____

Why?

_____

Experience 3 was:

_____

How did you feel?

_____

Why?

_____

If You Had God-like Powers

If you had the power to create any job at all, what would it be? It doesn't really have to be a "job" that you could apply for. Remember, in this exercise you have god-like power to *create* your job. Draw heavily from your list above. Write as much detail as you like.

_____

_____

_____

_____

_____

_____

_____

_____

_____

_____

_____

_____

_____

_____

_____

_____

_____

_____

_____

_____

_____

_____

_____

Deathbed Regrets

If you were diagnosed with a terminal illness and had one week to live, which is enough time to ponder your life but not enough to really do anything about it, what things would you regret not having done in or with your life? Forget about everyone else for the moment. What would *you* regret not having done?

_____

_____

_____

_____

_____

_____

_____

_____

_____

_____

_____

_____

_____

_____

_____

_____

_____

_____

_____

_____

_____

_____

_____

Your 80th Birthday

Envision yourself living to the ripe old age of 80. Someone throws a party for your birthday and invites friends and relatives. Everyone invited shows up.

Who would be there?

_____
_____
_____
_____
_____

How many would be there?

_____

What qualities would they cite in their little speeches about how they feel about you?

_____
_____
_____
_____
_____

How would you have been involved in their lives?

_____
_____
_____
_____
_____
_____

How would you like to be remembered by these people?

_____
_____
_____
_____
_____
_____

The $100 Million Jackpot

Let's say that you won $100 million in a lottery of some sort. Now, advance the movie by a year. You've bought all the houses, clothes, cars, and toys you could think of, did all the traveling you can stand for a while, and done all the frivolous spending that you can manage to do.

You have an unlimited amount of time and unlimited amount of resources. Now is your opportunity to do absolutely anything, there's nothing to stop you, and there's no reason to put it off any longer. What kinds of things would you do? What would you care to learn how to do? If you chose to take college courses (to get a degree or not), what field of study would you choose? What would you do to enhance your life and make it more interesting?

Free Personality Testing Resources

Taking personality tests is good way to help you identify your strengths. There are many web sites on the Internet that allow you to take personality tests for free. If you don't have Internet access at home, you can go to nearly any public library to gain free access.

The tests ask simple questions and your responses give an indication of your personality traits. These tests are helpful for those who are not quite sure about their strengths or how and where they can be applied in the world. They can also help confirm things you already know about yourself. Either way, they are free. You have nothing to lose and a good deal of personal insight to gain.

The personality tests typically take about 20 minutes to go through, but you'll probably find it very fascinating and want to take a number of them. At the end of the test, you receive results that illustrate how your traits line up with general career fields. Typically, the tests are based on widely accepted personality theories, so it's the sort of thing psychologists and counselors would use (doubtless, theirs would be more extensive and costly).

Below are four web sites you will find useful. If you want more information, you can go to a search engine and search for "personality test" to find more sites.

1. **www.allhealth.com/onlinepsych**
   Once there, look for these tests:
   - What Career Is for You?
   - The Colors Personality Test
   - Emotional Intelligence Test
   - How Smart are You?
2. **www.keirsey.com**
   This test will yield results similar to those on the web site above, but will ask a different range of questions.
3. **www.ncsu.edu/careerkey/career_key.html**
   This site will not only take you through a battery of questions, but will also suggest career fields and occupations based on the test results.

   The neat thing about this particular page is that it narrows down job fields to general titles. Once there, you can click on each of the titles and it will link you to a web page for the U.S. Bureau of Labor Statistics, specifically, the *Occupational Job Outlook Handbook.* There you will find some practical information about the career area in which you are interested.

The bad thing about being linked to this government handbook of career descriptions is that it is written with such practicality and dispassion that it can take the wind out of your sails. But don't let the writing style of a government bureaucrat dissuade you. Read the information, print it, save it, but take it all in. Having the practical details about a career area is always a good thing. Knowing this information will also keep you from appearing totally misinformed when talking to those in the industry.

4. **www.ansir.com**

   This site has a test based on a book called *Ansir for One,* which is also sold on the site. It has you take a battery of three tests of 50 some odd questions each. They are all descriptive phrases with which you agree or disagree as to how closely they fit you.

   What's great about this site is that they give in-depth descriptions of your personality type which are very complimentary. You can print the descriptions and keep them as an unbiased, objective reminder of your strengths. I recommend this site and test highly.

Think Like a Successful Person

Everyone has strengths. Unfortunately, if yours are not in academic areas, you and others in your life may have discounted their value. Don't let the disproportionate value that society places on academic skills dishearten you and make you think your strengths have no value. Society is comprised of people exercising strengths in all areas. You can too!

Everyone has faults. You are permitted to have them too. Faults are entirely opinions, whether your own or those of others. Don't take other people's opinions as gospel truth. Their interpretations of your behaviors and physical traits are based on a frail web of circumstantial beliefs. There are an infinite number of ways in which you will not live up to the expectations of others. People render judgements of you for their own benefit, not yours. They are in no position to judge you.

Discount the importance of your "faults" mercilessly. They have no value to you and can hurt you the more you dwell on them.

Strengths, on the other hand, are of extremely high value to you and help you tremendously the more you develop and exercise them. Your strengths will lead you to a more fulfilling and rewarding life, emotionally if not financially.

Without knowing your strengths and talents, you run the risk of getting stuck in jobs that are boring and monotonous. Clearly identifying your areas of strength and your positive qualities can help you focus your energies and find a job you love. When you do what you love, work becomes play and you naturally excel.

ROADBLOCK 7

Setting Goals

The lack of a direction and goals is a common barrier to starting on the road to success. So often we spend our lives driving in no particular direction. When we're headed nowhere in particular, we'll wind up nowhere in particular. However, once we set a direction and particular destination that we'd like to reach, almost always we wind up there. So, pick a place you'd really, really like to go, and don't be shy about it.

This is the most important chapter in the book in that you're going to take a crack at determining a future. Will it be set in stone? No. If you try one direction and it doesn't work out, you can change directions. But getting into the habit of setting goals is a big improvement over aimlessness.

Every great leader, everyone who has accomplished something fantastic, has stood where you stand now, on the brink of a new journey. No one is born with a direction, plan of action, and goal. We must all choose them ourselves. Those who do will often achieve their goals. Those who don't will likely drift, accomplish little, and blame everyone else for their poor circumstances. It is entirely up to you to choose what to do with your life.

Welcome to the threshold many great achievers have crossed before you.

The first six chapters of this book have been leading up to this very threshold by helping you recognize and tear down the barriers that have stopped you from trying.

First you saw the negative result of believing that success can be had only by those who possess a college degree. The evidence to disprove this conventional wisdom is enormous and undeniable. The lack of a college degree is not a genuine obstacle. It's the mental barrier—believing the myth—that is the obstacle. Abolish the mental barrier and you abolish the obstacle.

Next you started thinking about what success truly means to you. If you had never thought success could be yours, you likely didn't define it or you defined it in terms that you didn't fully analyze. Success can be yours, but it's up to you to determine just what it means.

You then confronted the biggest roadblock of all—your past, and the people who have crafted the person you believe you are. You now understand that they were but mere mortals with their own inadequacies and skewed perspectives and motivations. What they've made of you is not necessarily accurate. However, rather than expending time and energy blaming other people for your present state, you can leave it behind, and redefine yourself however you'd like. You can make it so simply by what you think.

By gaining a deeper understanding of your thought processes and beliefs, you realize the limitations you believe you have are not necessarily true. Those things which you have come to believe to be concrete truths about yourself are merely a vast web of interpretations based on historical circumstances. Your beliefs are up for question and can be redefined. You can rewrite events of your past to minimize their negative effects on you. You can teach your mind to build a library of strength, to visualize and prepare for your success in the future.

With this new understanding, you can open your eyes to the possibilities before you. As a human being, you are incredibly flexible and adaptable. You possess a mind that is the most powerful force on the planet. It can solve incredible problems like no other creature.

You, yes you, possess capacities much like those of all others who have achieved great things. The only thing that separates you from those who have achieved great things is what you think.

You live in a time like no other in the history of humankind. The possibilities are endless and the resources to help you achieve your goals are plentiful. Take advantage of your potential, your capacity, and the time in which you live.

And, finally, you started a new way of thinking, to minimize those things you consider faults and prevent them from overshadowing your strengths. The development and exercise of your strengths, both present and future, will make for a more rewarding and fulfilling life, emotionally if not financially.

So, here you are at the threshold of a new journey.

The limitations you felt you had are gone, or at least no longer a dominating factor in your life. Your potential is vast, your ability to achieve great things is limited only by your thoughts. It is now time to take the critical step and begin writing your future.

You are now at a point where you are free to determine what to do with your life. You are no longer shackled by your past. You may choose to celebrate and tell everyone you know. You may choose a peaceful, internal moment of calm to commemorate the truly monumental decisions you are now making. Your decisions are genuinely important. Not only are they important to you, but they are important to those around you, whether family, friends, or co-workers.

The effect of your decisions can change the lives of those around you.

The effect of your decisions could change the world.

Every person of great accomplishment has been at the very point that you are now. Many overcame great adversity. Many sacrificed a lot in making their decisions. But they have all stood where you stand now, on the brink of a new journey with little more than a dream as both their weapon and shield in the battles ahead.

Hesitation

In a study described in the book *Think and Grow Rich,* by Napoleon Hill, a graduating class from Harvard was surveyed regarding their goals. The study showed that only 3 percent had clearly defined goals, the others merely vague goals or no specific goals at all. Several years later, the 3 percent who had clearly defined goals had a combined net worth greater than the combined net worth of the rest of the 97 percent!

If setting goals works so well, why do we hesitate to set our own? How many times in your life have you been urged to set goals? But all too often, it's one of those things that we hesitate and procrastinate on. What's getting in the way? Let's examine a few reasons why people hesitate to set goals.

Embarrassment

Many people are highly influenced by those around them. If those around you don't set goals, they're likely to view your goal setting as wishful thinking and pie-in-the-sky dreaming. Those around you may chastise you and make you think goal setting is silly. If you want to live under the tyranny of fearing ridicule, don't set goals. However, if you want to take charge of your life, ignore the taunts of those around you and set goals, high goals.

Hocus Pocus

Setting goals and having them all come true often sounds like hocus pocus to many. This likely stems from past disappointments or failures.

Past disappointments

These can lead you to believe that things will never go in your favor, creating hard-boiled skepticism. It's easy to develop a belief that nothing will ever go right or that you have an inescapable cloud of bad luck looming over your life.

Without guidance, a few early mishaps or disappointments can set the stage for interpreting all future events against your favor. It merely "seems" like everything has always gone wrong. In reality it could have been interpreted either way and the negative way was always *chosen*.

Past failures

You might have tried a few endeavors in the past and failed. This leads you to believe you will fail again in the future. Or, it may cause you to fear failing again as it would confirm an overall suspicion that you are a "failure" in life. Such is not the case.

The number of successes is in direct proportion to the number of attempts, and so are the number of failures. A baseball player is considered a really good batter if he can average over 300. That means that only one in three times at bat does he get a hit. The other two times he fails. Out of 100 times at bat, he failed around 66 times! Successful people all realize that failure is just a part of the game. When a failure occurs, it is not a reflection of you as a person, but of the mistakes in the actions taken or not taken.

Lack of Goals to Set

If you never believe it can happen, you will never spend the time to think about it. This is much like asking someone what he or she would do with $10 billion. Since this is so far beyond what a person might reasonably expect to happen, how to spend $10 billion doesn't often cross our minds. However, because $1 million is easy enough to believe, whether by the lottery, inheritance, or earning it, we all have some ideas of what we'd do with a million bucks.

So, think in terms of, "if you set goals and they were guaranteed to come true, what goals would you set?" Take the time to think about it, even if it's for the first time.

Fear of Destroying the Fantasy

Besides the fear of failure, we sometimes fear our beliefs might be proven false. The fantasy of "what might be" is comforting and enjoyable, and we'd hate to see it destroyed. A person can while away the hours daydreaming about achieving this goal or that. But when the prospect of it really happening comes close, fear kicks in and they back off, or sabotage the effort, feeling that it's better to leave the fantasy unexplored rather than have it dashed on the rocks of reality.

The Hazards of Not Setting Goals

Whatever the reason, not setting goals leaves your life up to circumstances, chance, luck, and the benevolence of others. To leave your life to the benevolence of others makes you a slave to their whims.

Had you not taken the spoon and learned to feed yourself, had you not taught yourself to dress, or walk, you'd still be dependent on someone else for these basics. To rely upon someone else to fulfill your life, to make it meaningful, to make it enjoyable, makes you dependent on others.

Take responsibility for your life and set goals. It may be difficult at first, but will prove more and more rewarding as time goes on. Doing so gives you incredible control and a feeling of power, rather than helplessness. Frankly, I'd rather maintain control of my life than leaving it to the whim of fate, or worse, others.

How and Why Goal Setting Works

Okay, how does this work? You set a goal and it comes true. Like magic, right? Wrong. It's not magic at all. It is a result of the natural mental processes of human beings. These processes have always been at your disposal, in fact, you've been using them all along. You might not have realized this, but the same mental processes that you use every day to go to work, buy a car, buy a house, or move to a new town can be used to set incredible goals and actually make them happen.

There are very specific reasons why goal setting genuinely works.

It's the Bailiff's Job

Recall how we described the reticular activating system as the bailiff from our little courtroom scene. The bailiff is charged with allowing in only those inputs that are important to you. Well, we're going to assign the bailiff to looking out for specific inputs. With millions of inputs at any given moment, there is a good chance that an input pertaining to your goal is out there whether you take notice of it or not. If we don't tell the bailiff what to look for, important inputs might easily be missed.

You do this every day already. But without the direction of a goal, your bailiff is just picking out your favorite movie stars, songs you like, colors you like, cartoons, phrases, cool cars, and people who are attractive to you. In other words, the bailiff is picking out a whole bunch of miscellaneous stuff. These are all important to you in some way, but they're just not focused. Once you have a goal, not only will the bailiff pick out the miscellaneous stuff that you find important, but also those things that pertain to the goals you've set. It may be headlines in a newspaper or magazine, signs you see while driving, something mentioned on the news, or information overheard from people at the next booth in a restaurant. These inputs all existed already. But now the bailiff will pick up on these things too. It's just part of the bailiff's job!

> *Without a goal, opportunities will slip by unnoticed.*
> *With a goal, opportunities will be plucked out of the morass.*

Something Worthwhile to Chew On

Your mind is the most powerful force on the planet. It is an incredible problem-solving machine. It is constantly in use and constantly solving problems for you. The only problem is that you're not giving it much of a challenge. If the problems you give your mind to chew on are getting to work, going to the store, how to look cool in front of your friends, figuring out the crossword puzzle, or how to get your new puppy to stop chewing up your house, your mind is seriously underutilized.

The fact is your mind can solve nearly any problem that comes within its grasp and experience level. Now, this is an important caveat to spend a moment on. Your mind will have a hard time figuring out things of which it has no experience. For example, the average person would not likely figure out how to get to the moon. However, humans have solved that problem. The people who got Neil Armstrong to the moon went through a good deal of education, experimentation, and experience to make it all happen. It was a long road to get there, but it didn't just happen overnight.

Your mind will use what it knows to solve problems. If there are small gaps in experience or knowledge, your mind will figure out how to obtain the necessary information to fill the gap and solve the problem. It might be simply getting a phone number for a government office, or learning to write novels.

Now, let's say that the goal you set is to get some new wheels. Easy enough. You've driven by car lots before, so you go, yak it up with the salesperson for a while, you agree on putting together a deal, get financing, down payment, and voila, new wheels. Not a particularly tough problem, generally speaking.

Now, let's increase the goal. Let's say that it is to make a million dollars. Well, considering the difference between where you are now and having a million dollars is likely a big jump, you have two choices. One is you can quit and not even attempt it. This is what stops most people. They voluntarily turn off their problem-solving motor or refocus it on other things, like getting the neighbor to stop leaving the trash cans out front all week.

However, let's say that you leave your problem-solving motor going on your goal of making a million dollars. Your mind will automatically begin taking what it presently knows and breaking down the problem posed by the goal. Your mind will go through lots of different scenarios of how one might possibly get to a million dollars.

"Can I make a million by singing? By dancing? By playing an

instrument. By painting a picture? By being a movie star? By writing a novel? By becoming president of the company? By inventing a widget?"

Your mind will go through lots and lots of scenarios searching for ideas that match up with some capability, experience, or talent that you presently possess. It discards those that are beyond your capabilities or morals.

When your mind comes to a likely candidate, it sets about solving what it would take to make that step happen. Far too many people don't put enough value in their strengths or even recognize their strengths at all. So they jump at those things which can be had with no specific strengths at all, such as playing the lottery or gambling. What's unfortunate is that is also where many people stop. They figure that the only way to a million dollars is through luck. Again, they turn off their problem-solving motor, or refocus it on how to set the VCR clock.

But, because you have spent time identifying your strengths, you can combine your strengths, passions, and things you have enjoyable experiences with to bear on the million-dollar problem.

Until you deliberately tell your mind to stop trying to solve a problem, or you deliberately refocus your mind on a different problem, it will keep working at it. If there's a piece of information your mind needs to fill in a gap, it will direct you to do so.

Your mind never stops solving problems. What matters is the nature and magnitude of problems you give it to solve. It could be something as mundane as "Will these sunglasses make me look cool?" Or, it could be, "How do I use my strengths to achieve my goals?"

> *Your mind will continue to work on solving the*
> *problem of reaching your goal until you tell it to stop.*

Bringing Focus to Idle Moments

Without a goal you let your mind drift during idle moments. You watch the tube aimlessly, passively listen to the music or talk shows on the radio during a commute, and dwell on good things or bad when you're not mentally engaged. Basically, all that mental capacity is being wasted. This is much like flying the space shuttle to the store for a jug of milk.

It is estimated that your mind thinks at a rate of between 600 and 1,000 words a minute. If you spend an hour a day in idle moments, that's roughly 36,000 to 60,000 words worth of thought that are wasted on frivolous things.

However, setting a goal changes all that! Without a goal, your mind spends idle moments chewing on trivial things. With a goal, your mind chews on important things. Those idle moments then become productive, problem-solving moments. You'll think through what you know, approaches, strategies, what books to read, people you might be able to contact, and how to alter strategies given new events.

Count up the idle moments you truly have during the day. If you have a mentally active job, your idle time might be less than a physically active job. Let's say that between getting up, showering, getting dressed, eating, driving, getting coffee, taking breaks, coming home, and the time before you go to bed, and time at work where you're not mentally focused, let's say you have ten total hours of idle time being awake. We won't bother to count the ability of your brain to solve problems while you sleep.

That's TEN HOURS A DAY, or 3,650 hours idle time a year that your mind could be chewing on things pertaining to your goal! That's over 152 continuous 24-hour days worth of problem solving power! Factor in the number of words per hour at which the mind thinks, and that's 131,400,000 to 219,000,000 words worth of thought brought to bear on your goal.

What's great is that it doesn't take a lot of effort as it doesn't require focused energy. You won't even break a sweat. It can be very enjoyable, and even exciting! As you come up with solutions to problems, your goals get closer and closer. Life becomes exciting every day.

Big Gulps versus Little Bites

It's impossible to eat an elephant in one gulp, but it can be done one bite at a time. Too often people are scared off by the enormity of a goal, like making a million dollars. They just presume it's impossible, knowing what they presently know. But broken down into bite-sized problems to solve, it can be done.

The first bite-sized problem you might solve is how your

strengths could be utilized to make a million dollars. The next bite-sized problem might be calling people who have experience in those fields. The next might be studying up on the industry you've chosen, then learning how to put together business plans, where to turn for money and advice. Each of the little problems is often very easy to solve. Having a goal gives you a linear set of bite-sized problems to solve.

Even an elephant can be eaten one bite at a time.

Summary
Simply by setting goals, your mind automatically starts working on them. As long as you let the problem-solving motor run, it will keep chewing on problem after problem, eventually enabling you to achieve your goal. It is a natural part of your mind's processing anyway. So why not put this very powerful problem machine that's already running (and possibly under-utilized) to work for you?

Define Your Goals
Now it's time to get down to business. It's time to set some goals. If, after doing the exercises in the previous chapter and taking the free personality tests on the Internet, you still don't know what goals to set, then the first goal is to identify them.

There are some rules I'd like you to adhere to for this exercise.

1. Do it! Simply by writing out goals, your mind automatically starts working on how to get there. Without stating your goals, your mind will continue to wander aimlessly mulling over what TV shows to watch or how to look cool to strangers.

2. Don't be too shy or too practical. Don't feel like you're asking too much. If you want a million dollars, write it. If you want to be a movie star, write it. If you want to be President of the United States, write it. All of that problem-solving power working on that goal will, at the very least, get you in the ball park of your goal, which is much better than being nowhere in particular. Dream big and set your goals as high as you want! Be brave!

3. Put some deadlines on it. It's been said that goals are dreams with deadlines. We all seem to work better under the pressure of a deadline. Having many deadlines and milestones to achieve will keep you under self-imposed pressure, which is much better than the self-imposed limitations you've been living under thus far.

Hmmm . . . Self-imposed pressure to achieve versus self-imposed limitations that impede my happiness? I'll take the self-imposed pressure to achieve. How about you?

Define a Direction

You may already have a clear goal in mind. If so, jump to the section on "My Goal Is . . ." and write it out. If you don't already have a clear goal in mind, let's use the elements and themes from the exercises in the previous chapter. You'll formulate a direction by summarizing your strengths, talents, desires, and industries that interest you.

"My strengths seem to be in . . ."

_____
_____
_____
_____

"Talents I'd like to develop would be . . ."

_____
_____
_____
_____

"Things I like to do revolve around . . ."

_____
_____
_____
_____

"In ten years I would love to be . . ."

_____
_____
_____
_____

"My dream job would be . . ."

_____
_____

"Industries in which I'd like to apply my strengths are . . ."

_____
_____

"My Goal Is . . ."

Now that you have some direction it's time to start committing to some goals. Again, these are not set in stone, but write them out to get you going. Change them later as you need, of course, but do this exercise now.

In 10 years I will be a (descriptive term of what you will be doing). . .

_____

_____

_____

_____

_____

_____

_____

I will be earning/worth . . .

$ _____

_____

_____

_____

I will be living in (kind of house and where) . . .

_____

_____

_____

_____

_____

_____

People will know me for (strengths and talents you'll exercise) . . .

_____

_____

_____

_____

_____

_____

Milestones to get to my ten-year goals:

Eight years from now I must be . . .

_____
_____
_____
_____
_____
_____

Five years from now I must be . . .

_____
_____
_____
_____
_____
_____

Three years from now I must be . . .

_____
_____
_____
_____

One year from now I must be . . .

_____
_____
_____

Six months from now I must be . . .

_____
_____
_____

Don't Give Up!

Now that you've established some goals, promise to yourself that you will never give up. There may be distractions, tragedies, and misfortune that will come into your life. Don't let them stop you. Take a breather, deal with the issue at hand, but always come back to your goal. If your goal becomes absolutely impossible, you might need to change it, but always come back to pursuing a goal, some goal, any goal, as opposed to no goals at all.

Not long after I published the first edition of my book, my first wife asked me for a divorce. It took me well over a year to cope with all that entailed. But I eventually regained focus and resumed applying my energies to my project. I was determined to not let the personal tragedy of a divorce stop me. I used to tell my children that you can use this matter as an excuse for doing poorly or quitting, and no one will fault you. However, you will have to live with the result of quitting, whatever it is.

Choose to succeed *despite* any negative event and don't let it stop you.

Never, never, never quit!

Think Like a Successful Person

Many hesitate to set goals for any number of reasons, whether out of embarrassment, disbelief, not knowing what goals to set, or fear of destroying fantasies. While hesitating to set goals is not life-threatening or hazardous to your health, not setting goals will lead to a lackluster life of little accomplishment, and, likely, little enjoyment.

Take the time to set goals, even if it's to find a goal to set.

Your mind is a natural problem-solving machine. It is the most powerful force on the planet. Having a goal will automatically bring focus to the powerful abilities of your mind which are now being expended on the frivolous.

ROADBLOCK 8

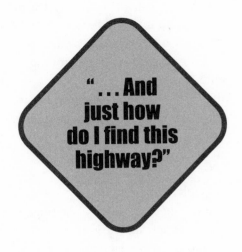

" . . . And
just how
do I find this
highway?"

Planning and Execution

Driving on the highway to success is challenging enough. But sometimes we have difficulty just getting to the highway. We know it's there, we can envision it. But getting there from where we are can sometimes seem like navigating through a maze of suburban streets.

"Where do I start?" you might be asking. After all, the goals you've set are quite grand, even monumental, seemingly impossible, are they not? It may seem quite daunting, even a bit scary. However, the process is actually quite easy once it's laid out for you.

"But I don't want to lose what I've got!" you might be fretting. Don't worry, you don't need to dump your present job or lifestyle to start pursuing your goals. You will begin by learning about things of interest to you, then exploring things in more and more depth. The process may take six months to a year, maybe more. You won't ever feel you're jumping, but rather, transitioning in a very methodical and comfortable manner.

The fastest planes, trains, and automobiles do not start out at full speed. Neither will you. You will first creep, then crawl, then walk, then run. Once you begin to move you will begin to build momentum, more and more as you progress, moving faster and faster. Pretty soon you will be unable to envision *not* moving forward. You will become unstoppable.

What's even better is that it's all very exciting. You will find that your life takes on a whole new dimension of excitement and satisfaction. You will feel purposeful and directed like never before. Other issues that have haunted you will now diminish in importance.

In this chapter we'll cover some small steps you can begin taking that will get you moving towards your goals.

The Vacation

Imagine taking a long vacation. You've decided to go somewhere, but you've not had time to plan. You have no idea of where to go or what to do when you get there. You only have X dollars, which you feel isn't really enough to do anything significant with.

So, you start off just driving in any old direction, not really seeing anything of interest just yet. It gets dark and you're still driving. It's getting very late, so you figure you had better find some place to stay. You find a motel that has a vacancy. It's so late and there's not a heck of a lot else in sight, so you take it. Well, the accommodations are substandard and you're pretty displeased. But, you don't want to take a chance on something else since there was nothing else on the horizon.

The next day you take off, again with no particular direction. You drive and drive until it gets late. Again, you get a motel room that's not what you had hoped for, but you stick with it for the same reasons.

The next day you set off, and along the way you come to the ocean. You hadn't exactly planned on going to the ocean, but hey, people have a pretty good time at the ocean. So you decide to start looking for a place to stay, this time while it's still light. You get an inexpensive hotel room. It's nothing fancy, not as luxurious as some that you've seen, but certainly not the kind of dumps you've been in the last two nights. Not wanting to goof up again, you book the room for the remainder of your vacation. It turns out you have just enough money for the room, for food for the duration, maybe some attractions, but that's about it.

You get home after the vacation and friends ask how it went. You tell them it was okay, nothing memorable, just okay. You grew tired of the beach after three days, walked around aimlessly looking for something exciting, but found nothing. You went to a wax museum which was okay, a house of mirrors, and two movies that were ho-hum. You spent a lot of time reading some cheap novels, watching the tube, or sitting on the beach killing time. You at least feel good that you managed to get home with a few bucks in your pocket.

Then another friend comes back from her vacation and tells everyone about the incredible time she had. She went to Hawaii, stayed in this luxurious hotel on Maui, met exciting people, did some surfing, snorkeling, and sailing with some friends she made. They all got together and went on a helicopter ride, saw some whales, and looked at an erupting volcano. She went hiking in the rainforest and went swimming in a tropical pool beside a hundred-foot waterfall. She had an amazing time and everyone was hanging on her every word as she told her story.

"That must have cost a fortune," you comment.

"Not at all, really. It only cost me X dollars."

Damn! That's what you spent! She had a great time and you had a boring time. It makes your vacation seem like a monotonous nightmare by comparison.

So, how come she had such a good time and you had such a lousy time?

Planning and execution!

Unfortunately, the boring vacation scenario is how most people spend their lives. They set off without doing a lick of planning or having any idea of where they should *or could* go. They think that certain lifestyles are just beyond their means, so they don't even investigate them.

They settle for jobs that are less than desirable because they had to take something at the time. They eventually settle for a slightly better job as it seems better by comparison. It may not be as fancy a life as they might really like, but they are afraid to try anything new because they don't want to screw up what they currently have. They settle for a certain monotonous lifestyle that's punctuated by a few ho-hum highlights. They feel lucky if they manage to save a few bucks when they hit sixty-five.

However, just as the friend in the story above was able to have a great time for less money because of planning and execution, you too can live an exciting and fulfilling life through careful planning and execution. Just as information on inexpensive travel and discount hotels is readily available if you were to only look for it, the information you need to plan your life is readily available. Look for it!

"But, that's just a story!" you might say of the vacation scenario described above. No. It really happened.

Go to the Library

Your library card is the most valuable card you have in your wallet or purse. Credit cards can buy things. A library card can get you unlimited amounts of information. It is this information that can help you achieve your goals and make your life more rewarding, emotionally if not financially. And a library card won't cost you a dime! What's even more interesting is that there are wonderful people at the library who are experts in how to utilize the resources, and who love nothing more than to help you.

Now that you've identified some strengths and talents, set some goals, and have begun envisioning how you might reach them, it's time to immerse yourself in information. Done right, it won't even seem like work.

When you visit the library you'll be looking for information on:
- your areas of interest
- your strengths
- the industry you'd like to break into
- companies in your industry

Revealing Your Areas of Interest

If, after going through the exercises in the previous chapters, you have yet to find what genuinely interests you, visiting the library will help reveal areas of interest you may not have thought of. You may have come up with areas of mild interest, but nothing compelling. Over the years you may have come across things that intrigued you, but you might have dismissed them at the time. Now that you know how people can make a comfortable living at nearly anything, you can look at things that intrigue you with a new eye.

You may not have been able to identify strong areas of interest because of lack of exposure. If you're just out of high school or haven't had many jobs, it may be hard to say that you've had lots of experiences that get you excited. Visiting the library can open your eyes to fields to which you have never been exposed before.

Do this!

Look at your calendar for the rest of this week. Find a time that you can spend two or three hours at the library. Commit to yourself to do this and *bring a notebook*.

Once you get to the library, browse around the non-fiction sections. Just look at the titles, pick out some books, look at the covers, flip through pages, look at pictures, etc. Don't feel you have to look for anything specific, just look at whatever catches your eye. Go through the entire non-fiction section, start to finish. You don't want to miss something that was just around the corner.

Write down anything that interests you. If a book title or topic compels you to write something, do so. If you don't feel compelled to write anything, that's a good indication too, so don't write things that don't compel you. Also, be sure to write down some of the call numbers on the binding of the books so you'll know how to get back to them.

Don't limit your choice of topics because you think they're an unrealistic way for you to make a living. If there are magazines or books written on a given topic, there are people making a decent living at it. You can too. So, nothing should be excluded from your list of things that catch your eye.

Don't check out any books yet. You'll find that many areas interest you. If you begin grabbing books, you'll wind up with an armload, feel like you're getting way too many books and quit partway through. What you're looking to do is expose yourself to lots of topics and you don't want to overload yourself.

By the time you're done, you will likely have a very long list of things that interest you. Take your list home and think about it. Your mind will automatically be drawn to things that genuinely excite you and begin weaving scenarios around them.

This should be a very easy and exciting first step.

Your Strengths

If you've been able to identify your interests, strengths, and talents, visit the library and/or bookstore to deepen your knowledge on the topic.

Your objective is to develop expertise on the topic through repeated exposure and different points of view. It has been said that if you read 12 books on any one topic, you will become an expert on that topic. Try it.

Another objective is to better understand those things in which you've developed strengths without guidance. For example, you may feel you're good at public speaking but never had the benefit of training. Doing more research on public speaking gives structure to what you've been doing. It will also give you more techniques to enhance what you currently do.

Later, as you begin to break into that field or talk to others in the business, you'll have a better base of knowledge, frame of reference, and ability to gain respect from others.

If you live in a highly populated area, your library probably shares its books with others and keeps record of them in an electronic catalog. If a book you want to read isn't at your branch, you can have it ordered and sent to your branch so you can check it out conveniently.

Libraries are free, but often times have dated material or less popular books on a given topic. Bookstores are not free but often have current and popular, high quality books on a given topic. Once you've narrowed down your fields of interest, you might choose to spend the money on current, quality materials that you will be able to keep.

Do this!

Schedule time to visit the library again. Go with your list of interesting topics. Choose two or three of your favorite topics to start with. Pick three or four books in each one of those topics. You may want to bring a grocery bag to make carrying them easier. You'll likely wind up with a dozen or more books. Take as many as you like as you won't have to read them all.

Bring the books home, and, over the next few days, plan some time to just browse through them. Your objective is to find things that draw your attention. Read section headings, look at pictures, read captions, skim paragraphs that might seem interesting. Each book should take you less than 10 or 20 minutes.

Over a few days of this activity, you will become aware of what is truly of interest, and what is of only mildly appealing. What you will also discover is that by simply skimming the books, you actually start learning about the topic. Repeated exposure to similar points, terms, illustrations, etc., begins developing your expertise. Decide which topics interest you most and read the books a bit more in depth.

Go back to the library, return the first set of books, and get a new set. Get more books on the topic you found most interesting, but also get some books on other topics that wound up on your list. Your objective in doing this is not only to develop more depth on one topic, but also not to leave other stones unturned. You may discover that other topics are even more compelling. Or, if they are at all related, your depth and breadth of knowledge will be enhanced. You may also discover a way in which the two topics can be related, and, potentially, come up with a market niche for you to fill.

Continue to visit the library as often as necessary to go through your entire list of interests or to develop expertise in one or more areas.

As you start narrowing your focus of interest, begin studying these areas in earnest by reading the books in depth. Take notes on things that strike you as important, write down titles, author names, and page references. Later you may find these references useful and this will make it easier to retrieve the source of your information.

This process should take three to six months. While it may sound like work at this particular moment, when you're discovering more and more about your strengths and areas of interest, you will continually grow more and more excited. Having more information on a topic tends to make the idea of making a living at it all the more real.

The Industry You'd Like to Break Into

A natural next step to developing expertise in a specific area is discovering more about the industry to which the topic pertains. The library is once again a great place to turn. Here are some of the valuable resources you will use:

Magazines. While books might describe specifics about topics, magazines offer opinions and interpretations of industry conditions and problems. On top of that, advertisers promote their solutions to industry problems.

News articles. Libraries keep entire newspapers on micro-fiche going back decades. Sometimes it's just local papers, sometimes nationally distributed papers, such as the *New York Times* or *The Wall Street Journal*. These articles can give you a deeper sense of the industry's history and major players.

Reference librarians. It takes a good deal of education to become a reference librarian, and these people know their stuff. Their whole purpose at the library is to help you use it. They will know where to find things or be able to suggest alternative resources. Treat them well and show appreciation for their help, and they will help you in every way they can.

Catalogs. There are lots of catalogs on a variety of topics, including trade associations, clubs, and more. These catalogs will put you into contact with people working in your area of interest.

Free Internet access. If you do not have a computer at home, the library has computers set up that are (typically) continually connected to the Internet, often with high-speed access. (More on the benefits of the Internet in the next section.)

Talk to Those in the Business

If you've done some of the research suggested above, chances are you're going to know as much, and sometimes more than many people actually working in the industry! Lots of people get jobs working at companies but don't really have a good idea of exactly what the company does. Think about your current job for a moment. Even if you know what the company does, do you understand problems in the industry, competition, or other related issues? Well, the same is true for many people you will encounter for the industry into which you will be calling.

In my 15 years in the computer software business, I discovered that people are often so narrowly focused on their own specific task that they haven't a clue about the big picture.

By having developed expertise in your area of interest, you're going to have some significant advantages when calling on those in the business:

- You are going to know about industry problems and issues.
- You are going to know about competitors in the industry.
- You are going to know about people who sell to those in the industry.
- You will be able to communicate with those at higher levels in the organization who are more in tune with the big picture. By talking to those at higher levels, you're talking with people who have the power to hire you with or without a position open.
- You may even be able to help them with information, insights, and observations.

The Internet

The Internet gives you direct access to players in the industry of your choice as well as letting you check out what people are currently saying on your favorite topics. You'll see what's happening in the industry domestically and internationally. You'll learn not only what companies say about themselves, but what others say about them in news articles and email forum exchanges.

If you've invented a product, the Internet will help you check out competitive or similar products, or check out potential buyers of your invention.

Associations

Nearly every industry has a trade association for people to get together to discuss issues of that industry and how to solve problems. Nearly every library has a catalog that gives information about trade associations, as well as contact names, addresses, and phone numbers. Nearly every trade association will welcome you to a meeting with open arms and will gladly introduce you around. They are looking for more members and will give you the royal treatment.

You can easily explain to the members that you meet that you're interested in launching a career in that particular industry and you want to know what it takes to be successful. You can ask for names of people to contact that might offer you more insight, or even where there might be openings. Just about everyone at the meeting will give you a card, so you can call them back later when you have more questions.

Calling, Writing, Emailing

You will want to use one or more of the following ways to communicate with those at the highest levels of an organization. The objective is to arrange any kind of face-to-face meeting with someone high in the organization. The smaller the company, the easier it will be to get to the top. When you start at the top, if the top person doesn't have time to meet with you, he or she may forward your inquiry to someone who has time. Instructions to meet with you coming from the president usually get followed.

The approach you will use for each of these methods of communications is slightly different.

Calling

Here you'll be on a name-finding mission. You may want to hold off on actually trying to talk to your target contacts for a bit, and I'll explain why.

Receptionists and executive assistants are trained not to let callers get through to executives. However, they will very often at least tell you who the executives are. Also, from a psychological perspective, receptionists and executive assistants are easier to talk to. Getting through to the head honcho on the first call can be unnerving and make you stumble and fumble around with your words.

Questions to ask on your name-finding mission:

"What is your mailing address?"

"Who is the president of your company?"

"Can he or she be reached at the address you just gave me?"

"Can I get an email address for this person?"

If you desire to talk to a specific person in an executive position, say the VP of Marketing, ask for the name of that person instead of or in addition to the president.

Writing

Once you have the name and address of the highest person in an organization, you'll want to write them a letter asking them for a meeting. It's important to get their attention with some kind of benefit you can provide them if they respond to you.

A typed letter is more formal and professional looking. Handwriting will also do, but is less desirable. The upside of a typed letter is that it conveys that you're very serious about your endeavor. The downside of writing is that it can be easy to goof up, either with bad formatting, writing style, grammar, punctuation, and typos. Little mistakes on a printed piece of paper create a very poor image. If you're very good at writing business letters, write one. If you're new to it or not quite sure, try emailing.

Emailing

Emailing has become a very easy way to get right to the people you need, those at the top of an organization. It is non-intrusive, typically not screened (the way phone calls and mail are), and executives will typically read and respond to their own email.

Another upside to email is that it has evolved as a legitimate form of communication without a lot of formal structure. There are thousands and thousands of books on how to write a proper (printed) business letter which emphasize proper formatting, salutations, number of paragraphs, and sentences per paragraph. But such is not the case for emailing.

People at all levels of business are so used to getting sloppy emails from others inside the company and out, that if you goof on an email, it won't be so critical. Certainly, make your email as neat and brief as possible (nobody likes to read an email that's bigger than one screen), but typos, punctuation errors, and poor formatting are more easily overlooked.

The Nature of Your Communication

Remember, the objective of communicating with a company is to arrange a face-to-face meeting with anyone high up in the organization, as high as possible. You'll need to provide a reason for such a meeting, and it helps if the reason can be of benefit to them.

Be a writer doing research

You can say that you are doing research, which you genuinely are, on players in that industry. You can say that you are writing a freelance article or a book on the industry, which, if you think about it, you're well qualified to do. You may or may not actually write the article/book and get it published, nor are you obligated to do so. However, if you do write an article/book and it actually gets published, you'll enhance your credibility and expertise tremendously.

In the letter or email, describe some general observations you have on the industry, then ask to meet with someone regarding something specific. *Benefit to them:* People may be more open to meeting with you if they feel they could wind up in print. Free publicity never hurts.

Be an inquiring mind

Describe in your letter or email that you've been investigating the industry as a career option. You might cite some of the books and articles you've read to suggest that you're serious about this.

Ask who might be the most appropriate person to talk to about the realities of being in the business before you dive in. The more specific you are, the less likely you'll wind up being directed to the personnel department. Emphasize that you're not looking for a job just yet, that you're merely exploring the industry. *Benefit to them:* They can check you out as a potential employee without having to run an ad.

Be a solution provider

In your letter or email, you might describe that you have a solution to a particular problem that you have observed in the industry. Ask if the problem you have observed applies to them without being specific about your idea or invention. *Benefit to them:* They may be anxious to find out what you think is a problem that they could possibly learn to avoid by visiting with you—for free, no less.

Visiting Businesses

However you couch your reason for meeting someone in a company, be sure *not to ask for a job* during your initial meetings. Your objective is simply to gather information.

Offer to meet them after hours, when you have time and when they have time.

Ask the people with whom you meet about what it's like to be in the business, problems they encounter with customers, competitors, or the government. Ask for their opinions on where they think the industry is going and what innovations they see on the horizon. Indicate that you've done some study on the industry and share observations you've made. Don't speak about specific competitors as this will be a clear signal that you will do the same about them.

Ask those you meet with for any advice on where to turn for more *information* (let me emphasize, *not for jobs*). They may be able to refer you to others in the business or related businesses. Having an introduction, such as "My name is <your name>, and Joe Bloggs at Ajax Wax suggested that I call you . . ." is much better than a blind call. Not only will they immediately be more open to talking to you, but also will have a sense of obligation to Joe Bloggs.

A meeting where the company contact does not feel imposed upon will lead to another meeting should you request it. The more meetings you can arrange with either the one company or competitive companies, the better. When you start getting to know the players, you will start to be able to see opportunities to solve problems for them. This is where you will eventually get a foot in the door of the business.

Remember, until then, you're just gathering information, not asking for a job!

Breaking Into the Line of Work

Here are three strategies for breaking into a particular line of work. The more you know about the business before you attempt to do so, the better your chances of success.

Get In at Higher Levels

After meeting with several people in the business you might start getting job offers. Why?

You have specialized information and knowledge about the industry and competitors. You may even have more knowledge than many of the people who work for the companies you meet. Competitive information or your "outsider's" perspectives can be very valuable to an organization. Information helps people solve problems, and that's what our entire economy is all about, solving problems for one another.

If you've been able to meet with executives, you have information from an executive's perspective. Demonstrating that you understand their problems and have ideas about how to solve them puts you in their league, if not significantly higher than the average new hire.

You have shown ambition enough to do this kind of legwork. Ambitious people are a *rare commodity*, let me repeat, a *rare commodity*. An ambitious person is much more valuable than a non-ambitious person. People who have founded organizations or worked their way up to become an executive recognize this kind of ambition *immediately*. You would stick out like a golden nugget amongst pebbles. Combine an ambitious person with industry-specific knowledge, competitive knowledge, and ability to discuss issues at an executive level, and you become a jewel! Any executive would be a fool to not snatch you up! Even if they don't have an immediate opening, they will often create one for you until they can figure out a title. I have seen this happen more than once!

Do Part-time Work

Maybe you have chosen to not meet with all those people in the industry as described on the previous pages. Some folks are just more shy about doing things like that, so if you're one of them, don't feel bad. However, you can also get a part-time job in the field.

This will give you a realistic picture of what the business is really about. A part-time job will:

Establish contacts: You'll get to know not only those running the business, but vendors and service people who help to keep the business going.

Tell whether you like it: Probably the most valuable bit of information is whether or not you genuinely like the business. You may have illusions about how great it would be. A part-time job will show you the reality. I would highly recommend this before getting involved in any kind of franchise operation.

Build your resume: All of the experience you gain from a part-time job can be put on a resume to help you get other jobs in the same field or when building a business plan to raise money for your own venture.

"Where do I find the time for a part-time job?" you might be asking.

Most people have an average of three to six hours a day of disposable time between finishing a full-time job and going to sleep. In addition, most people have two full days off a week, so that's another 32 hours of disposable time on the weekend. In all, there's between 47 and 62 hours a week of *disposable* time in which the average person is not obligated to a full-time job.

"HA!" you say, "I have no *free* time *at all!*" It may seem like such because you have chosen to spend it hauling kids around, running errands, and so on. But in actuality, it is disposable time, regardless of what you've chosen to fill it with.

There is a big difference between genuine obligations and a sense of obligation. Hauling kids, running errands, attending PTA meetings, and the like are not genuine obligations and, with some creativity, could be delegated to someone else.

"I couldn't deprive my kids of that time," you might say. I understand what you mean as I have three boys of my own. However, ask yourself what will provide them with a better role model as they become adults, someone who lives a life pursuing a dream or foregoing it; someone who is fulfilled or dissatisfied with life?

Try the part-time job for a transition period. In a few months, you will decide either to make a career out of it or to get out. You may even find that the more limited time with the kids or spouse will become more quality time, rather than merely watching TV with them.

Try Consulting

If you've done a good deal of research and met with lots of people in the business, you have highly specialized information. You can write articles, even books, based on your observations and including your suggestions on how problems should be addressed.

You also have the ability to share your observations for money, otherwise known as consulting. If you've had the benefit of talking with the big players in an industry, smaller players would love to know what you know, how they compare to the big players, and what they can do to improve. You can consult with them for weeks or months to understand their operation thoroughly, then make your recommendations based on previous knowledge and what you've learned from them.

When it's time to approach the next company in that industry, you now have intimate knowledge of working for one of the competitors. Should you choose to open a competing business yourself, you now have months of practical experience and observations to cite when building a business plan to raise money for your own venture.

Use What You Know to Solve Problems

Our entire economy revolves around solving problems for one another. When you gather lots of information on any given industry, your observations become valuable as they can help to solve problems for a business. Whether you write about your observations, get a job with a company to help them solve a problem, become a consultant and help many companies solve problems, or come up with an invention or new line of business, *you're solving problems!*

Make it your mission to solve problems. Look for ways to improve practices and procedures. Keep a notebook of what you have done in the way of solving problems for a business, not just in your dream job, but in the job you have now. Write down all things that you do to help improve business, document the results of your efforts whenever you can. This becomes great material for a resume for getting more and better jobs.

Understand that you are solving problems in all that you do. If someone is paying you to do something, anything, you're solving a problem for them. Look for more and more ways to solve problems. The bigger the problem you solve, the more valuable you become, to your present employer and the next. The more value you have to employers by solving bigger and bigger problems, the higher you will go in your career and income. The closer your problem-solving is to your areas of interest and strengths, the more your heart will be fulfilled.

Think Like a Successful Person

Much like the many other hesitations described in this book, if you don't believe that you can find your way into a job aligned with your strengths and areas of interest, you won't give it much thought. Without forethought, it may seem impossible and not worth pursuing. Without planning and execution, you will likely live a ho-hum life.

But once you identify your true areas of interest, with a bit of enjoyable research into the field, you begin acquiring information that is of high value to others in an industry. The more information you have, the better able you will be to solve problems, and problem-solving is what our economy is all about.

Finding your way to the road to your success is as far away as the nearest public library and is absolutely free. Give it a try. It won't cost anything but a bit of time and gas money.

Get planning!

ROADBLOCK 9

"I don't need no need no stinkin' oil!"

Self-Sabotage

Choosing to drive a car without oil is asking for trouble. In fact, it's insane. We just know it's going to ruin the car. Yet we sometimes do and say things to ourselves that are also asking for trouble and ruin our chances for success. We engage in habits that sabotage our best intentions and undermine our goals. We do these things intentionally even though we know it's bad for us. You may not even realize it, so learn to recognize these habits so you can be sure to avoid them. The road to success is tough enough without you undermining your own efforts.

Your Worst Enemy

Imagine someone moving into your neighborhood. You meet this new person and at first things seem okay. But after a while you find this neighbor to be pretty irritating.

Whenever you come up with a good idea, this neighbor shoots it down, "Naw, that would never fly!" the neighbor tells you frankly. By way of casual conversation, you mention to this neighbor that you've read this book.

"Oh, all those books are the same with their happy B.S. They're so far from reality it's not even funny," the neighbor says.

Unperturbed, you tell this neighbor that this book has helped you set some goals, you want to be rich.

"You! Rich? Ha! You ain't never gonna be nothin'. Stop wasting your time with that pie in the sky crap."

You give it a try and start a small business.

The neighbor comes to visit, "Well, how long do you give it before you close up?"

Things don't go 100 percent and the neighbor tells you, "See, I knew it was just a matter of time. Better start getting some names of bankruptcy lawyers now when you're not in such dire straights."

Business begins to wane, and you realize you're going to have to give it up. The neighbor tells you with a bit of glee, "Oh, I knew all along you wouldn't make it. Face facts, you're a loser!"

Sound pretty crazy? What kind of creep would do that to you? Would you even let the neighbor in your home with an attitude like that? Would you even want to talk to the neighbor on the street? Well, chances are that only a genuine creep would treat you like that, and there are some out there in the world.

But doesn't all the neighbor had to say sound a bit like the troubling yamma, yamma that goes on in your head all day long? You may have even seen where I was going with this because you recognized the nasty neighbor within yourself.

Think about the things you say to yourself. If someone else were to say to you the things you say to yourself, would they not become your worst enemy? You'd likely throw them out the door. You'd avoid them at all cost. You'd plan to seek revenge on them, wouldn't you?

Yet that's how we treat ourselves all the time and we don't think twice about how harmful it is to us. That's right, *harmful!* In fact, sometimes we turn on the sad music to emphasize our mood and feel sorry for ourselves. We think about what miserable wretches we are. We work hard to recall all the other times we've screwed up. If someone tries to cheer us up, we resist, "Just let me be alone for a while!" We want to be alone so no one will interfere with the beating we're inflicting upon ourselves.

Sometimes we tell others, "I'm my own worst enemy," or, "I'm my own worst critic." We openly admit how much we *like* to beat ourselves up. It's a double whammy, "I always beat myself up and I admit I'm stupid for doing so."

It's almost crazy how we treat ourselves. If we do it too much it *can* drive us crazy. We convince ourselves that we're beyond hope and worth nothing. It can make us perpetually depressed, make us physically sick, or even drive us to suicide.

It's all happening in our heads, and we do it to *ourselves*—voluntarily!

Why would we do such a thing? Why would we want to make ourselves so depressed, sick, and suicidal? Because we're being controlled by a negative belief we have of ourselves. We had all these other experiences that meant we were bad, so interpreting this situation any differently would seem like a lie! That's why. It doesn't matter that it's self-destructive, as long as it agrees with our past interpretations. "See, I told ya!" we hear echoing in our minds when we try something new but fail.

Now, it's not always that extreme. Sometimes we're not so harsh on ourselves. We don't continually beat ourselves up, at least not to the extreme illustrated here. However, some studies have shown that most people have *over 5,000 negative thoughts per day.* They don't have to be extreme. It can be just a gentle reminder like, "I can't do that."

Negative Self-talk

Negative self-talk is a very difficult habit to overcome. If you do it now, chances are you've been doing it your whole life. It might be mild or it might be drastic negative self-talk. It can be everything from, "I can't do that," to, "I'm a failure," to, "I'm a worthless person."

Seldom do we have someone in our lives who can convincingly steer us away from negative self-talk. Some are busy doing it to themselves and don't know any better. Others may try but are unsuccessful at convincing us because their kind words disagree with all the memories and meanings dredged up by our subconscious.

In my research on correcting negative self-talk, I've seen many instances where the advice is to write out positive affirmations (phrases), and put them on the wall, on the mirror, carry them on an index card in your pocket, and to look at them, or read them aloud three times a day (or more). This reflects the notion that if you hear, read, or say something frequently enough, you will begin to believe it. But remember we saw that interpreting events in your favor may seem like a lie if it disagrees with previous interpretations. Just the same, a positive affirmation will seem like a lie if it disagrees with previous negative self-talk.

Being directed to repeat to yourself several times a day, "I am a winner! I am a winner! I am a winner!" may not convince you that you are a winner. If you don't have lots of previous experiences to support the statement, you may be inclined to follow up such a phrase with the thoughts, "Oh, B.S.! This stuff isn't working!" And that gets stored away too. The next time someone suggests that you say, "I am a winner," the "Oh, B.S.! This stuff isn't working!" is very likely to come right back with it from the previous experience.

Reversing this habit

My advice to you is different. I recommend that you take a look at the phrases highlighted throughout the book. Each one of these phrases is designed to give you a thought that you're less likely to disagree with due to your past interpretations. For example, instead of "I am a winner!" try, "Hurtful words come from a troubled soul." Or, "The human mind is the most powerful force on the planet."

Review this book looking for the highlighted phrases. Write them out on a piece of paper, index card, or poster. Put them on the wall, mirror, or in your shirt pocket. Repeat these phrases to yourself as a transition from predominantly negative thoughts to more positive ones. They are designed to illustrate ideas about the nature of humanity and of your potential. They should not conflict with your past interpretations, and, therefore, won't seem like lies.

Not only will these more positive statements displace negative thoughts, they will also stimulate positive thoughts and interpretations, therefore building a library of strength.

You don't have to be your own worst enemy. Take control! The next time you find yourself about to say something self-critical, whether out loud or just in your mind, stop yourself. Remind yourself that you're causing yourself injury and hurting your future. You wouldn't tolerate that from anyone else, so don't tolerate it from yourself.

> *There will be lots of people in your life who will gladly put you down. Don't be one of them!*

Self-Imposed Deterrents

Self-imposed deterrents are things that you say to yourself that deter you from trying. You put these handcuffs and shackles on yourself! No one has to do this, but we do it just the same with great frequency.

Limiting Labels

One of the many ways we sabotage ourselves is by establishing and believing limiting labels for ourselves. We openly tell others about who we are and traits we have. We tell everyone things like:

"I'm lazy."

"I'm not very smart."

"I'm forgetful." Or, "I'm always late."

"I'm not very good with numbers."

"I'm a slob."

"I can't lose weight."

"I'm unlucky." Or, "That's just my luck."

"I'm hopeless." Or, "I'm just a loser."

There are, of course, many more labels you can think of. What labels do you give yourself?

We do this readily and frequently. We can observe a behavior of our own two or three times, sometimes only once, and we'll affix a label to it and say that it is true of us. We may be late for an appointment on three occasions and we'll conclude, "I'm always late." From that point onward, we whip out that label whenever it's convenient. We begin to think of ourselves as "always late," and it becomes true.

We pick up and keep labels like they're collectors' items. Why? Why do we label ourselves in such negative ways? We do this for three main reasons:

To avoid embarrassment

We will give ourselves labels to avoid potentially embarrassing situations based on past or imagined experiences.

At sometime during our lives we may have been in a situation where we felt ridiculed, laughed at, or just plain stupid. We might have been in a school play as a kid, and froze, or forgot our lines. The tension of the moment is indelibly etched in our memories and we will label ourselves, "I'm not good in front of an audience," to avoid ever having to get up in front of an audience for any reason—all because of one incident.

Sometimes when faced with a situation, we don't even need a real experience to cause us alarm. We may be asked to do something outside of our comfort zone and we'll conjure up an experience in our minds. We'll see ourselves in the situation making a fool of ourselves, then quickly decline so as to avoid the imagined experience.

To avoid having to try

We may be asked to do something and we'll offer up a label for ourselves simply so that we won't have to do it. The reason doesn't have to be fear based on real or imagined experiences; it may be something we just don't care to do. For example, we may be asked to baby-sit for a friend's children. We'll say, "Oh, I'm not very good with kids," to get out of it. Chances are, we'll remind ourselves of that label quite often and eventually come to believe it is true.

More often, it is something we feel is something beyond our capabilities. We may avoid a business proposition by labeling ourselves as, "I'm not very business savvy."

Whatever the reason, we're simply looking to avoid having to step out of our comfort zone and do something that we normally wouldn't do, fear based or not. If it seems at all challenging, we just throw out a label to avoid having to try.

To avoid responsibility

There are times when our labels come in pretty handy, as when we're looking to avoid responsibility. We'll escape blame with a label because something about ourselves is permanent and beyond our control. For example, if we forget to turn in a project on a deadline or bring an important report to a meeting, we'll claim to be forgetful. We can't help what we are, right?

Another commonly used label is, "I just can't lose weight." This label gives us the convenience of not accepting responsibility for our overweight condition. It helps us to believe that the little snacks now and then, or scavenging off the kids' plate after dinner, has no bearing on our weight.

We give ourselves labels far too quickly and based upon little supporting evidence. They provide us with convenient explanations and excuses when posed with something new. Most dangerously, *we come to believe* the ever-growing collection of labels as true about ourselves. We eventually become extremely limited in our abilities. We stagnate, become miserable, and feel we can do nothing.

Reversing this habit

Just as we give ourselves negative labels, we can give ourselves positive ones. However, this is much more difficult than it sounds.

Negative labels provide us with convenient excuses to not do something. Positive labels compel us to do something new and to expend effort.

We might try a new label like, "I never procrastinate." Whew, boy! Now we have to buckle down and do something to prove it. That's a lot of effort!

However, rather than trying something the extreme opposite of a negative label you've used in the past, try a compromise label. The extreme opposite of, "I never like doing new things," would be, "I always dive right in to new things." An extreme jump like that might be too hard for you to realistically accept. Instead try, "I'm always open to new ideas." Instead of an extreme statement like, "I never procrastinate," try, "I don't always procrastinate," or, "I don't procrastinate on things of genuine interest. I need to develop more interest in this task."

What's most important is that you take on new labels that you can believe, accept, and will stick with. Break away from the limiting labels, but do it gradually. Begin by developing the habit of taking on simple labels that you can stick with. You will eventually get to the point where you are able to take on new, more ambitious labels.

> *Negative labels limit and weaken us.*
> *Positive labels enable us to grow stronger.*

"If you want to learn something thoroughly, teach it to others." You've probably heard this phrase a time or two, and it's often quite true. Use this truism when it comes to labels. There are lots of people around you spouting off self-limiting labels all day long. This will provide you with plenty of opportunities to suggest that they not label themselves in such a negative way, and point out some positive truth about the person. This reassuring gesture may help you win many friends. Besides, your friends will be sure to point out when you spout off a limiting label about yourself.

"Can'ts"

"Can'ts" firmly establish something that we don't even want to try or don't think we can succeed in. We readily whip out a "can't" for many things in our lives and leave it at that. We don't even try, we don't have to, we're off the hook!

It may be something mundane, like, "I can't read backwards!" Which is entirely untrue. That's right, untrue! Given enough practice, anyone can read backwards as easily as reading forwards and still make sense of it. But, chances are you just never tried to read backwards before.

It might be something a little bit more, like, "I can't play basketball." This is an example where you might have tried something a bit, weren't all that good, and never tried again. But given enough practice, with the right coaching, you might even prove to be pretty good.

It may be something like, "I can't lose weight." This is an example where you might have tried several times unsuccessfully or with meager results, and just chocked it up to something genetic, that is, beyond your control. Deprived of food you would most certainly lose weight. Or, more realistically, given a change of eating habits and lifestyle, rather than temporary diets, you will lose weight.

If anyone else in the world can do something, chances are that you can do it too. Human beings are the most adaptable creature on the planet. Any time we say that we can't do this or that, it is not genuinely true. Whatever it is, it *can* be done, with the right set of circumstances, conditions, and instructions.

"But maybe it's just something I choose not to do," you might say.

Aha! Now we're on to something.

Whenever you come up with a firm "can't" statement, change the word "can't" to "I choose not to," and look for a reason why you would choose not to do something.

To say, "I can't climb Mount Everest," would be untrue. A simple examination of the statement would reveal, "I can climb Mount Everest, but *I choose not to* because it's a monumental task and I just don't feel it's important for me."

To say, "I can't play basketball," would also be untrue. You might discover, "I was not well coordinated when growing up, and due to subsequent embarrassment in school when attempting to play, I've never developed much skill in the game. Because of fear of embarrassment and ridicule, *I choose not to* play basketball."

To say, "I can't lose weight," is, again, untrue. With close examination, you might come to realize, "I've already convinced myself that I'm not such a good person which is why I've let go and gotten into this overweight condition in the first place. Periodically, I try a diet when I get really motivated, but I give in to cravings. I become discouraged not only with the effectiveness of the diet, but with myself. I figure the diet's not going to work and I'm doomed to be an overweight person anyway, so I give up trying."

To say, "I can't do math," is also untrue. When given some thought, you might realize, "Due to anxieties created by parents, teachers, and other kids in school, I didn't pay much attention in class. But because understanding math is cumulative, I fell behind and I was too embarrassed to get help. Besides, I became preoccupied in my teen years with my identity, social acceptance, or confusion about where I fit in the world. This led to more pressures to measure up, which became more and more difficult. How could I understand advanced math when I still didn't get the basics? So I learned to avoid it and convinced myself and everyone else that I was just no good in math."

Reversing this habit

The truth is that there are many things you say or feel you can't do of which you are entirely capable. Given the right set of circumstances and coaching, you can do nearly anything.

The key is to discover why you would choose not to do something.

"I can't" is really a cloak for the phrase, "I choose not to."

Change any "I can't" phrase in your daily vocabulary to "I choose not to." Then ask yourself why you would choose not to. By examining the reasons why you choose not to do something, you can correct those reasons and do it. Or, you may decide the reasons are ridiculous or not longer pertinent and do it. Of course, you may decide the reward of something is not all that important to you, like climbing Mount Everest, or learning a foreign language. At least you can choose not to do it with a clear conscience.

However, if it is something that truly is important to you but feel you can't do, discover why you've chosen not to, then seek out ways to correct it. Remember, people without legs have run in marathons.

"Shoulds"

"Shoulds" are tasks or behaviors that someone has said is important but that you're not doing or are putting off for some reason. This someone might be parents, teachers, others in your social circles, society in general, or even you. However, you're resisting doing the task or behavior for *a reason*. You are not giving the task a priority as high as others think you should.

If you felt the task or behavior was genuinely important to you, you'd be doing it! For example, a father who spends a lot of time with his kids doesn't go around saying, "I should spend time with my kids." He's doing it! A woman who saves money out of every paycheck doesn't walk around saying, "I should save money out of every paycheck." She's doing it.

When something is of high priority for you, you just do it. If someone tries to set a high priority on a task or behavior for you and you don't go along, it becomes a "should."

These tasks and behaviors that "others" feel are important for you can be called "expectations." Everyone has expectations of one another. We often have expectations about how the world should run, too. Most importantly, always remember that you have not been put on this earth to live up to the expectations of others. Everyone has their individual belief systems, which are a vast web of circumstantial interpretations. That does not necessarily mean they are right for you.

The problem with "shoulds"

Enslavement. One of the biggest problems with "shoulds" is that some people let them rule their lives. They spend all their time trying to live up to the expectations of domineering parents, siblings, bosses, spouses, or the "rules." These people may never spend time figuring out what they want out of life. Because of their enslavement to "shoulds," deciding what they want to do in life may come in a confusing explosion of a mid-life crisis.

Guilt. People have enough things to worry them and cause them to doubt themselves and their worth. Guilt stemming from not doing things they "should" only adds to this self-doubt. This guilt may cause people to adhere to the "shoulds" at the expense of their own dreams.

Opportunity lost. Imagine the difference between spending ten years doing things others expect of you versus ten years focusing on your goals, exercising and developing your strengths. What kind of person would you be in the first scenario versus the second? How happy would you feel? How successful would you be? If you were to become a lawyer or doctor because your parents felt you *should*, you'd likely be well off, but would you genuinely be happy?

Masking a real priority. The fact that you're not doing something that someone thinks you should might be an indication of something else that has yet to be resolved. A parent may not share time with children due to unresolved issues from his or her own past. Until those issues can be brought to light and resolved, the parent may never be the best parent he or she can truly be. A spouse may have hidden issues that prevent the marriage from being entirely successful or mutually satisfying. A good employee may suddenly put in only marginal effort because certain contributions have gone unrecognized.

They're handed out free and are worth every penny. Sure, we all have our thoughts on how the world should run, almost always without considering the ramifications if our wishes were carried out. Likewise, we often have opinions on how others should run their lives, again, without giving much thought to consequences. Just as we hand out opinions about how others should run their lives, others do the same to us with the same lack of regard for the effects on you. They don't have to live in your shoes, you do!

Resolving this issue

Listen to what's in your heart and scrutinize "shoulds" with a critical eye.

Certainly there are "shoulds" that, if not followed, would have dire consequences. These might include paying your taxes, paying your debts, feeding your kids, etc. But there are a whole host of "shoulds" for which the consequences of not following are guilt, a brow-beating, or someone being displeased with you. If a "should" is going to distract you from your goals, examine its worth as well as the consequences very closely.

> *Don't become a slave to "shoulds" at the expense of your goals.*

Be wary of becoming a slave to the expectations of others. Consider putting a higher priority on the pursuit of your dreams than on pleasing others.

Don't let the time you spend living up to the expectations of others detract from pursuing your goals.

Comfort Zones

We all carry the question in our hearts, "Am I good?" Many things we do are an attempt to answer that question.

We surround ourselves with people who help us to feel okay. We choose to associate with people of the same ethnic heritage, with similar values and outlook on life. When we cross ethnic lines, we still choose people of similar professions, social class, political or philosophical views. We choose friends and mates who make us feel good about ourselves, or at least accepted. When others make us feel bad about ourselves, our choices, or our views on the world, we often avoid or dislike them.

We make decisions and choices in accordance with our unique belief systems and what we feel is true of us. People get to where they are in their lives through deliberate decisions and choices. To believe it is the result of fate is a deliberate choice as well.

Too often the decision many people make is to stay within a known comfort zone. They know the people, environments, and activities, and feel some certainty that they will be made to feel okay or accepted as long as they stay within those controlled parameters.

Meeting new people often makes us feel uncomfortable. We don't want to be judged, especially negatively. Going to a party where we know only a few people can be especially challenging because we know we'll be subjected to judgements by many, many people.

The uncertainty of new places can sometimes make us feel uncomfortable. For someone living in rural areas, going to "the big city" conjures up fears of getting lost, getting ripped off, of muggings, or of getting shot in the an alleyway. To a city dweller, going camping in the mountains conjures up fears of bears, wolves, snakes, or breaking a leg and being stranded in the middle of nowhere.

To be asked to engage in new activities or events can also make us nervous. We don't want to appear incompetent or look like we don't belong. Someone who has never gone to church may feel awkward when invited to a friend's church. A junior level manager may feel uneasy when asked to be on a discussion panel at an upcoming convention.

A very common example is making a speech. Most people would rather die than get up in front of an audience and talk. Under the spotlight of everyone's attention we feel our true selves will become blatantly obvious, that our incompetence will be undeniably exposed for all to scrutinize and judge. Even speaking up in a meeting, our voices become quivery, and our hands shake in fear. We're not even standing or making a formal speech, we're simply in the spotlight.

In normal interactions with co-workers and peers, we can more easily choose to engage with people with whom we feel emotionally safe. If someone makes us feel good or accepted, we chat. If someone makes us feel judged, we avoid them.

But in front of an audience, we feel out of control. We sense the scrutiny of many eyes over how we look, what we say, and of our nervousness. We fear negative judgements of us, especially when we're so out of balance. We misinterpret feedback from the audience and blow it out of proportion. Our eyes focus on those falling asleep, the argumentative audience member, or anyone looking bored or unfriendly, and interpret it all to mean that we are terrible. The audience, however, rarely thinks such things and is more often sympathetic to such situations.

The less certain of we are of ourselves, the more we dread new situations or being evaluated negatively by others. We fear the answer to the question of "Am I good?" is going to be answered, "No, you're not good. You're a fool!" So we choose to stay in our comfort zones where our worth will not be scrutinized and judged.

Resolving this issue

Outside of our comfort zones is where there is growth for us.

Expanded comfort zones. Going to new places, meeting new people, and engaging in new activities *and surviving* the experience enables us to expand our comfort zones. When we are more comfortable doing new things, we will engage in an ever expanding repertoire of things we are able to do. We become capable of much more.

New contacts and resources. Meeting new people means discovering who else out there can help you toward your goals.

New ideas and perspectives. When we interact with new people, we learn new things, gain new ideas, learn of new resources and ways to solve problems. Being exposed to new ideas may mean discovering a missing piece in a puzzle for us, or totally ignite a new thought process for us.

> *Just outside your comfort zone is where*
> *you will find growth and opportunity.*

It is not necessary to jump way out of our comfort zones. Stepping just a bit outside helps us to take on challenges slowly and grow accustomed and confident. We become a person we never imagined we could be.

Forfeiting Control

If you don't command your life, someone else will! Without a goal or direction in life, we're inclined to ask others what we should do. There are many who will gladly tell us. The only problem is that it is generally what *they* want us to do. Unfortunately, this is all too commonplace.

> *By asking others for our direction, we begin to live*
> *the life they construct for us, rather than a life we*
> *construct for ourselves.*

Let's take a look at the people who we typically believe have control over our lives.

Parents

We tell our parents we don't know what we want to do, so they make lots of suggestions. Sometimes they don't give us a choice in the matter and begin telling us early on that we're going to be such-and-such. The only problem is they might want us to become something *they* are proud of, regardless of what we feel. If we don't comply, we become black sheep and failures. Even if we wind up being successful, we still disappoint them. Parents like this won't feel we've grown up unless we take their advice.

Authority Figures

We tell our high school counselors and teachers we don't know what we want to do, so they make lots of suggestions. They'll give us *sensible* advice that sounds good because it has a future, and we can potentially make a decent living. The counselors believe they're successful when we leave the office feeling like we've made a decision. Teachers feel fulfilled with the excitement of helping to shape someone's life. But the counselors and teachers don't have to live with the consequences of their advice and our choices, we do. Be extremely happy that you don't have to live forever with the consequences of the choices you made in adolescence based on what was cool at the time. There's always time to change. Mankind is nothing if not adaptable.

Our Employers

We go to employers hoping a job will hold some kind of future for us and that a direction will become clear. However, employers hire us to solve a specific problem and are seldom interested in our finding a direction and pursuing our goals. We become dissatisfied when we do not discover our calling on the job, or resentful if employers don't paint a progressive future for us.

Who Is Ultimately Responsible?

If we leave the decision up to someone else, they will gladly direct our lives for their own benefit. You have the power to choose your own direction in life. Exercise that power, or someone else will exercise his or her power *over* you.

Blaming Others

It is far easier to blame others for our failures or lack of achievement than it is for us to accept responsibility. To accept responsibility means we have to put forth effort, risk failure, and admit mistakes and shortcomings. Blaming others means we're off the hook. We can easily paint a picture in which any given task is impossible for us if there is another person, group, or organization that is out to stop us. The more convincing the picture we paint, the easier it is to escape having to try.

For example, you could say that you will never be rich because aliens abducted you and put a computer chip in your brain that shocks you each time you try to improve yourself. It will be difficult to find someone to relate to your experience, so very few people will believe or support you.

However, blame your inability to get ahead on big corporations and the rich people who run them and you'll have a lot of others agreeing with you. Many of your friends and relatives have tried to get desirable jobs in big companies and have been rejected. They all share your reaction and belief that rich people are out to "keep you where you are." They support your belief and you support theirs. Everyone's satisfied to have an explanation for their semi-miserable situation in life.

The targets of blame can range from parents, siblings, teachers, rich people, people of another ethnic background, to big corporations and the government. An overriding tendency of human beings is to blame others for their own problems. It makes us seem less responsible for our own failures, creates support amongst others like us, and assures us that we are right.

It is a natural instinct for people to want to associate with those who are like themselves. It is easy to be convinced that people who are different are somehow responsible for our problems. Racism is essentially blaming an easily identifiable group for your own problems. Yet, even if we were all the same exact color, we'd find other ways to categorize one another into groups. We would find physical features, ways of dress, accents in speech, and local customs to identify "others" and lay blame for our problems upon them.

Beneath all the blame is an excuse for our lack of achievement.

Whether the excuse sounds legitimate or absurd, it is an excuse just the same.

> *Being defeated by an excuse, no matter how good it sounds,*
> *still means that you are defeated.*

Yet, no matter whom we blame and how convincing a story we paint, the result is the same—we've accomplished nothing. We might twist and weave a convincing story about how a person or group of people are out to oppress us, but we are ultimately responsible for accepting such a story. By making the deliberate choice to believe it, we make a deliberate choice to oppress ourselves.

There is an old saying, "We have met the enemy and the enemy is us!" This usually refers to groups of who people have a tendency to get so wrapped up with infighting that they become their own biggest obstacle in achieving their mission. They defeat themselves by fighting one another.

I'll alter that saying as it pertains here.

> *I have met my oppressor and my oppressor is me!*

We expend so much of our energy finding others to blame for our failings and reasons why we cannot succeed that we become our own greatest obstacle.

We are the only ones who keep us down.

We are the only ones who decide when to give in.

We are the only ones who choose not to think of ways around obstacles.

We are the only ones who declare defeat against real and imagined oppressors.

We are the only ones we can blame for our fate.

Sometimes we blame other ethnic groups for working against us. However, many others have been opposed by those same groups and won.

Sometimes we blame big corporations for taking unfair advantage. However, you can move swiftly and outwit large, bureaucratic, and lethargic corporations and seize the opportunities that they miss.

*Would you rather fight, win, and enjoy the victory,
or quit and have only blame as your prize?*

Think Like a Successful Person

There are times when we are our own worst enemy. We engage in negative self-talk and beat ourselves up endlessly. There are plenty of people in your life who will gladly tear you down. You don't have to be one of them.

We randomly pick up self-limiting labels and believe them to be true about us. We can alter that same behavior and give ourselves more positive labels that leave an opening for improvement.

We have a long list of "can'ts," all of which we really can do. When we change the phrase "I can't" to "I choose not to" we can begin to discover why we are choosing to avoid a particular behavior.

"Shoulds" are the expectations of others which can easily enslave us with guilt. But expending all our energy on things other people feel are important for us to do at the expense of our own goals is hazardous. "Shoulds" need to be scrutinized with a critical eye and discarded if they detract from our goals.

Comfort zones help us to feel okay about ourselves, but they keep us from growing. Stepping outside of our comfort zones, little by little, helps us to gain the confidence to continually expand our comfort zones and our abilities.

When we forfeit control to others, such as parents, counselors, or the government, we also give them permission to control our lives. We will wind up living a life they create for us for their own benefit, not ours. Maintain control and you will live a life of your own design.

We can blame others for our problems and lack of accomplishments all we want. But no matter who or what we blame, whether ridiculous or believable, the end result is the same.

ROADBLOCK 10

"Where'd all these back-seat drivers come from?"

Resistance from Others

If you look around, you'll probably notice all the back-seat drivers in your life. Your parents, siblings, and friends have a habit of telling you how to drive. It is so common that you may not even realize they're doing it. Getting them to stop isn't so easy. Here we'll learn what to look for and how to tune out their unsolicited inputs and manipulative behaviors.

Resistance from Friends

So, you've decided to pursue your dreams, to take charge of your life, to be rich. You make a big announcement to all your friends and expect them to wish you well.

But wait, they're laughing. They're chiding you and telling you that you're a fool. How can that be?

"Am I crazy? Am I kidding myself? Am I just dreaming?"

No, you're not crazy, kidding yourself, or just dreaming. Expect this kind of reaction from friends. It's bound to happen for some very predictable reasons.

Current Friends Equal Old Thinking

You've surrounded yourself with people who make you feel okay about yourself. They think like you and you think like them. If you've been friends a long time, they likely still have your old ways of thinking. Unless they're reading books like this along with you, they're not changing as you are. You are outgrowing them. You have new thoughts, they still have their old thoughts.

This may seem like a very tough thing to swallow, and I may seem harsh for saying it. However, as you grow, and you will, some of your current friends may not understand. The more you grow and the more they stay the same, the greater the gap will be in your ways of thinking. Surely there will be common ties of experiences shared, but you will be changing.

Expect this change to come about with your old friends.

> *Don't expect old friends to accept your new ideas.*
> *Seek new friends who share your beliefs and attitudes.*

It Unsettles Their View of the World

Your friends may have a more absolute view of the world, that this is just how life is and there's no changing it. They don't believe that people have the power to move from where they presently are to anything different. They don't believe that they have the power, and therefore neither does anyone else they know.

I experienced this when I wrote the first edition of this book. People couldn't believe that I could write a book. They thought I was joking or that it must not be worth a damn. Why? Because they never knew anyone in their lives who ever accomplished anything of significance. They couldn't imagine writing a book themselves and couldn't imagine someone just like them writing a book either.

Someone just like them was breaking out of the limitations they felt kept them captive in their situations. When you have lived for so long with the feeling that fate is in charge of your destiny, seeing someone else like you take control of their own destiny is unsettling. It can make you question your own reliance on fate and wonder if you're squandering your time on the planet.

You're Getting Ahead, They're Not

Friends may resist your new ideas because they see that you just might get ahead. This would make them realize that they are not and make them feel worse.

"Everyone else seems to get ahead, but not me," they may think to themselves.

The ribbing and attempts to make you feel like you're kidding yourself are really pleas of, "Don't leave me behind. Stay here and keep me company, make me feel that I'm okay as I am."

Don't let pressure from friends hold you back.

Defense Strategy

A friend is someone who makes you feel good about yourself. You meet them largely by chance or by being brought together for a common purpose. You might sit next to them in a class, or you live next door, or down the street. You might meet them in the military, a summer youth program, or at work. Once together, you are drawn to each other because of things you have in common.

Whenever someone is similar to you in some way, whether clothing style, looks, attitudes, points of view, you like them. The similarity makes you feel okay about yourself. They reassure you that the choices you make are right, and it makes you feel comfortable to have them around.

While clothes and looks may be an initial attraction to those similar to you, it is attitudes and points of view that will build the strongest bonds. People often bridge the visual gaps of clothes, looks, and even ethnic lines with a common attitude, perspective, philosophy, or ideology. It is the way people think that is most important to them. When someone agrees with you, you feel right and good, and will likely bond with that person, regardless of all other factors. When someone disagrees with you, you will likely distance yourself from that person, regardless of all other factors.

Some friends may change with you or at least be supportive of your new ideas. Others may reject them, think you're being unrealistic, and be unsupportive. The unsupportive ones may have to go. This may sound sacrilegious, but it does you no good to cater to those who do not support you. Don't hold yourself back just to maintain their friendship. Even if you try it for a while, you will begin to resent them, realize you're cheating yourself, and end the relationship anyway.

It will be easy to spot the nay-sayers in your circle of friends. They will argue with you over your abilities, try to make you feel foolish for thinking new thoughts, and blatantly shoot down ideas. You'll likely not have many problems letting them go.

It may be trickier to differentiate between friends who are acting in your interests and those acting in their own interests. Friends who urge you to *not* try may be acting in their own interests. Ask yourself what might be motivating their non-support. The friends who support your efforts and will be there for you no matter what are the ones to hang onto.

Unlike your family, you can pick your friends. Do yourself a favor and pick only supportive friends and let the relationships with unsupportive friends go by their natural course.

Seek Out New Friends

As you grow and change the way you think it will be inevitable that you will seek out new friends. When you set out to achieve incredible things, you may need reassurance from those who believe incredible things are achievable. If you want to build a business, don't consult your current friends. They don't believe they could do it themselves, so how can they give you advice? Consult with others who have built a business and they'll tell you a great deal. If you want to be a millionaire, talk with someone who believes it can be done, like another millionaire! Reach out to them in some way and they will likely welcome you. Why?

One, because they know that they have gotten to where they are by the deliberate choices they've made. You will remind them of themselves and they will admire that. You are as rare as they feel.

Two, because they like to surround themselves with others who want to accomplish something great in their lives. It feels better to be around positive, ambitious people than around non-ambitious, negative people. They will want to have you around.

> *To achieve something incredible, surround yourself with those who believe incredible things are achievable.*

Resistance from Family

Family members are more likely to try to disrupt your plans than are your friends. Family members feel at liberty to manipulate your life for their own benefit, or at least for their own beliefs. It's as if you have a responsibility to them to conduct yourself in certain ways. Change the picture and you're likely to encounter some serious resistance.

In her book *Emotional Blackmail*, Dr. Susan Forward describes the many ways in which family members manipulate each other to get their own way, using emotional arm twisting rather than brute force. Seemingly submissive behaviors such as crying, pouting, the silent treatment, grumbling, simmering anger, or just bolting from the room or house unexpectedly are all effective ways to exert control over another without resorting to arguing and/or violence. Of course, there are those cases too.

People will sometimes resort to extreme measures to get you to behave the way *they* want. It may come as a surprise to you that family members will offer resistance to your desires to get ahead, but they will. Be prepared for and understand their reactions.

Parents

Parents go right to the top of the list of those who expect us to live our lives for their benefit. They created us, and society generally regards children as a reflection of the parents, so they're much more inclined to manipulate us. What we do reflects either positively or negatively on them.

Parents seldom encourage children to be "what ever you desire, as long as you're happy." Sometimes it's "I want you to become something you're proud of," which *really* means "something *I'm* proud of." When you choose to do something that contradicts what they want, they'll argue fervently with words like "be realistic," "don't embarrass yourself," "you'll never be happy doing that," "what kind of job is that?" "When are you gonna grow up?" They'll accept our choices only when we choose what they had planned.

Many parents genuinely do have your best interests at heart, which is truly admirable. Their main concern is that we find a line of work that's safe and practical. If what we choose seems extreme or risky, they envision our failure and potential embarrassment. What is "risky" can range from the obviously dangerous, such as hang-gliding or mountain climbing, to the mundane like taking night courses in something with which they are unfamiliar. They don't want you to jeopardize the relatively comfortable lifestyle that you've managed to acquire. They may not outright tell us not to do something, but they'll ask us, "Do you think that's really wise?"

There will be significant resistance if what you want to be embarrasses your family. After all, they're only human and are also mortified if they think others will laugh at them, or even whisper behind their backs. So don't fault them for their human instincts.

Then there are parents who outright shoot us down and taunt us with words of certain failure. It seems odd that someone would do this, but some parents experience great difficulties of their own and don't like the idea of their children doing better than they did. They may feel that life has dealt them a losing hand.

Taking charge and trying to win runs contrary to their belief that you can't control fate, and that any attempt to do so is hopeless.

Siblings

Brothers and sisters have a tendency to feel they are cut from the same cloth. If your brother or sister were to become a doctor, lawyer, or a person of fame or power, you would likely borrow upon his or her accomplishments for your own sense of worth. However, if your brother or sister were to do things that embarrass you, you would likely feel that is a reflection on you. Imagine if someone in your family were to become an axe murderer. How would you feel?

Siblings want you to behave in ways that will not embarrass them. And because they're siblings, they're much more inclined to suggest, advise, or flat out tell you how to run your life.

Spouses

Some spouses may also offer resistance. Your plans may threaten to disrupt their world. Whether they succeed at stopping you depends on the relationship you have. A spouse may *seem* less dominant but have alternative methods for getting his or her way. But spouses can emotionally blackmail us into cooperation.

Just as with friends, you choose a mate based on similar values and views. When your values and views of the world change, it may no longer agree with your mate's. Your mate may have a vision of living in your current neighborhood and lifestyle for the rest of his or her life and believe that is all that he or she *deserves*. Whether you paint a picture of minor changes or of grand achievements, your mate may think you're crazy and try to resist your ideas and efforts, whether overtly or covertly.

Remember, we surround ourselves with people and possessions that reflect what we believe to be true about ourselves. What you wear, the place you live, the jobs you pursue and settle for, the way you speak, and the friends you choose all reflect what you believe about yourself.

If you live in lower economic circles, it is because until this point in your life that's all you believed you could get or deserved. If you met and married your spouse in these circumstances, that is what your spouse believes to be true about him or herself too. Just because you are developing a new belief about yourself doesn't mean your mate is growing in the same way. If suddenly you start getting ahead and significantly improving your lifestyle, if it is beyond what your spouse believes he or she deserves, they may resist rather strongly.

Imagine going from where you are now to a shantytown with no indoor plumbing, heat, ragged clothes, etc. You'd likely feel very uncomfortable and out of place because that is much less than you believe you deserve. You'd likely struggle very hard to get back to an environment in which you feel you belong.

To move from a mobile home park to a mansion and country club may seem to be universally desirable. However, if you're not the instigator of such a transition, such a move may be beyond what you think you deserve and make you feel out of place. If your spouse is not learning and growing with you, the plans and transitions you will make in your life may also make them feel uncomfortable.

If you are married, as you grow and change, it is very important that your spouse also grow and change. Otherwise, expect resistance.

Family Tradition

We are born into a set of family rules and values. Generally these rules are established by someone of dominance in our families. The dominant members may be male or female, and they may have lived generations ago, yet their "word" reigns over our lives today.

Those who follow the rules and exhibit the values get the admiration from others in the family. Those who defy the rules and exhibit behaviors contrary to family values will get criticism. "What is your Aunt Mary going to say when she finds out such and such?" The threat is not so much of what Aunt Mary will think of you, but how much you'll embarrass your parents when Aunt Mary implies your choice is proof of your parents' failure.

Who are these people and why should they rule your life today? What business do they have governing your life? Did these "rules" spring up from issues in the troubled lives of your ancestors? And why should you be shackled with them? Just because they are your ancestors does not make them right or smart. Their dominance simply made their ideas and philosophies prevail.

Stand up and establish your own family tradition.

Defense Strategy

Remember, it is your life to live, not anyone else's. Do what makes *you* happy and live *your* life. Living a life someone else has orchestrated for their own benefit may make them happy, but you'll be miserable. Living to please someone else will build resentment and dissatisfaction in your life, perhaps causing you to explode. Then you'll make drastic decisions and big mistakes that will not only disappoint your family anyway, but leave you with potentially harmful consequences. Constructing your life to be as you want it to be, rather than as someone else wants it to be, will give you the time to craft your life carefully and successfully. Don't give into their pressures and guilt. Everyone will be happier in the long run.

Resistance from Experts

You may seek advice from "experts" whom you may know or not know. These "experts" are those who are genuinely experts or merely more experienced in the field that interests us. We may get negative feedback from them by their telling us, "You can't do such-and-such," and it discourages us. "They know more," we figure, "so they must be right." We're inclined to give up on our endeavor at that point because the "expert" said we "can't."

They may not come right out and tell us we can't. Sometimes they do it indirectly. Instead of saying, "You can't become a millionaire," they'll say, "Have you ever thought about the sacrifices you'll have to make to become a millionaire?" Or, if you have a product idea that you think will sell millions, they'll ask, "Have you figured out your target market? Have you considered the demographics? Have you located a good attorney?"

They may come across like they're doing you a favor by pointing out flaws in your ideas; however, they may be subconsciously trying to burst your bubble. They want to say "can't" but have to find another way to say it. Yet the extinguishing effect it has on our enthusiasm is the same.

But why would an expert tell us we can't do something? They did it, so why can't we? Consider this:

> *Anyone who tells you that you can't has a hidden motive.*

The word "can't" should be a red flag for you, an alert to make you skeptical and closely examine their motives. Why would someone you don't know tell you that you can't? How could they know your abilities, your dreams, and your drive? What would motivate them to tell you that you can't?

"I couldn't, and you can't either."

They may have tried and failed. But that does not mean you will fail too. They may tell you about how hard it is, try to give you good advice so you won't make the same mistakes they did. It may be reasonable advice, but they may not have had the sort of drive and persistence that you possess. They may not have had the clear vision you have. Your experience might be totally different from theirs because you are uniquely you and unlikely to make the same mistakes they did (you'll make plenty of your own).

"I could, but I had to work real hard to get here."

Someone may feel what he or she has achieved is incredible, and that to say anyone can do it would cheapen the accomplishment. Some protect the mystery and awe of their accomplishments to make themselves out to be superior to all others. However, you may approach things differently. You don't have to go the same long and difficult route they took. The more innovative your approach, the more likely it will make it and shoot to the top.

"I've been there and know what it takes, and you don't fit the mold."

You don't have to fit the mold. Innovators are the ones who stand out in any field. The ones who fit the mold may be well known in their own time but forgotten in history because they're so indistinguishable from everyone else in the field. Those who are different shake up the business and make it better.

Take a look at Steve Jobs, founder of Apple Computers (also without a degree). Doubtless he's faced his share of "higher ups" who thought he was unfit to run a business, but he's done a marvelous job launching (and later resuscitating) Apple.

"I know what is right and therefore you are wrong."

Just because a person achieves something positive does not guarantee he or she will be a benevolent person. Sometimes they are downright ornery, rude, arrogant, and contemptuous. Just when you thought you'd get encouraging words from an expert, he or she shoots you down and shows little remorse. Hurtful words come from a troubled soul, even if they've been successful in their field.

"I'm having a lousy day, so I'll pass it along."

Many things affect what someone says. Your ideas may be perfectly sound, but you happen to catch someone on a bad day.

We attribute a god-like quality to those who have accomplished something significant, believing that they are all knowing and have their world in complete order. We believe that they don't suffer from troubles and self-doubts like we "mere mortals" do. We don't suspect that they might have a lousy day or that they might have internal troubles. When they brush us off with a "can't," we take it to heart and become discouraged.

Defense Strategy

Many unknowns can affect an expert's opinions and advice to you. Your only clue that something is wrong beneath the surface is the word "can't" coming from their lips. Anyone who is genuinely successful and has no hidden motives will gladly try to encourage you and give you positive rather than negative advice.

Try not to let an expert's opinion disrupt your plans. Certainly take them into consideration. Listen to what they say, balance it with what might be causing them to tell you that you can't. Be skeptical of their negative advice and store it that way in your memory. But don't let it stop you!

Handling Feedback from Others

We've seen how others will resist your goals and dreams. It's also important to consider how to deal with those who attack you.

Negative feedback can be discouraging in itself, if not devastating.

As you move ahead you will still have many years of conditioning to overcome. The person you are is largely shaped by the feedback and reflections you get from others. It is often difficult to shake old habits.

You may continue to get negative feedback from others, just as you may have in the past. The danger is that it can cause you to say, "Oh, who am I trying to kid? See how people treat me? I'm no different than before!"

You may have heard of "Pavlov's dogs." Pavlov, an early psychologist, who formulated the theory of conditioned stimulus and condition response, was experimenting with several dogs. Every time he would feed them, he would ring a bell. After several days of doing this he merely had to ring a bell and the dogs would salivate despite the absence of food.

Similarly, you and I have been conditioned to interpret certain signals from others as having a particular meaning. In early childhood, for example, others may have teased and laughed at us. Later in life we interpret people laughing at something we *do* as laughing *at us.* We take offense, become humiliated, and relive the torment from our youth. Conditioned stimulus, conditioned response. This may not have happened to *you* as a child, but doubtless you have your own set of conditioned stimuli to which you have your own unique set of responses.

When you're done reading this book, you'll be thrown back into the world of those same conditioned stimuli as before. In order to change how you think of yourself, it will be important to change your conditioned responses that you would normally have.

Again, how you interpret events is entirely under your control. If you choose to interpret events against your favor, you hurt yourself. If you choose to interpret events *in* your favor, you benefit yourself and improve. When your subconscious mind revives old, hurtful memories, re-label them, give them new meaning, then store them back that way.

Everyone Is Imperfect

Everyone has faults—everyone! From the President of the United States to your own parents, no one is exempt from faults. When someone hands you some feedback that hurts you or makes you mad, consider that they are flawed human beings too. They are likely attacking you to shore up their own wounded feelings. Even if they are legitimately pointing out one of your faults, so what? Everyone is entitled to have his or her faults. The fact that they are attacking you is blatant evidence of the inadequacies they feel toward themselves.

Every Interaction Is an Evaluation

In every interaction with others you are continually evaluating yourself as compared to them. You will either be dominant, submissive, or evenly matched. Or, you may think in terms of superior, inferior, or equals. Whether you realize it or not, you're doing it nearly all day long.

We "people watch" and evaluate how we compare with others we see. We pick out and pick on characteristics of others and they do it to us.

When we talk with people, we're well beyond communicating for survival. We verbally interact with one another to elevate or diminish ourselves, or maintain equal standing with the other person.

We elevate ourselves by showing others how smart we are, using big words, talking about big, important topics, bragging, being louder, dominating conversation, trying to express ourselves more intelligently or logically, and trying to win arguments. We gossip about other people to make them look worse, thereby making us look better.

We diminish ourselves by keeping quiet, by not challenging, agreeing despite disbelief, giving in to arguments, avoiding arguments, or outright admitting that we're wrong or inferior.

We maintain equal footing with one another by using kind or non-threatening words, by joking around, by pulling back when we tread on sensitive ground, and by withholding judgement. Overt attempts to elevate yourself in a relationship where you're supposed to be on equal ground creates resentment.

Whenever you're feeling singled out, picked on, or discouraged because of interactions with others, do not take it as something wrong with you. This is just a natural tendency of people being people. You're not being singled out. Accept the fact that it happens and it happens to us all.

Arm Yourself

To guard yourself against feeling singled out or inferior when you interact with others, remember some of these phrases. Write them down on a piece of paper, stick them in your pocket, and look at them a few times a day. Memorize them so that you'll be able to spot a conditioned stimulus, recognize it, and interpret it correctly— *in your favor!*

- **Hurtful words come from a troubled soul.**
- **People try to elevate themselves at the expense of one another.**
- **When people are handed emotional pain and anger, they will pass it along to the path of least resistance.**
- **Those who judge me and my worth are doing so for their own benefit.**
- **Everyone is imperfect. No one else is qualified to judge me and my worth.**

Think Like a Successful Person

Your goals, dreams, and journey will not come without encountering resistance. It happens for predictable and very human reasons.

Surprisingly, those closest to you may resist your changes, what you want to do, and where you want to go with your life. Disrupting their comfort zones and their beliefs about the world may make friends feel that they are wrong, or falling behind.

Family may resist your changes if they've have *your* future already planned. They do it for their own sense of pride or to avoid the embarrassment of having your choices reflect negatively on them.

However, you're not in this world to live up to the expectations of others. It is your life to live, not theirs. Don't let feedback from others stop you from trying and achieving.

People are resistant to change unless it comes from within. As you read, learn, and grow, others may not be changing along with you. You may think the changes you're experiencing are wonderful, but others may not understand. The changes you speak of may be a threat to them and the way they think.

Expect it, understand it, and accept that it is inevitable. Most importantly, don't let the resistance you feel from others cause you to doubt yourself or stop you.

ROADBLOCK 11

"But, I'm already halfway down this highway..."

Improving Your Current Job

So, changing roads just isn't possible at the present? You may have other commitments that are keeping you on your present road. Or, you may already love the line of work you're in and just need ideas on how to get ahead. That's okay because there are ways to make the drive down your current road a bit smoother and speedier.

The bulk of this book has been geared toward discovering your strengths and establishing goals. It may seem that I'm suggesting you look for something other than what you are currently doing. However, there are many ways you can establish goals in the context of what you're doing now. You may not have to switch roads at all to exercise and develop your strengths and talents.

Until now, you may have suspected the only way to get ahead in your current job is to work harder or take college courses, earn a degree, and hopefully get promoted. The most valuable thing you can do to boost your career, not just in the short term, but for a lifetime, is improve your interpersonal skills. That's right, people skills!

All the world's commerce is about solving problems. To effectively solve problems, you must interact with people. Sure, there are the macro problems of a business involving the product or service the company sells. Then there are the micro problems of working inside the business. The concept of "internal customers" within an organization has been well established and accepted for some time now. People must solve problems for other people within a business. The more effective your people skills are in helping others to solve problems, the more valuable you are to your company. The good news is that your people skills are entirely portable from one company to the next and one industry to the next.

This chapter covers the many ways you can work your way up by strengthening your interpersonal skills. It has a list of tactics and strategies that you can employ to improve your value to a company, whether working in an office, in shipping, in retail, or construction.

Answer the Question

As I have mentioned many times, everyone walks around with the question in their hearts, "Am I good?" Answer this question for them by suggesting, "Yes, you are good," whether in obvious or subtle ways.

Since we're all wandering around fending for ourselves, very few people think to give positive feedback or acknowledgement to others. When you do, you will stand out in the minds of all those you encounter. They will appreciate you, respect you, and desire to get more positive feedback from you in the future. They will, as a result, support you, talk well of you, and want to keep you around.

Imagine for a moment going around giving everyone a gift. Each gift is appropriate and individualized to the person receiving it. Each gift is one you *know* they will like and even cherish. As you pass them, you hand it to them, smile, and go on about your business. Imagine how others will view you. Answering the question they carry around in their hearts is just that kind of gift. It's appropriate just for them, they will like it, and may even cherish it.

Here are a few simple tips.

Acknowledge Others

Whether it's just saying hello, smiling, or inquiring about them, people like to be acknowledged, to feel important enough for you to break the ice with a friendly gesture.

All too often when we pass others by on the street, at the store, or in the hallways at work, we experience tense moments where we don't know whether to nod, smile, or say hello to someone, whether we know them or not. If it's a friend, no problem. But for everyone else, we hesitate, wait, wait, wait, and pass. If they make the first move, "Whew!" we're off the hook. They broke the ice and we merely need to respond, which is much easier.

The tension comes from our fear of being judged by others. We don't know whether this stranger or person we barely know will return a nice gesture or snub us. We hate to be snubbed because it makes us believe that we were just judged as unworthy or unimportant by them.

Envision how, in times of physical chaos and uncertainty, we would become very cautious toward anything that threatens our physical safety or possessions. Just the same, we become cautious around anyone who threatens our sense of emotional safety. This is especially true for someone who has been emotionally harmed, either traumatically, or by being picked on over the years. When you've been told all your life that you're not good, by many, many people, everyone is a likely threat to your emotional safety.

Like you, most people fear the threat to their emotional safety. By offering a friendly gesture, you say, "I come in peace. I will not harm you. I think you're a good person."

By positively acknowledging other people, you are releasing their tension, and letting them know that you are emotionally safe for them. You give them permission to respond in kind without fear of being snubbed by you. And, if they venture a bit more, they may even get a compliment from you.

Think about it, have you ever known someone who goes around and smiles and says, "Hi!" to *everyone*? Such people are often *liked* by nearly everyone because of that simple gesture! And what about the personal sense of relief you feel when you're around them? Would you like others to have that same feeling toward you?

Make the first move, break the ice, let them know you're not a threat to their emotional safety. Make a nice gesture of recognition and make it easy for them to respond. You may get snubbed occasionally, but more often people will respond in kind, with a smile, a nod, a hello.

Compliment Their Displays

People surround themselves with people and possessions that reflect what they feel about themselves. They put evidence of themselves on display. These displays are extremely important to them as they feel it represents them. This explains why people can become so traumatized when their home is burgled. Pieces of them have been trashed or stolen.

Whatever it is that people put on display for you, find some way to acknowledge it, if not compliment it. If they wear clothing that catches your attention, compliment it. If they have pictures in their office, compliment them, whether children, cars, houses, or whatever kind of picture it is. If you're unsure, inquire about it.

That's easy enough when it's something you like. But what if their kids are ugly, their car's a junker, and their taste is odd. Often an acknowledgement like, "very nice," will do. At the very least, inquire about it. If it's their kids or spouse, find out about things the kids/spouse do and compliment that. If it's their possessions, find out the reasons behind their acquiring it and compliment that.

If it's on display, it is something about them that they want recognized.

Give feedback using positive words of approval and praise. Instead of just nodding your head and mumbling a bored, "uh huh," to show that you're listening, say things like "interesting," "excellent," "brilliant," "fascinating," "clever," and so on. You don't have to exclaim these words and overdo it, but use a subtle substitute for "uh huh." People will feel excited after talking to you that someone found them to be so interesting and worthwhile.

Make Others Feel Important

Consider the word "respect." This is another one of those concepts that we talk about frequently, but many find it hard to put a finger on exactly what it means. What is it that makes you respect another person? What is it that makes them *earn* your respect? What can you do to earn the respect of others?

Respect is simply making others feel important. There are no unimportant people in the world. Who is to say who is and is not important? We might feel people are less important than us because of the human tendency towards self-elevation. Just as you may think you're more important than others, others think they're more important than you. But who is really in a position to judge a person's worth or importance?

Absolutely everyone has an ability to *hurt* you or *help* you in some way. Show someone you feel they are important and you will stand out from the crowd in their eyes. They may do you a favor, go out of their way to help you, or simply show you respect in return. Show someone they're important and you will earn their respect for quite some time. Make them feel important in small doses over a long time, and they'll likely respect you forever.

People whom you make feel important will talk positively about you to others. They will defend you in your stead if someone else talks badly of you. When their source of feeling important (that's you) is threatened, they will come to your defense.

Convey that someone is unimportant, that is, disrespect them, and who knows to what lengths they will go to in retaliation. If you're lucky they will merely dislike you. If you're unlucky, they may talk badly about you or find some way to get even with you. This can range from spiteful acts that will somehow cause you difficulties to *outright violence*.

Conveying to someone that they are important is an incredibly small investment of your time, but can pay off dividends dozens, hundreds, or thousands of times over. The payoff might simply be positive feelings toward you, or it could be in real dollars. It may come to you directly from the person you make feel important, or it may come indirectly when they influence another person in your favor.

Ask Them about Themselves

How can you make others feel important if you barely know them? Strike up a conversation and you'll find dozens of opportunities to make them feel important. Simply asking them to talk about themselves makes them feel important.

People are often starved for attention. Sure, there are those who get lots of attention without even trying. But the vast majority never get enough recognition. It may be days, weeks, months, or even years between the times when someone asks to hear our views or how we feel. If *you* ask someone what they think, you stand out in a vast desert of non-recognition.

How do you feel when someone asks you to express your thoughts and share your views? Pretty good, huh? There's an old saying, "How positively a person feels about a conversation is in direct proportion to how much they get to speak." If you engage someone in conversation, get them to speak about themselves. They will, in turn, feel the conversation went great, and view you as an interesting person. You make them feel good about themselves, and they'll want to engage you again.

Most people have difficulties striking up a conversation. They feel at a loss for something interesting to say, like it's a burden on their shoulders. That's an easy problem to solve. Just ask open-ended questions about them. Here are five easy questions or directives that can get a conversation going.

"What brings you to (blank) today?"

"Tell me about yourself."

"Tell me about your family."

"Tell me about where you're from."

"Tell me about what you do for a living."

If you usually feel uncomfortable at striking up conversations, write these down on a slip of paper, stick it in your pocket, and memorize them. It's a fairly easy task that will pay off in improving how well you relate to others.

These conversation starters have definite advantages.

They're open ended. They make the other person reply with more than just a short, "yes" or "no," or any other one-word conversation stoppers.

They're non-threatening. They don't assume anything about the person you're engaging that might embarrass them. You are not asking them to reveal something that may be uncomfortable. They can regulate how much they reveal without feeling awkward.

They will provide you with many bits of information to further fuel the conversation. Get the other person to expound on topics which they bring up or for which they show enthusiasm.

"Tell me about (something they've mentioned)."

"How do you feel about (something they've mentioned)?"

Repeat back a phrase from what they've mentioned.

For example, the person says they work in glass art. You can easily get them to talk their heads off by saying, "Glass art?"

Spend most of your time finding out about them. They will be ecstatic to tell you, they will end up liking you, and you didn't have to do much of any work.

Assume Equality

In the spectrum of people we encounter, there are those we feel are superior to us, such as company presidents, bosses, managers, politicians, famous people, wealthy people, extremely beautiful people, etc. Because they have accomplished something we believe to be important, great, admirable, and so on, we often think them better human beings. We mentally put them on a pedestal, as if they are more than mere mortals, and know far more than we do. We also assume that they don't have the same kind of worries and problems that mere mortals have.

The downside of this is that we grovel in their presence. We act is if we are less than they are. What we fear is that they will judge us negatively for all to witness. So we are on our best behavior, "Sir" or "Ma'am" them to death, and exude such politeness our mothers wouldn't recognize us.

The truth is that these people are just people. They very often don't feel any different than you or me. They very seldom feel superior to you or anyone else. Oh, sure, there are arrogant jerks from time to time who use their position as a prop of self-importance. Ignore them. But for all others whom you might assume are "superior," treat them just like you would an equal.

For example, here's Fred, a famous actor. Fred goes out in public and adoring fans approach, gush, and fawn all over him. Fred doesn't necessarily look down on these people because he knows that he's just a person and the fawners have yet to recognize that. Fred remembers when he used to be non-famous and how he felt just like his fans do.

Then Alice comes up and treats Fred like a normal person. Fred says to himself, "Hey, here's someone who's gotten past all that pedestal stuff. She gets it." Consequently, Fred treats Alice like an equal!

The same will be true for you when you assume equality with all those folks you previously felt were superior and from which you feared judgement. Treat them like an equal and they will view you as an equal.

The very same can be said for those who are in any kind of "lesser" role than you. They may look at you as their superior and presume you know much more than they do. Treat them like an equal and they'll have admiration and respect for you.

Give Praise in Private

This is often done best in private so as to risk as little embarrassment as possible for you and whomever you're praising. Compliment them on something they have done, achieved, or a decision they have made. Don't praise them on physical characteristics as they had no choice in that matter (except for hairstyles). Appeal to their choices, decisions, insight, and character. Tell them that you recognize the challenges they face and how well they've handled the situation and that you respect them for it.

If someone is new to you or has not demonstrated anything readily worthy of praise, you can appeal to a "sense of something" about them. "You know, I can't quite put a finger on it, but I get this sense that there's something exceptional about you."

Remember, you've graduated to the "Yes, I am good" phase. They're still in the "Am I good?" phase. They will think that you're an angel swooping down from heaven to deliver that very message. Why? Because they think that there's something very important inside of them, but they can't quite put a finger on it either.

Who Needs This?

EVERYBODY! Everybody walks around with that question in their hearts! Everybody needs and appreciates this kind of treatment. From the people at the entry-level positions right on up to the president of the company. Your subordinates need it, your boss needs it, your customers need it. Oh, by the way, your spouse needs it, your parents need it, your kids need it, your brothers, sisters, and cousins need it.

When you give people the answer to the question in their hearts, they will like you, do favors for you, and want to keep you around. Just do it!

Attitude Is Everything

To many people, "attitude" is a four-letter word. They've been told all their lives, "You've got an attitude problem," in one way or another. They've got an attitude, they lack attitude, they need an attitude adjustment, and so on.

Many feel, however, that attitude means, "Swallow whatever it is I'm telling you and like it." Unfortunately, when "attitude" is used as a hickory stick like that, people tend to distrust the word and anyone wielding it.

However, attitude *is* everything. Attitude will open doors for you, people will go out of their way to help you, and people will want you around. Why?

Put yourself in the boss's position for a moment. Let's say that you're dealing with employees, Chris and Pat. Chris has a positive attitude, Pat a negative attitude. You're paying both the same and they're in similar roles.

Chris shows up for work, does the job assigned, is happy to do so, and readily takes on new assignments.

Pat, on the other hand, shows up late, barely gets work done, complains about the work assignments, makes excuses, blames everything else for not getting assignments done, and acts imposed upon when given new assignments.

As a boss, it's easy enough to see that you'd rather keep Chris around and ditch Pat. You would likely begin giving Chris more important tasks that you need to make sure get done. You fear that if you give anything to Pat it wouldn't get done or it would get screwed up, for which Pat would likely try to escape blame, of course.

But, it gets worse.

Pat likes to share this attitude with everyone else. Pat tells everyone how much the job sucks, how stupid you (the boss) are for a variety of reasons; is extremely good at finding the negative side of everything, and convincing others of the same. Pat likes to infect everyone else with this attitude. Not only that, but Pat likes to paint Chris as a brown-nosing lapdog so that no one else will care to emulate Chris's behavior. Even worse, the majority of people who get hired don't have a particular direction in life, and don't have a really strong positive attitude. They are often neutral at best and they are more likely to be influenced by people like Pat. Pat is not only an unproductive individual, but an insidious drain on your organization.

As the boss, you begin to cherish Chris and anyone else like Chris. Act like Chris and your boss will likely begin to cherish you. Not only will your immediate boss see this, but your boss's boss too. You will stand out as someone to keep around.

So how can you improve your attitude without coming across as a "yes man," brown-noser, lapdog, or suck-up? Here are some tips:

Don't Be Negative

Probably the easiest thing to do to be positive or at least neutral is to avoid being negative about anything or anyone. Simply decline to participate in negative discussions about the company or other people. Of course, this may be hard to avoid in all circumstances, but wherever possible, make a point of avoiding negativity.

Not only will this help your reputation in the long run, but it will likely help you to feel physically better. Negativity on the job can lead to depression, a sense of futility, and a lack of control. This can lead to worsening attitudes and physical symptoms. You wouldn't eat spoiled food when you know it will make you sick. So avoid negativity because you know it will only make you sick.

Avoid Negative People

When others spew their negativity, they are not intentionally trying to make you feel ill, but the result is the same! What ever it is they're interpreting in a negative fashion is just how they see things. They're interpreting things today in accordance with how they interpreted of events from *their* past. They wish to share their interpretations with others to get support, not only with current events, but retroactive support for all the past events that are just like it.

Negative people don't see themselves as being negative, but as being realistic and right. They try to persuade others to be "realistic" and agree with them that they are right. They believe they are trying to help you see reality.

> *Don't become a victim of someone else's past.*
> *Avoid negative people.*

Recognize that negative people will inadvertently infect you with a negative attitude, which can easily lead to job dissatisfaction, poorer performance, emotional distress, and potential physical illness. Poor performance and job dissatisfaction are a recipe for getting passed over, demoted, or losing your job. If and when it's time for the bosses to clean house, they're going to get rid of the "dead wood," or negative people first. Negative people can, quite realistically, cost you your job! On top of that, when you take this bad experience to the next job and see anything remotely similar, you'll likely develop a negative attitude on that job as well.

Look For the Positive

As we've already seen, any event can be interpreted in any number of ways and still be true. The only thing that makes an interpretation *seem* true or false is whether or not it agrees with previous interpretations.

Interpreting everything in a positive way, however, may make you feel gullible, naïve, unrealistic, and vulnerable to being blind-sided by reality. Here's a remedy for that.

As a challenge or even a game, take any event that you encounter at work. Do your best to come up with both a negative way and positive way to interpret the event. By doing so, you will *acknowledge* that the event has more than one possible interpretation. Open your phrases and comments like this:

"If I were to interpret this negatively, it seems . . ."

"If I were a negative person, I'd say . . ."

"A negative way to look at this is . . ."

"On the negative side, it might appear . . ."

This also tells people in advance the interpretation has a negative slant, rather than being absolute truth or what you genuinely believe. Then proceed to point out some positive interpretation of the same event.

By examining both a positive and negative interpretation of an event, you and others will be less likely to feel gullible.

Identify and Solve Problems

Every business has its problems. You may have heard the phrase, "the grass is always greener on the other side." When you're with a particular company very long, you get to know the problems of that company intimately. People often come to believe that only their company has problems and that all others operate more efficiently. When you look at another company from the outside, you can't see all the problems it has. But once you get there, the problems soon become apparent.

Since every company has people and people are imperfect, company problems are inescapable. This may sound like bad news; however, it is very good news.

People pay to have problems solved!

When you're just breaking into the job force or have an entry-level position, you may think that your company was "kind enough" to give you a job. However, at whatever level you are within the company, you're solving a problem by being there. Without question, they are paying you to solve a problem for them. The bigger the problem you solve, the more they will pay.

Now, when you were hired, your employer had a very specific problem in mind for you to solve. As long as you continue solving that problem, they'll continue paying you, probably at that same wage. However, seldom are there rules against you discovering and solving more problems than you were hired to solve. The more problems you solve, the more value you have to the employer. Again, the bigger the problem you solve the more they are likely to pay.

When most people see a problem on the job, they just moan and groan about it and talk about how stupid other people are for not doing something about it. What a waste of opportunity!

Rather than moan and groan about problems, come up with a way that you can see to solve them, as cheaply and easily as possible. The cheaper your solution is and the easier it is to implement, more likely it will get done.

People at all levels of management have problems presented them all day long. If you merely point out a problem without any solution, that means more work, headaches, and a possible chewing out for them. However, presenting a problem with an economical solution makes everyone look brilliant.

Start with small problems that you can solve on your own. When you're done, just tell you're boss what you've been up to and mention the problems you've solved. When you see a really big problem, write it up and propose how you will solve it.

Solve many problems and you will gain a reputation as a problem solver, a troubleshooter, or a "go to" person. You increase your value to your employer, secure your job, and move up to bigger and bigger problems to solve. The bigger the problem you solve the more they will pay.

Support Others

It's easy to develop a sense that bosses, managers, and executives at a company are all of one mind. When you see them at meetings, they sing from the same hymnbook and they all look so unified. You never see disagreement between these people when they're pitching the latest company strategies.

However, the reality is that it's often hard to get people to agree on anything. Within the executive ranks of any company, there is often a good deal of disagreement, different philosophies, infighting, or out-and-out battles. Managers and executives are always having to deal with one kind of disagreement or another. Everyone else has their opinions and interpretations about how things should get done.

Executives and managers often feel alone in their ideas. They believe they are right and everyone else seems to think they are wrong. What they welcome, more than anything, is support for their ideas. Give it to them.

You may or may not have clout within your company, but even *your* support is better than no support at all. Even if it's only moral support, providing them a chance to tell you about why they believe they are right can help them. They'll feel better after venting. They may discover new angles, approaches, and arguments in the telling. You can agree on points and add to them. You can disagree on points and challenge their line of reasoning to strengthen it (play the devil's advocate). No matter what, you're helping them.

When you support others, they will want to keep you around. Even if they leave, no matter the circumstances, they may take you along with them. If they are at higher levels in the organization, you will have their ear and their trust to make suggestions on how you would solve problems.

If you work for a small company, stay late and talk to the top person directly. Chances are they're still there after the executive secretary is gone. Act like an equal and they will view you as an equal. Solve big problems for them and they will give you big problems to solve.

Project the Right Image

Imagine how you would feel if a newspaper article about you were to come out with a headline that was inaccurate and made you look foolish. You'd be in a panic thinking that people were all getting a very wrong impression of you. Be careful that the image you project accurately reflects what you want others to *read about you*.

People read volumes about you and make some strong assumptions when they first glance at you. These assumptions may be totally inaccurate, but others will believe what they see before you've had an opportunity to say a word. Take a look at yourself and ask if what you project is what you want others to see. Don't assume the attitude of, "If people don't accept me the way I am, too bad for them!" No, too bad for you! People will *accept* you however you are, but they will make assumptions about you that may be wrong or contrary to what you want.

Whatever image you want to convey, you can improve your receptivity with others by how you appear. Without even saying a word, people will like you more if you are well groomed, your hair is cut or styled nicely, your clothes are neat, and you refrain from frequent use of bad language.

Grooming

You *don't* need to get a military haircut to project the right image, just keep your hair style well groomed. If you want to wear your hair long or wild as part of who you want to become, great, as long as it's well styled. Keep it neat and clean, otherwise people will be distracted by bad or ugly hair. You want them to focus on you, not your hair.

For men, facial hair should be monitored. Beards and mustaches are okay, but keep them groomed. Studies show that people generally trust clean-shaven men more. If you can gain more trust without the facial hair, it may be worth the sacrifice. It's up to you and what's appropriate for your line of work.

Clothing

Don't change your clothes radically or wear things that do not suit your present occupation. Wearing a suit to a construction job will have others thinking you're wacko. All you need do is dress just a little better than your peers. If you're in the blue jeans and tee shirt crowd, wear clean blue jeans and a collared shirt. If you're in the clean jeans and collared-shirt crowd, wear casual dress slacks and button-down shirt, and so on right up to the suit and tie crowd. Dress just a bit better than your peers and you will stand out in people's minds without looking ridiculous. People will view you as better than your peers without being able to put a finger on just why.

Moreover, the world is very uniform conscious. For example, if you were to get all cleaned up, conservative hair style, nice slacks, lab coat, stethoscope, clip board, and go walking around a hospital, people will all assume that you are a doctor.

Use this automatic reaction to your advantage. Dress in the uniform of the position to which you aspire. I'm not saying that you should dress like the president when you work on the shop floor. Dress in the uniform of the level just above your present position.

Finally, everyone who dresses well agrees that when you dress better, you feel better. Dressing well can give you more confidence. It is a constant reminder to you that you are on your way up. When you think that way all day long, you will behave accordingly.

Language Etiquette

Nearly everyone I know swears, even tells raunchy jokes, right on up to presidents of companies. So, I'll not try to convince you to never use bad language. However, discretion is the key. Be careful about when you use it. In the bar with friends, okay. In a meeting with co-workers or customers, don't do it. There is great risk of making a bad impression if you use bad language. Unless there's something very specific you're out to achieve, is it really worth the risk?

Consider, too, the things you talk about. The easiest way to avoid mistakes is to get the other person do all the talking. You just ask simple questions, they blab on and on, and end up thinking you're brilliant. Avoid giving your opinion about anything they say unless it's positive and praising. Remember, you're not engaging people to merely express yourself or pass the time. You're engaging people to find out about them and get them to like you.

The bottom line is to adopt the look and attitude of what ever social group you're looking to make your fortunes in. There is no one who can say what social groups are right or wrong, but pick one, walk the walk, and talk the talk. Appear and behave differently than those in the group you choose to move up in and they will focus on your differences. Appear and behave the same and you will remind them of themselves and accept you.

Confidence and Authority

When you project the image of what you desire to be, do so with conviction and confidence. Don't project uncertainty and hesitation. If you've decided to be a famous photographer, don't say things like,

"Gee, I'm hoping to someday, maybe, um, be, um, a photographer, if I can, um, make money at it." People will believe that you genuinely want to be a photographer, but will also believe that you will probably cave in and give up.

Project confidence in yourself and your goals. Say, "I'm going to be a photographer, I'm going to be world famous, and I'm going to make a lot of money doing it." People will respond to you, not only with belief that you will be one, but that you are bound to become famous with such a confident attitude. They may even feel a twinge of excitement that they're getting to meet you in person, even before the fact.

Develop Your Repertoire of Talents

Volunteer for Committees

Being on committees gives you the opportunity to wear new hats and interact with others. Wearing new hats outside your day-to-day role expands the list of things you can put on your resume, increases your value to the company and in the job market. In addition, you are exposed to things you like, dislike, are good at, and not so good at. This helps you to better determine where your strengths and talents really are.

As you interact with others in your company, you will get to know them, giving you a chance to develop rapport throughout the company. This improves your job security, as well as suggesting places to move if you want to change your present role.

Volunteer for Unwanted Tasks

Unwanted tasks are problems that need solving. The more problems you solve, the greater your reputation as a problem solver, troubleshooter, and "go to" person. People will want to keep you around and give you bigger problems to solve. The bigger the problem you solve the more they will pay.

In addition, you will be developing new strengths and talents as with committees.

Volunteer for Charitable Events

Some companies engage in charitable events in the community. In addition to giving back, it helps the company's image. If you're part of that, you're showing you care about the community and the company image.

Again, you will be developing new strengths and talents, as well as meeting new people outside your organization who may be able to help you.

Change Companies

You may not want to change your line of work, but you might consider changing companies. Chances are the skills you're developing at your current company are portable and beneficial to another.

Also, changing companies can be a good way to get significant increases in pay. Bosses, managers, and executives can become complacent with their current resources, that is, they take the current situation for granted. When it comes to giving you a raise, your unhappiness with a smaller raise than you'd like is not much of a problem to them. However, a vacancy at another company is a problem that they must solve in a hurry! They're more likely to pay what you want in order to solve the problem of a vacancy.

From Big to Small

When you start with a big company and go to a smaller company, you have a lot of reputation that you can borrow upon. The smaller company will feel like they have a genuine asset from the big company, someone who knows how the big company does things.

From Small to Big

When you come from a small company, chances are you had to wear many hats. This increases the variety of jobs for which you can apply. When a big company is looking to fill a spot, usually it is very specific. If you have any experience doing that specific job from the many hats you've worn, you have something specific to offer.

From Competitor to Competitor

If another company has a vacancy, they have a problem that must be solved! If you come from a competitor and already have industry knowledge and experience on the job, you can solve the problem for them immediately. The more skills required for the job, the less training they will have to put you through and the quicker you will get down to the business of solving their problem. Be sure you haven't signed a "non-compete" contract with your present employer, however.

Think Like a Successful Person

The easiest improvement you can make in order to accelerate your career is developing your interpersonal skills. The interaction between people is what makes a company function well, internally and externally. Your interpersonal skills are portable skills that will help you in what ever job or industry you choose.

Learn to give positive feedback to other people on a routine basis. Most people are starved for such positive feedback and appreciate you for giving it to them. They'll help you, support you, and generally want to keep you around.

Don't let attitude be a four-letter word to you. Those with a positive attitude help the company accomplish its goals. When it's time to promote someone or fill a new position, your attitude will help tremendously. Those with negative attitude become an insidious drain on the organization. When it's time to cut back, the "dead wood" goes first.

Solving problems is what the world's economy is all about. People pay to have problems solved. The more problems you solve, the more you will come to be known as a problem solver, troubleshooter, and "go to" person. The better you become at solving problems, the bigger the problems they will give you to solve. The bigger the problem, the more they will pay to solve it.

Supporting others is beneficial to those you support and increases your value to others. Key people in your company are faced with problems all day long. Everyone has their ideas about how to solve them, and often they conflict. More than anything, what people need is support for their ideas. Even if you presently have no clout, your support is better than no support at all.

Projecting the right image is one of the easiest ways to improve your position within the company. If you want to be a manager, look like a manager. If you want to be the company president, look like a president.

Expand your skills, strengths and talents by volunteering for things outside the normal scope of your job. Even the unwanted tasks improve your reputation and value to a company.

ROADBLOCK 12

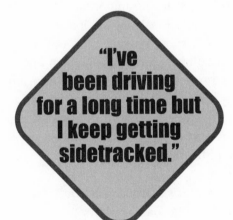

"I've been driving for a long time but I keep getting sidetracked."

Detours Along the Way

Even when your goals are clear, any number of things can distract you from them. These detours may seem important at the time, but often they do little to advance your life and help little toward your success.

You've probably had days where you start out on one task or project but you get interrupted with a seemingly more important one. You focus on the interruption only to have *that* interrupted. This happens again and again throughout the day. If you manage to make it back to getting a little something accomplished on your first project you consider yourself lucky. You wind up spending more time dealing with the interruptions than getting anything productive done. You stay late or come in on the weekend to have uninterrupted time to focus on the important things. In the meantime, the genuinely meaningful tasks of the job slip away.

The same is true for life. We may start out with some hopes and dreams of what we'd like to accomplish. Then one interruption after another takes us further and further away from our dreams. If we get to spend any time at all in pursuit of our dreams, we consider ourselves lucky. We work extra hard to make enough money to pay for our dreams in the form of hobbies, if at all. In the meantime, the genuinely meaningful things we wanted to do in life have slipped away.

The holiday classic *It's a Wonderful Life* draws this picture for us very clearly. Poor George Bailey wants to travel and live a life of adventure. But one crisis after another keeps cropping up and prevents him from having the life that he wants. While this is a touching tale about how one man can affect the lives of many, it's also a dismal portrait of the life most of us live.

Just like George Bailey, we start out with hopes and dreams, but we get sidetracked, maybe not because of a crisis, but with settling for less than we had hoped for. We tell ourselves that what we hoped for wasn't really practical anyway. We try to content ourselves with what we wind up with and suppress thoughts of what might have been. If we're lucky, like George Bailey, we come to a point later in life where a momentous event makes us happy for the life we've had despite having missed out on the life we wanted. If we're not lucky, we grow old, bitter, unsatisfied, and filled with regret.

We'll take a look at those distractions that can easily interrupt us or keep us from pursuing the life we really want. While they seem like significant aspects of life, we sometimes give them more importance than they deserve. However, when we manage to put them in the proper perspective, *we can keep them from derailing us*, while enjoying them to boot.

Emotions

Emotions are the spice of life, the feelings that make life interesting and enjoyable. They can also make life miserable and unbearable. Without them, life would be tediously boring—but endlessly more productive.

Emotions can take us on a wild roller-coaster ride where it seems like we have absolutely no control. We behave in ways we normally wouldn't and say things we later regret. If we could only be like Mr. Spock of Star Trek fame, we'd do what was logical and best with uncanny focus. But emotions are there to distract us, make us think twice, make us decide things against our own better judgement and long-term goals.

I'm not suggesting that we become automatons, emotionless robots bent on the pursuit of money. I am suggesting, however, that when we better understand our emotions, we can keep them from overwhelming our lives and better judgements. We can maintain control and help ourselves to stay on track.

Love

Let's address the most significant emotion in life first. Certainly love is what we all seem to want. Many of us are lucky enough to experience it at least once in our lives, some of us on a regular basis. Still others spend their entire lives not really feeling love at all.

Ask anyone what love is and you'll get a variety of vague answers. Some will tell you God is love. To others, love is caring for someone. There are many different kinds of love, we're told: love for your parents, love for your children, love for your spouse, romantic love, companion love, friendship love, and spiritual love. Sometimes we have the darker side of love, such as lust, love of money, love of objects, and even nagging love-hate relationships.

Endless reels of movies depict the quintessential love. Endless scores of songs tell of the joy and the pain of love. Billions and billions of dollars are spent in pursuit of love. Many lives are sacrificed for love, endless years spent in search of it, or many grow empty and bitter without love.

With such an everyday use of the term, you would think that people would be able to clearly identify love with a concrete definition. Yet its definition seems to elude us and keep us guessing. Love gets a disproportionate amount of attention for being so ill-defined and fleeting.

When we think we're on the verge of love, we're inclined to make stupid decisions quickly before love gets away from us. If we better understand what love is, we can keep it from distracting or destroying us.

> *Love is a degree of attraction to someone or something based on how it makes you feel about yourself.*

Love is fairly simple when defined this way. The essence to remember is how someone or some thing makes you feel about yourself.

Love for parents. If we're lucky, our parents make us feel good about ourselves when it seems the bullies of the world are out to get us. They take our side when we have a conflict with others, be they neighbors, teachers, sometimes even the law. They stand by us and make us feel worth something when no one else does. We love parents because without them we may not have anyone else in the world who will be so loyal to us.

Love for children. We feel a strong attraction to our children when they exhibit our finer qualities. They are a reflection of ourselves and our ability to produce other human beings. If they excel they make us proud and we love them more. Sometimes they frustrate us by defying us and our teachings and values. Sometimes they hurt us by making us feel inadequate or that we've failed somehow in rearing them.

Love for siblings. We have love for brothers, sisters, and sometimes extended family because they accept us, or at least put up with us when we're rejected by the rest of the world. Often times they're forgiving and will tell us we're okay when we've failed. If we're lucky, they may even lend or give us money when we're down on our luck when no one else in their right minds would.

Romantic love. In the endless sea of faces, the people we know and don't know, we're lucky just to have friends. We are luckier still if someone feels strongly attracted to us and feels that we are somehow special. If we're strongly attracted to them as well, we fall in love. There is a mutual belief that each is lucky to have the strong attraction of the other. The person to whom we are attracted accepts us as we are (or at least as much as we'll show them at the outset). The other person thinks we're special and that makes us feel joyous. Sure, our parents believe we're special, but that goes with their job. When someone else believes we are special, particularly if the person is attractive, it makes us feel fantastic.

Companion love. This is where two people mutually accept and like each other over a long period of time. Each partner is attracted to the other and both are forgiving of flaws and faults. This is the kind of love felt in long-term marriages. There may no longer be the hot, romantic love they had at the outset. That kind of hot, passionate love is more associated with the newness of discovering someone, and the ardent effort to stimulate attraction. The mutual acceptance of one another is what keeps companion love going for the long haul.

Love of things. Sure it's possible to love things. A fancy car, luxury boat, an expensive house, or suit of clothes can make a person feel particularly special or important. A person can therefore feel a great degree of attraction towards the object depending on how strongly the object makes them feel about him or herself.

Love of a job. Just as *things* can make you feel fantastic, so can a job. We can be engaged in employment that utilizes our talents and skills and it can make us feel great. If we're so lucky, work becomes play, and we excel because we're passionate in our execution of the job. Play, incidentally, is an activity that makes us feel great and utilize our talents and skills. Imagine that!

Love for pets. We can feel a strong degree of attraction towards pets as well. Pets can't criticize or judge us. They accept us as we are. All we need do is show them some attention and they'll be loyal to us no matter what.

Giving love to others. Simply showing others how highly we regard them creates a sense of worth in them. They, in turn, feel a degree of attraction to us based on how good we make them feel about themselves.

Unconditional love. We're advised as parents to give our love unconditionally to our children. We convey a positive feeling toward our children no matter how they behave, whether their behavior is in accordance with our wishes or against. It's easy to feel frustrated toward children who defy our wishes, and very difficult to convey positive feelings in the face of their defiance.

One-sided love. This happens when someone is attracted to us, but we're not attracted to them, or vice versa. In one-sided love, one person admires another, but the feeling is not mutual. The admirer imagines how wonderful and special he or she would feel if only he or she had the same admiration in return. This is most common in infatuation with movie and music stars. "Wouldn't it be great if (Mr./Ms. Bigstar) were to like me? Just imagine what all my friends would think then!" We envision that we'd be on top of the world.

Love-hate relationships. We sometimes hate another person we're close to. But because of the nature of the relationship, we feel obligated to say we love them. The guilt of saying that we hate them is overwhelming, so we deny the negative emotion and say we love them. This is most common in parent-child relationships where the idea of "you hate your mother?" brings about such strong feelings of guilt that it's easier to say, "No, I really do love her, we just have a love-hate relationship." In a marriage, love-hate relationships often wind up as hate relationships and end in divorce as there's little societal guilt for getting divorced.

Self-love. You have the ultimate control over how you feel about yourself. By focusing on your good qualities and accepting your bad ones it's very easy to be happy that you're "you" and that you're alive.

Many motivational and inspirational books talk about self-love as the top priority in achieving success or in loving others. They say, "If you can't love yourself, how can you love others?" This can be perplexing if you don't clearly understand love. Besides, a lot of people are uncomfortable with the idea of self-love, believing it means vanity and selfishness.

Once you put love into perspective, it's easier to maintain control. If you can first make yourself feel great, or at least okay with yourself, you can pick and choose what relationships you establish with others. If you have no self-love and feel desperate or deprived of love, the first one to come along and show any attraction to you can send you off on a whirlwind ride. You could easily give up everything you have in pursuit of that feeling. You can be easily tricked when someone attractive to you pretends to love you.

If, on the other hand, you have the self-control to make yourself feel great and worthwhile, you'll have the control to assess what the other person really means to you and what sacrifices, if any, the other person will cost you. At that time you can make more clear and reasonable decisions.

Love is a fine thing. It feels great when someone we're attracted to values us so highly. But if we cannot make ourselves feel great, we may be at the mercy of the other.

Attraction

What is attraction? Like love, it is something that we deal with every day, but we don't always understand it or why it has such power over us.

Attraction is envisioning how the close association with someone or something highly valued by society will elevate our own status.

There's a mouthful, so let's break it down.

We can be attracted to things, such as fancy cars, houses, boats, and so on. We envision what it would be like to own them and how we believe others would regard us. The higher the elevation in status, the stronger the attraction.

Often, we won't jump to extremes, but desire the "next upgrade" from where we presently are because it's believable and achievable. If you have to stretch to make a $99 a month car payment, the idea of acquiring a $100,000 Mercedes Benz seems incomprehensible, so we put it out of our minds.

When it comes to being attracted to people, we are able to determine our attraction to them amazingly fast. When we see someone, our minds quickly evaluate how closely their physical features match those that society regards highly. If a person looks like an attractive movie star, rock star, or model, we envision how a close relationship with such a person would elevate our status. This desire to elevate our status is not conscious. The words, "being involved with *that* person would *really* elevate my social standing," don't likely go through your mind. Yet the feeling that you're somehow more special than you were before can be traced back to the idea of social elevation if you give it some real thought.

We can be attracted to people for many reasons.

Popularity. Whether we're young or old, we may be attracted to someone simply because they seem to be able to attract lots of friends. They may establish their popularity through good looks or charm, but we hope that an association with them will help us to acquire some of their friends, or at least be viewed by their friends as someone worthy.

Sex appeal. Each society clearly depicts what is physically desirable in a man or woman, what kind of facial features, what kind of curves, and where. Those who match that closely are highly regarded. Even those who possess just a few of the desired physical qualities are valued highly. Being able to win someone who possesses these qualities helps to elevate our status. When someone highly valued is attracted to us, it reflects well on us.

There are many who will argue that sexual attraction is instinctual, that we're simply trying to identify the best candidate with whom to reproduce. If that were so, we'd be sexually attracted to everyone, and only those of the opposite sex. We'd disregard physical features and simply be attracted to someone healthy and able to produce offspring. Yet we can still feel incredibly attracted to someone who is physically disabled or of the same sex. The argument for instinctual attraction goes right out the window.

Social status. Of course there is a direct connection between regard for high social status and our attraction to people who have it. Their social standing may be the result of having lots of money, power, or strong influence with other people. They need not be "attractive" in the sex appeal sense, but may command great respect in society. To be recognized by them as being someone special or important is a secret but strong desire. Pick a president whom you admire, whether the president of a company or the President of the United States. What would it be like to get to know him or her on a personal basis? How would you feel about your social standing then?

Mutual attraction. There are times when we feel attracted to people who are attracted to us. Not all of us have the good fortune of looking like movie stars and models. Many of us feel unattractive and are glad when someone finds us appealing for any reason. They make us feel we have worth and are special. We may still be attracted to the movie stars and models, but the idea of actually being involved with them would make us feel awkward and out of our "league." We feel happy with someone who is consistent with our own self-perception, that is, in our own league.

While this is not an attraction due to a desire for social elevation, it is based on how another person makes us feel about ourselves.

Remembered attraction. We can feel a strong attraction to someone who reminds us of someone else who made us feel good. We can be attracted to women who remind us of our mothers, or attracted to men who remind us of our fathers. We can be immensely attracted to a person we've never met because he or she reminds us of an old flame.

Sex

What is *"sex"* doing in a book on success? What do you spend a great deal of time thinking about? If you're like most folks, you spend a a lot more time thinking about it than actually doing it. It is probably, therefore, a big distraction. It's been said that, "sex takes so little time but causes so much trouble." I'm not suggesting for a moment that you abstain from sex, or even from thinking about it. However, the better you understand it, the less likely it will consume your life.

When we're engaged in sex we're communicating so many things to one another on a very intimate level. The intimate communications of sex are the closest we come to sharing our true *self* with another. We read many signals and make interpretations about our worth as a human being. This is why men always want to be "the best" and why women want to be loved "as a person" rather than just for their bodies. This is also why rejection in sex can be so devastating.

We may read signals that tell us we are virile or beautiful and have great sexual appeal and prowess. We may have a strong desire to get these signals, not just from one person, but from many. The more attractive the partner is, the more meaning and value the signals have to us.

We may read signals that tell us we are impotent, unworthy, or less of a man or less of a woman. Sex in fantasy becomes emotionally better than sex in reality as we envision ourselves with more sexual appeal, prowess and of having greater sexual worth. We envision sex with beautiful people, yet without our imperfections to make us feel inadequate. We envision pleasing them, thereby getting positive signals about our intimate worth.

We may read signals that tell us that we are special to our partners. The signals tell us that we are neither fantastic nor poor sexual partners, but good enough to keep our partner happy.

Certainly the physical pleasure of sex attracts us, but if that were all there was to sex, we'd either be happy by ourselves, or with any partner at all. But sex is more about intimate communication about our unprotected, undeniable selves.

We seem to have an insatiable drive to receive these intimate sexual signals to elevate or reassure us of our worth. However, you can control and can interpret what sex means to you.

Are the conclusions drawn from the signals we get from our partners worth the lengths we will go to get them?

Will you allow your worth as a person to be defined by the worth you feel during sex?

Is sex really all there is to life? It's certainly important, but it's not all there is.

This is an endless topic and there are many aspects of sex that go well beyond the scope of a book on success, but I'll leave it at this. I once heard a woman in the audience of a television talk show speak up that, "sex is about what's happening between your ears, not what's happening between your legs." I couldn't agree more.

It's all between your ears

Love, attraction, and sex *are* all about what's happening between your ears. By demystifying them, you will feel in more control when these emotions come over you. Many poor decisions in life are made because of them. I hope you will be able to avoid big mistakes because you now have a better understanding of them.

When you're grasping for someone to give you a sense of worth, you will likely end up in a relationship for all the wrong reasons. If your sense of worth is tied to how a particular person views and treats you, you become enslaved to them and are at the mercy of their whims.

Success brings about self-confidence and a better sense of doing what is in your best interest. Having a strong sense of worth puts you in a position of strength. You can better evaluate those relationships you currently have as to which ones are healthy to maintain and which ones are harmful and should go away.

If you're going to make an emotional investment in someone, make the investment in yourself first. All other relationships in which you engage will be healthier for you and others.

Hate

Another big distraction in our lives is hatred. Even though our mothers taught us that hate is an ugly word and that we shouldn't feel hate toward anything, we still do.

> *Hate is a degree of repulsion toward someone or something based on how it makes you feel about yourself.*

The same ideas expressed for love can be inverted and expressed for hate.

We hate the bully who makes us feel inferior. We hate the lover who makes us feel inadequate by cheating on us. We hate the swindler who makes us feel stupid after they take our money. We can also hate someone or something, not because they makes us feel anything less of ourselves, but because they make us angry or are contrary to what we believe to be right.

Anger

> *Anger is the frustration you feel when things don't go your way, no matter how hard you try.*

We get angry with other family members because they tease us no matter how much we ask them to stop. We get angry with our children for acting up no matter how many times we tell them to behave. We get angry with big corporations or activist groups because they continue to exist no matter how much we wish them to go away. We get angry with criminals who get away with their crimes, no matter how much *we* obey the rules. We get angry with the politicians we voted against because they defied our vote or because we gave them our vote in exchange for a promise that they've broken. We get angry at the courts when they hand down seemingly absurd judgements and rulings.

We believe things are right or wrong based on whether or not they agree with our beliefs and past interpretations of events. How we interpret events is a reflection of who we believe ourselves to be. When events go against our will, it is an affront to what we believe is right, an affront to us and the meaning of our very existence.

When we see someone dressing or acting radically different from us, we are affronted that someone would do such. It defies how we believe people should dress or behave based on our historical interpretations. It challenges what we believe is right and we don't like being told, if indirectly, that we are wrong. We don't like the suggestion that our historical interpretations are wrong because our historical interpretations constitute our very self-perception. We don't want to be wrong or bad. We want to be right and good.

Consider, however, that even if those things that anger us were to finally go our way, something else will crop up that goes against our will and beliefs. There will always be things that don't go our way. There will always be people who challenge us, not for the sake of making us angry, but because that is what they believe is right. Everyone has their own interpretation of what is right based on their own vast web of historical interpretations. We challenge them, their belief in what is right, their historical interpretations, their very sense of self and what is good and right, just as they challenge us.

Who is right and who is wrong? There's no telling. Any event can be interpreted many, many ways. There is no right or wrong interpretation of an event. What makes the interpretation seem right or wrong is whether it agrees with our own, personal web of historical, circumstantial interpretations.

When we realize that it's not always important for things to go our way, we can alleviate much of our anger. When we can examine the real meaning of things that go against our will and how they do not really reflect on us, we can free ourselves from anger.

Imagine yourself on a trip to Mount Everest by way of Japan. Right away, when you fly into Tokyo you see many things that are totally foreign to your experience and sense of what is right or wrong, based on your upbringing. As you travel through Asia and visit many of the countries, again and again, you come across things that "just wouldn't be that way" in your homeland. By the time you get to Tibet you have seen lots of poverty and people treated in many ways that would be unacceptable back home.

If you were to try to right all those things you saw that were wrong, you'd never make it to Mount Everest. If you were to get angry or fret over all that you saw, you'd be a miserable mess and distracted from your ultimate goal.

You cannot possibly right all the wrongs that you see in the world. Unless righting all the wrongs is your goal, don't let those things that contradict what you believe is right consume you or distract you from your goal.

Other Emotions

Jealousy is when you feel someone else is getting something you deserve.

Envy is when you feel someone else *is* what you wished you were but feel you'll never be.

Happiness is when you feel good about yourself.

Joy is when you feel ecstatic about yourself.

Fun is when you're engaged in an activity that makes you feel good about yourself.

Sadness is when you feel the answer to the question, "Am I good?" is "No, you are not good."

Misery is when you feel extremely bad about yourself and don't see a way out of that state.

Sorrow is when someone who has been a source of positive feelings for you goes away or dies. People who are not particularly close to their parents feel perplexed at their lack of feelings when the parents die. They're supposed to feel sorrowful; however, they may have never received positive feelings from them, so the loss goes without sorrow.

A friend is someone who makes you feel good about yourself. An enemy is someone who makes you feel bad about yourself. A friend can quickly become an enemy by saying something that makes us feel bad when we trusted them to always make us feel good.

Television

Millions of dollars have been spent researching and arguing over the negative effects of television. Most of the focus has been on the sex and violence. Does violence on TV translate into violence in the viewers? I have only one question in response. What did criminals do for inspiration before the advent of television?

What all the research and debate seems to overlook is the incredible amounts of time people spend watching. It's been said that Americans average 25 hours a week watching television. For some, watching television consumes the largest portion of time during their waking hours.

For example, let's say that a teenager watches an hour of TV in the morning before school, and four hours after school. If you know how teenagers can be, this sounds pretty conservative, right? Add approximately 16 hours over the course of a weekend, and that adds up to 43.5 hours in a week. That's more than a full-time job! A daily average of 6.2 hours times 365 days a year and you have 2,263 hours a year, or 94 days of *pure* television. If you factor in 8 hours a day to sleep, that stretches it out to 141 days of pure television. Can you imagine what you can do with 141 days, or 4.7 months worth of time?

Forget about the sex and violence, there are three other harmful aspects of television that the experts fail to point out.

Activity Displacement

When we watch TV it means, typically, that we're doing nothing else. Let's say for the moment that there's nothing genuinely harmful about what you watch. Let's also say that you watch as much as the teenager described above, or an average of 6.5 hours a day. That breaks down to the numbers below.

Activity	Hours per Year	Days equivalent	Months Equivalent	Percent of total
Work (40 hrs/week x 50 weeks/year)	2000	83	2.72	23%
Commute (30 min. each way twice per day)	250	10.42	.35	3%
Sleep (8 hours per night)	2,920	121.67	4.0	33%
Television (6.5 hours/day)	2,263	94.3	3.09	26%
Other (dressing, eating, other entertainment, house/yardwork, and doing nothing)	1,327	55.3	1.81	15%
Total Year	**8,760**	**364.69**	**11.97**	**100%**

Next to sleep, television dominates your day! Even more than work!

Now, let's say that you decorate your television tube with a sledgehammer. That changes the percentages above in one significant respect. Your television time goes to zero, and your "other" time goes to 3,590 hours a year, 149.5 days, 4.9 months, or 41 percent of your year. What can you do with that time? Read books, listen to educational tapes, explore your abilities, take up hobbies, try things that are new to you, find things out about yourself that you did not know. Right now, television is likely preventing you from doing all the things that will improve yourself.

Here's a brief exercise. It won't require you to write or say anything, just use your imagination.

Imagine how you feel after two hours watching television, not anything specific, just channel surfing. Do you feel exuberant, excited, proud of yourself, a better person? Now, how do you typically feel after reading a book like this? Do you feel better after reading a personal improvement book for two hours than you do after two hours of TV?

Now, imagine keeping up the habit of reading personal improvement books, or even just books on your favorite topics (but not fiction) for two hours a day instead of watching TV. How would you feel after two years? With 1,460 hours of learning under your belt, you'd probably be pretty much an expert on your favorite topics, wouldn't you? You'd be a heck of a lot smarter on that subject, and you'd probably be able to launch a business with what you know!

How about after two years of watching the tube? You probably wouldn't be much of an expert on anything. Okay, you might be a whiz at TV trivia. Sell that to someone. There are tons of people with that useless skill. They don't call it a "boob tube" for nothing.

Manipulative and Harmful Messages

Take a course in Marketing 101 and one of the very first things that you learn is how to convey a message to the receiver. Marketers work very hard to subtly convey that you'll be somehow better off if you buy their products. In fact, they get paid huge sums of money to do exactly this. If they don't, they're out of a job. The converse of their efforts is, of course, if you don't buy the product, you're worse off. You're not as attractive as you could be with the product. You will smell badly, you will be dumber, poorer, less sophisticated, less "cool," less of whatever it is that the marketer embeds in the message. Since we cannot afford to buy everything, we can wind up with feelings of inadequacy because we cannot have what the marketer tells us will improve our lives.

Don't underestimate the power marketing has over you. The power is incredibly effective, manipulating your emotions, values, and beliefs about what is right. We are bombarded with these messages all day long. On the average half-hour television program, only between 17 and 20 minutes is the actual programming you tune in for. The remainder is *carefully crafted marketing messages indirectly telling us that we're inadequate* because we don't have their products. That's as much as 43 percent of the time you spend watching TV. If you're anything like the teenager in the example above, you might be spending as much as *973 hours a year being indirectly told that you're inadequate!*

If you've made the decision to stop saying negative things to yourself, you might want to switch off the tube as well.

A Flood of Conflicting Impressions and Values

Television provides nothing if not an endless variety of things to watch. With this variety comes thousands and thousands of messages about what is right, what is important, what is of value, and what is "cool."

The influence over our lives of what we see on television is undeniable and the impressions become deep and permanent. If I were to sing the words "the Professor and Mary Ann" most any American will immediately be able to identify the television program, if not sing the entire song.

People wear clothes, hairstyles, adopt ways of speaking, ways of living and thinking that reflect what they've learned from television. If it were all positive and consistent, it might be a good thing. But all too often it is valueless. And the messages are inconsistent! What is depicted as having worth changes from season to season and at the whims of programmers looking to come up with something new and different. They're more concerned with getting ratings than they are with what effect the messages they convey will have on you. Take a look at most of the talk shows that air throughout the day. Bizarre behaviors, absurdities, and things contrary to most value systems are highlighted and touted as something normal and fascinating.

Certainly there is educational programming that can be very good for you. However, with the number of hours, the quality of programming, and negative aspects of television that most people watch, the positive programming hardly makes up for it. This would be much like saying drinking a beer a day is good for your health, then ingesting a case of beer and a bottle of hard liquor every day.

The vast majority of what is on television is mental junk food. The programming we watch and the manipulative messages can leave us feeling empty, inadequate, if not anxiously confused or depressed about our lives.

The time you spend watching television is time not spent finding out about your strengths and abilities, your likes and dislikes, or determining what you'd like to do in life.

You may not be ready to decorate your tube with a sledgehammer, but consider cutting back and doing some personal improvement work and see how you feel.

Escapist Reading

Like watching television, we can engage in other escapist activities that seem to be good for us. I'm thinking specifically of reading fiction.

Watching theater movies is escapism very much like television, without the commercial messages. They too distort reality. They are also heavily laden with messages about what is right and what is wrong, what is cool and what is not cool, what is good and what is evil. Fortunately, they are expensive enough to limit the amount we go to see them.

Reading, on the other hand, is valued highly in most any society. If all of the reading were good and productive, it would genuinely be great. I will give reading of fiction the credit for exercising one's mental faculties. I will also yield that the escapism of fiction can help to relieve stress. But rarely does most fiction improve you as a person. Time spent reading fiction is time spent not improving yourself.

I will not suggest that you stop reading fiction; we all need to escape once in a while. Be careful that it does not become the only thing that you read. Do the mental comparison of how you feel after reading a novel for two hours over reading a personal improvement book or a book on your favorite topic.

Politics

Many take up a passive interest in politics. They justify that it's important to keep informed and know what's going on. They get riled up with beliefs about how the world should run and how others should think. They also get angry that the opposition party just won't go away.

Everyone wants to be right. It's nearly impossible for any two people to agree on everything. Since everyone wants to be right, the other person or party must be wrong. By expressing their opposing ideas, they send a message right back that you are wrong and it can be angering. Try as you might, you can never seem to convince the other party to think logically (like you do) and see how your view is right. When things go against your will no matter how hard you try, your anger grows.

Politics at this level is endlessly frustrating and ultimately futile. Unless this is your chosen direction in life, frustrating yourself with a passive interest in politics is pointless.

Consider this: if the opposing political parties were to vanish overnight, there would be some other group that did not believe as you do. There will always be others who do not see the world as you do.

In *The 7 Habits of Highly Effective People*, Stephen Covey talks about "circles of influence" and "circles of concern." There are things within your immediate world over which you can have direct influence and control. These would include the job you choose, the quality of service you provide, the attitude about yourself and others that you maintain, and the way you think. This is your circle of influence.

There are others things within your world over which you have very little influence and control. This includes what goes on in government, the news, and the rest of the world. This is your circle of concern. Certainly you can take an *active* interest in politics and bring it within your circle of influence. However, frustrating yourself with a passive interest is pointless and a waste of your valuable energy.

Concentrate your energies on those things within the circles of your influence, rather than the circles of your concerns.

The Major Inhibitors in Life

Thus far in this chapter we've discussed those things in life that seem important but can easily draw our precious attention away from our goals. They can occupy the limited time and energies we have for pursuing our dreams. When not fully understood, distractions can derail us or destroy us and we don't know what happened.

This next section is about those things that stop us cold. They prevent us from doing things we might like, or from even trying.

Self-doubt

Far and away, the biggest show stopper is self-doubt. Although we've already talked about it, it's important enough to repeat.

We can have fantastic ideas, lots of people supporting us, a plan, goals, tremendous enthusiasm, and momentum. But self-doubt can bring everything to a halt. Maybe not a screeching halt, but self-doubt can cause things to start going wrong a little at a time, to erode and wash away little by little.

Self-doubt lets the idea of eventual failure creep into our minds. If we believe that we really can't do something, we'll begin to see errors in a flawless plan. Little things will be taken as an omen that worse things are sure to happen. Even if things begin to right themselves after some setbacks, future setbacks will convince us that the omen was true.

We will give more weight to our weaknesses than to our strengths and allow them to cripple us.

Self-doubt is the dream killer!

Self-doubt is at the root of things such as fear of failure or fear of success.

Self-doubt is what causes us to interpret things against our favor.

Self-doubt is the cause of all failure.

Conquer self-doubt and you can conquer the world. Obstacles will not stop you, because you have an incredible ability to solve problems.

The only thing that can stop you is you (and death). Everything else is just an obstacle that can be overcome.

Busy Work

Busy work fools us into believing that we're being productive when we really are not. Because we believe we're being productive, we don't do anything else to improve our situation. Instead, we pat ourselves on the back for keeping busy and looking productive and fail to recognize that we're not going anywhere.

There are two kinds of busy work. One is busy work on the job. This can be activities like making some phone calls, checking email, reading the business section of the newspaper, filing, organizing, paper shuffling, sweeping, stacking, and straightening.

Most people do just enough genuinely productive work to keep their jobs. The rest of the time they're either engaged in busy work or plain old goofing off.

There is another kind of busy work that has much greater personal impact. We take jobs that pay the bills, jobs that make us look like and believe we're being productive. We are gainfully employed but typically unfulfilled and doing little to improve our lives. Consequently we do just enough to get by, hate Monday mornings, and live for the weekends.

Because busy work lulls us into believing that we're doing something worthwhile, we don't realize that there's something wrong. Sure, there's the general dissatisfaction with our jobs and lives, but that's just how life is! Right?

Pretty soon, television helps us to escape our dull and dreary lives. That's when we begin going nowhere fast!

Pretty soon, 10 years have slipped by and we're not much further along than 10 years before. We've gotten 10 years older, heavier, and gotten a lot of dull and dreary experience under our belts. Then 20 or 30 years pass in unsatisfying busy work that pays the bills, and we become old, bitter, and disappointed at how dreary life has been.

However, you don't need to ditch your busy work job on principle, at least right away. Busy work can have its uses for you as well. Busy work can pay the bills until you set some goals, come up with a game plan, map out what you'd really like to do. The average job consumes roughly 2,000 hours of your year. Turn off the boob tube and you'll have around 3,500 hours of disposable time in which you can explore your interests and create a game plan.

You can also learn a great deal from your busy work. It can teach you what you do and don't like doing. It can teach you about interacting with different kinds of people, what business practices work well and what doesn't work well. It can teach you about some of your own strengths, and also provide a testing ground for talents you'd like to develop.

View your busy work as a means to an end. Learn from it what you can and don't lose sight of your dream.

Comfortable Living

Comfortable living is very closely related to busy work. When we've achieved a little bit in our lives, enough to feel comfortable, we settle for second best. We put off trying to do what we really want to do.

There are two things working against us in comfortable living. One is that we don't want to jeopardize what we've managed to acquire and build. We've gotten ourselves a house, cars, boats, and family. Our jobs are stable and we don't want to risk losing what we've gained. Our subdued level of dissatisfaction could never be as disturbing as the thought of bill collectors calling at 3 a.m. The thought of losing what we've managed to acquire deters us from ever trying to pursue our dreams.

Comfortable living makes the payoff for pursuing what we want seem very distant and uncertain. The reality of a comfortable life is here and now for us to enjoy.

If we put off pursuing our dreams, nothing in our comfortable life will go wrong. We won't lose our houses, our jobs, our cars, our dignity, or self-respect. We easily convince ourselves that the dreams could never have been, so we don't feel so bad. That is, we don't feel bad until we grow old, sit around, and realize that all the houses, cars, toys, and sometimes family, don't mean nearly as much as the life we always wanted but never had a chance to live.

This is much like the feeling we get when watching George Bailey in *It's a Wonderful Life*. Towards the end when things look really rotten, we keep saying to ourselves, "He should have just left town after his old man died!" But no matter how many times we watch the movie, it never changes. Imagine how rotten you would feel at age 65 if you should come to the same conclusion. How will the dread feel when you realize that you can't go back and change your life and live the life you really wanted. Will you say to yourself, "I shouldn't have worried so much about losing things. At least life would have been exciting and worth living!"

Weigh the two risks for yourself. What would be worse, losing a few possessions in the short term, or the regret of never having lived a life you enjoyed? You can always buy new possessions, but you can't relive your life.

Often times the people who hit rock bottom and lose everything will turn their lives around and do what they wanted to do in the first place. They have nothing to lose, they've already lost it all. Because they begin to do what they love, they do it extremely well and become incredible successes. Why? They have nothing to lose and everything to gain by pursuing their dream.

Comfortable living is very often second best and not what we truly want. We enjoy what we have managed to achieve, but we're still not performing at our optimum. Like doing busy work, we do enough to get by, have a vacation once in a while, do things we like on the weekends, but we're shortchanging ourselves. We put aside a life of fulfillment and excitement in exchange for a life of safe mediocrity.

Do you have to bring yourself to the brink of disaster before you begin pursuing your dreams? No! With careful planning, you can take the 3,500 hours of disposable time you have per year and spend it in pursuit of your dreams. This compares to the roughly 2,000 hours you spend on a typical 40 hours per week "day job." You can continue to hold down your day job while you launch a dream on the side.

Will you work yourself to death? No! You'll likely begin to tolerate your day job as a means. You'll also begin to love the task of pursuing and building your dreams. You'll derive greater fulfillment in becoming your best and infinitely more successful than you would in a day job that you must tolerate.

Don't let comfortable living lull you into inaction. Take action toward your dreams, even if it's only reading books on your favorite topics. You will eventually begin to build momentum and inertia. Provided you conquer self-doubt, you will be unstoppable.

Think Like a Successful Person

Just when you've decided to go for it, life offers up some very tantalizing and irresistible distractions.

Emotions such as love, attraction, sex, anger, and hate all seem very important, and they are. But with a foggy understanding of them and why they affect us so strongly, we find they can easily overwhelm our lives.

If emotions aren't enough to sidetrack us, television and other escapist activities occupy our time, vast hordes of time, time we're not spending on pursuing our goals.

The ever futile politics keeps us wrapped up, makes us angry, and saps our energy, but for no tangible benefits.

Then there are those things in life which stop us from even trying. Self-doubt, busy work, and comfortable living may seem harmless but can be devastating to a dream of a fulfilled and rewarding life. These inhibitors make us feel comfortable and safe, but they result in lives of mediocrity and dissatisfaction.

Put these detours to your success in perspective and keep them from overwhelming your journey.

ROADBLOCK 13

"I just can't seem to get my butt in gear!"

Motivation

To many people the term "motivation" is a four-letter word, much like "attitude." Motivation is what they seem to lack or have too little of. Those who lack it are made to feel guilty or bad for not having any.

Is it just something that some people are born with and others are not? Is being motivated a sign of strength and good character, and the lack of motivation a sign of weakness and bad character? It certainly seems that way from looking at the way in which the term is used. Like "attitude," the term "motivation" has been used like a hickory stick to get you to do what someone else wants.

Everyone has motivation for something. However, you may feel a lack of motivation for what is important to *other people* or society in general. The trick is to find something exciting to you, and you will find motivation in abundance.

Why Some Seem to Lack Motivation

"So, what is motivation and why don't I seem to have any?"

Well, you do have motivation. Motivation is the urge or desire to do something. Everyone experiences feelings of "motivation" at some point in their lives. It just may not be for the things others have expected of you or when they expected it.

Imagine yourself in a museum that doesn't particularly interest you. If you're like me, most museums seem dull, so this exercise should be easy. Choose a type of museum that interests you least, whether art, culture, ancient history, science, farming, trains, sports, etc. Pick the one you like least and imagine yourself there.

You wander around looking at the exhibits, occasionally glancing at the descriptions to see if anything catches your interest. You walk from room to room, you see things that are different, but they're the same—boring. You wander, wander, wander but never find anything of interest. Pretty soon, you just sit on a bench and wait for something to happen, but nothing does.

Someone comes along and tries to help you with your problem. They try to stir your interest by pointing out things they find interesting. Yeah, okay, you see what they're describing, but it still doesn't strike your fancy. This person suggests reasons why you should be interested in all of the artifacts collected there, how important this is to society, and how important it is to you. But, sorry, still no interest.

The person takes you to a specialist, the curator, and tells the curator to help you come to an appreciation of the artifacts. The curator tries to point out little known things about the artifacts, and aren't you just lucky for knowing them.

You part with the curator and go back to sitting on the bench. People who *are* interested in the museum openly wonder what's wrong with you. How can you *not* find an interest here?

Pretty soon, it comes down to name calling, labeling, and chastising you for having such disregard for the museum and all the artifacts. You should have an interest, there's something wrong with you if you don't even try to develop an interest. Lazy, shallow, uncultured, unsophisticated, unappreciative, and so on, they call you. *Unmotivated!*

Now, are you truly unmotivated? No! You may have been trapped in a museum of things that hold no interest for you. You may be trapped in an environment or culture that holds no interest for you. It's easy to see how it would be hard to work up motivation for anything in such an environment. It's hard to get excited about something unless it excites you first.

And what of the environment and society into which you were born? You may have lots of people around you who are enthusiastic about this particular "museum" and are upset that you are not. Is there something genuinely wrong with you because you don't find what they prize very exciting at all? Likely not. Contrary to what you might have been led to believe, we are not all cut from the same cloth, family or not. We all find different things appealing, we all have different strengths and talents which are utilized and triggered in different ways.

What should you do? Stick around and pretend to have an interest? No! But that's what a whole lot of people do, and they wind up living tediously boring lives that end in pitiful regret.

Try finding a different "museum." There are no rules that say you must stay in the one museum. You don't even have to know what museum to visit next. When you get to the next one, if you like it, stay. And if you find that one equally boring, move on! Keep moving until you find something, whether a museum or something else that captivates you. The change in "museums" might be as simple as a new job, or a new town, or a new state. It might be a new country, or even a new continent. It might be a different field of work, or it might be paragliding in the mountains. There are no rules to hold you down, only the expectations of others.

Fumbling Around for the Right Fit

For some strange reason, we have evolved a "requirement" of sorts that a person begin trying to figure out what they want to do for a living sometime around adolescence. Around age 13 or so, we begin telling kids to start thinking about what they'd like to do—*for the rest of their lives!* To a teenager who hasn't had enough exposure to the real world it's nearly impossible to come up with any ideas. Some know without a doubt that they will become a doctor, lawyer, businessperson, and so on, but those are rare. The vast majority of teens are clueless and made to feel like misfits because of it. Oh, sure, we take guesses at things based on our extremely limited exposure, but those kinds of guesses are often premature.

One thing that I have found common among happily successful people is that they often times couldn't agree with what they were told by their parents.

They knocked around for some time in their late teens and early 20s, which can be maddening to a parent. Many had one or more menial labor jobs, like dish washing, working in lumberyards, sweeping floors, working stock rooms, lugging groceries, tending bar, selling newspaper subscriptions, selling vacuum cleaners door-to-door, being a "girl Friday," and so on. (I had sixteen such jobs between my teen years and finally getting into something I felt was a career path I could be proud of. These were certainly not jobs to write home about.) They visited many "museums" before they found one that was right. And when they did, they excelled.

If you haven't found something that excites you yet, that's okay. You're not required to stay in that museum. Even if you've made it to your late 20s or 30s, keep trying. There are a number of actors who got into acting in their 60s! It's often a good thing to try many different things until you find something that suits you best.

What Creates Motivation?

Again, motivation is the urge or desire to do something. But what creates this urge or desire? Certainly, there are the physical needs for food, shelter, and basic comfort. But beyond that, what seems to motivate us is the pursuit of those things that answer the question, "Am I good?"

As children, we seek attention from parents. "Look at me!" we shout from the top of playground toys. "Look what I can accomplish. Aren't I good?" When we can't readily get positive attention from our parents, we'll take any kind we can. As most parenting books say, "Negative attention seems to be better than no attention at all."

Through our youth we yearn for acceptance amongst peers. We want desperately to fit in, to not stand out, to not be chastised, to avoid being told by peers that we are different or *not* good. At times we find we're outcasts, so we make a stand and attempt to form pride in being different, and assert that "different" is good.

Later in life, we try to find ways in which to gain recognition for our good qualities, through work, through play, through social interaction.

Some attempts are petty and at the expense of others. We figure that the only way to gain recognition for our good qualities is by finding fault in others.

Some of us seek recognition of our good qualities by amassing money, seeking fame, power, through competition, or by association with those of high social status.

Still others seek recognition and acknowledgement by developing and exercising their strengths and talents.

At times, however, we find that what we're currently doing is unsatisfying. What we thought would make us feel good about ourselves did not deliver all that we had hoped, or carried with it unforeseen negative aspects. It seems many lawyers find they are unhappy, despite having achieved in a prestigious field, making good money, and acquiring coveted possessions.

Sometimes what made us feel good in years past no longer satisfies us. We have mastered the exercise of a particular strength to the point where it is no longer challenging, if not boring. We can no longer muster any motivation to carry on with this line of work.

At other times what makes us feel good about ourselves is the approval from parents, family, and friends for following their plans and living up to their expectations. However, that sense of satisfaction from the approval of others can grow old and no longer make us feel good. We wake up on the brink of a mid-life crisis yearning to discover what truly makes us feel good about ourselves.

What makes us feel good about ourselves can and does change from one stage of life to another. Don't be surprised if and when this happens to you.

What Causes the Lack of Motivation?

It's plain difficult to get excited about something that doesn't excite you first. If you can't see how something is going to make you feel good about yourself, you will likely find a lack of motivation to do it.

Don't be ashamed or feel guilty that you have no motivation for something someone else feels important. Everyone has their beliefs about the way things should be and how the world should run. Just because another person is a parent, elder, teacher, or authority figure doesn't mean that they are right or smart. They will gladly guide your life in ways that will make them happy. But you have to be more concerned with how you feel than how they feel. It is *you* who must live *your life*, not them.

Here are a number of things that might be the causing a lack of motivation to do something someone else wants.

- You don't see or believe there is a benefit to you.
- It does not utilize your strengths, talents, or skills.
- It does not work toward resolving your negative core belief.
- It risks exposing or accentuating your flaws or making you feel bad about yourself.
- It does nothing to make you feel better about yourself.

Pursuing things that make you feel good about yourself is not a crime. When someone urges you to "get motivated" for something they feel is important, it is an attempt by them to have you do what makes them feel good about themselves. What's the bigger crime? It is your life to live.

Ways to Get Motivated

If you don't yet have a direction and goal, make your first goal that of finding one. Once you have a goal, it is much easier to avoid the distractions of everyone else telling you what you should or should not do. If a task or activity is aligned with achieving your goal, do it. If not, toss it.

If you have set a goal but still do not find yourself motivated to pursue it, it may be one of the following.

Don't Settle for Second Best

You may be curtailing your dreams and goals because of the practicalities and realities of everyday life. You might wish to be a teacher, but because of traditionally low pay, you take a job in construction instead because of the better pay. But does "second best" due to practicality really excite you?

Put your practicality-based goal on hold for a moment and concentrate on ways to make enough money as a teacher. For example, you might choose to teach adults computer technologies, which pays considerably better. Maintain your "first choice" goal for a while and let your problem-solving mind come up with some way to solve the practicality issues.

Believe It Can Really Happen

There are many, many like you who have started from humble beginnings yet have achieved magnificent things. Look for examples of such stories and you will find them everywhere.

Your goals may seem far-fetched or unachievable. It may be hard to believe that you could be a millionaire (if that's your goal) when you're making $8.00 an hour. Have faith that setting a goal gives your problem-solving machine of a mind something to work on. It will keep on working on the problem until you tell it to stop. Believing a goal can be achieved is the "on" switch. Believing it cannot be achieved is the "off" switch.

Believing I can enables me. Believing I can't disables me.

Visualize a Path

It may be a long road between where you are now and where you would like to be once you reach your goal. Continually work on building a logical, believable, and achievable path to get there. Don't count on luck, magic, or the benevolence of someone else to make it all happen. Once you have a path defined, you can work on achieving the individual steps along the way. Your path may change frequently as you progress, but that's okay. Without the logical path in the first place, you would never be able to convince yourself to start. You would never flip the "on" switch to the problem-solving machine.

Write Out Your Strengths

You have strengths, whether you know what they are or not. If you know them or as you discover them, write them down. Continually remind yourself of these strengths and their value. It is the exercise and development of your strengths that will lead you to the most emotionally rewarding, if not financially rewarding life. Find ways to utilize the strengths you have toward reaching your goal. If there's a strength, talent, or skill that you will need to acquire to reach your goal, learn it, and you will be all the stronger.

Use Musical Triggers

Pick out a new song on CD or tape that you really like. It should be a song that's fairly new to you so it won't have a lot of memories associated with it. It can be whatever music genre you like: rock, classical, country, gospel, as long as the song by itself gets you into an uplifted mood.

Don't play it until you are really pumped up about your goals. When you get super pumped, play the song again and again. Keep playing all the time you're in your super-pumped-up state.

Now, remember how your subconscious mind recalls meanings and emotions along with various inputs? Next time you hear the song, what do you suppose is going to happen? You will recall the emotions and visions of achieving your goals that have been ingrained in your memory along with the song. Instant motivation!

Associate with People who Have Achieved

Unless your friends are achievers, don't bother to bounce your ideas off of them. What will they know that can help you? Seek out people who have achieved in your area of interest. Talk with them, get ideas, bounce your ideas, and work out problems with them. Because they have achieved the same or similar goals, they will further convince you of your goal's achievability. Learning of their path to success will help you visualize your own. They will help to educate you on aspects you need to know, how to approach things, and people who can help you.

Write Out Words of Wisdom You Like

When you find quotes and phrases you like or are particularly motivating to you, write them out and put them in places you will see them often. Choose things that you can believe wholeheartedly. Don't put up things about which you are doubtful as that will only serve to reinforce something negative. Most successful people I know have some kind of "words to live by" in their repertoire. You can easily do the same.

Listen to Audio Programs

There are lots of self-improvement audio programs on the market or available at your local library. Listen to them when you're driving, doing hands-on work, or exercising. You will learn a great deal in a passive way. The more information you are exposed to, the more tools you will have for solving problems.

Most libraries have self-improvement and educational audio programs available for free! If your library is part of a big network, chances are you can look for titles throughout the network and have them mailed to your library for you to check out. For example, I checked my county library system and found over 350 titles available on cassette. Check out this resource!

Coping With the Negative

Allow for Bad Days

Bad days happen. Expect them. Things just go wrong or differently than you might have expected. Tragedies happen. People die, get divorced, wind up in hospitals, and so on. When these things do happen, and they will, allow for it. Don't let it totally disrupt the pursuit of your goal. You may have to put your pursuit on the shelf for a while and get back to it later, whether in a few days, weeks, months, or years. But don't give up on your goals.

Expect to Fail Sometimes

Part of the learning process is trial and error, and learning what not to do. Getting it right the first time is a rarity. Failing and living to tell about it lets you know that failure won't kill you. Anything that doesn't kill you makes you stronger.

The hazard in failing is developing a sense that *you are* a failure. Such a belief can make you think that future endeavors are bound to fail, and so they will.

Understand that failure is a natural part of attempting, and not a reflection of your worth as a human being. If and when you do fail, be proud of your bravery in the attempt, of what you've learned through the failure, and of your courage to try again.

Disappointing Others

You will inevitably disappoint others with your choices and your decisions. This will put a lot of pressure on you to comply with their wishes. Carefully weigh the "shoulds" with which others will eagerly shackle you. Carefully scrutinize whether their expectations will divert you from your goals. You are not on this earth to live up to the expectations of others. They are not gods, nor masters, and you are not their slave.

Things to Avoid

Television

Your mind is continually solving problems. If you're watching TV the problems your mind is trying to solve are:

- What's the "before and after" phrase on "Wheel of Fortune"?
- The question to "The first man to wear a bow-tie" under "Historical Nerds" for $500.
- Will Fonticia finally dump her hubby, Chiselchin, when she finds out he's cheated on her *yet again?*
- How's the hero/heroine going to get out of the mess the villain has created in the latest mini-series?
- What's that tantalizing tid-bit on the "News at 11:00" teaser all about?
- What the heck else is on?
- I wonder where I can get that deodorant stick?

If television is all that you engage your brain with, that's the kind of stuff your brain works on. Rewarding, isn't it?

Negative People

Negative people can be very convincing and very persistent. Their motivation is not to make you a negative person, but to get you to agree with them and see "reality" as they see it. Don't become a victim of someone else's past. Avoid negative people.

Escapism

Sure, everyone needs escapism once in a while. Everyone needs salt, too. But don't eat a whole bag of salt. If escaping from the real world is your second full-time job, how will you ever learn to cope with the real world? Everything in moderation.

Busy Work

Pat comes up to Chris who is busy looking around under a street light at night.

"What are you looking for, Chris?" Pat inquires.

"I dropped my keys over there," Chris replies, pointing toward the darkness.

Don't let busy work fool you into thinking you're being genuinely productive. At the very least, recognize that you're doing busy work and that it is not genuinely important to your goal.

Passive Politics

If you really, really, really care about political issues, jump in and make a difference. Otherwise, save your energies and spare your blood pressure for things that really, really, really matter to you and your goal.

Worrying Over Things You Can Do Nothing About

I have never experienced anything as horrible as what I've imagined in my worries. Worrying about things you cannot take action on or have an influence over expends precious problem-solving cycles. Spend those wisely.

Things to Indulge In

"I like the stuff you have to say. But do I have to be 'rah, rah' motivated all the time?"

Absolutely not! Some of the things I will suggest below may

seem like a dentist or dietitian recommending lots of candy. There are lots of things that I highly recommend doing that I call (and I'm inventing a word here) "nonconcentrative."

When I say nonconcentrative, I mean any activity that does not occupy your powers of concentration. Writing, talking on the phone, doing math problems, and sword-fighting are "concentrative" in that they require a great deal of focus and concentration.

Any activity that is nonconcentrative allows your mind to wander, to solve problems, to absorb new inputs and information, to come up with new ideas, to visualize a path to your goal, to visualize having achieved your goal, or just a necessary break from your concentrative tasks.

Hanging Out, Socializing

Socializing with friends helps you to keep your sanity and feel okay with yourself. Besides, they may give you good ideas, or you may meet in places where there are lots of inputs to stimulate new ideas or solutions.

Doing Nothing

Just sitting around watching the sunset, the scenery, or nothing in particular is a form of meditation. With nothing to concentrate on, your mind can hash out problems, visualize, come up with new ideas, solutions, or just visualize.

Escapism

"Wait a second! You said escapism was something to avoid!"

Too much escapism, yes. But once in a while, you really need to let go, see a movie, read a book, watch the tube. Everything in moderation.

Sleeping

Believe it or not, your mind will continue to work on problems when you sleep. Many dream experts tell us that dreams are the result of the subconscious mind hashing out experiences of the day or worries of tomorrow. If you don't give your mind something specific to work on, it will meander through issues of concern. However, if you concentrate on a problem you're trying to solve before you go to sleep, you ought to have an answer by the time you wake up. When you're going to bed, the lights are down or off, it is quiet (hopefully), and no one is trying to distract you. This is a great time to concentrate on a problem or to visualize.

Exercising, Walking, Running, Pumping Iron

Exercise time is a good time for problem-solving and visualization. Also, if your exercise routine takes you outdoors or to a health club, the additional stimuli may jog something loose for you.

Gardening, Yardwork, Building Things

Again, more problem-solving/visualizing time. Be sure to plan on a problem to solve or a situation to visualize yourself in.

Shopping

Of course browsing through bookstores goes right to the top of my recommended list of places to shop. There are tons of topics that are bound to catch your interest or stimulate your mind as you look around the shelves. What ever catches your interest is something you should pay attention to.

But even if you don't get around to bookstores, any kind of store is okay. Just getting out, wandering around is good problem solving/visualization time, as well as time for exposure to stimuli. If you're going to be near a bookstore along the way, stop in to see if anything stimulates your imagination while you're shopping for what you'd intended.

Traveling

Talk about a great way to stir up new ideas! Go someplace you've not been before, whether across town, across the state, across the country, or around the globe. You're brain will be inundated with new stimuli, new ways of looking at things, new ideas, new people, and new sights. If you don't come up with something at that particular time, you may later when you have a problem to solve, and you think, "You know when I was in Rome, they did . . ."

Flipping Through Magazines

Certainly reading magazines takes concentration. But flipping through them exposes you to lots of stimuli, like pictures and headlines. If an article headline catches your attention, read it. Articles are usually about a problem and how someone solved it. Or, maybe it's about an issue, which is really a problem that has no solution yet. You might come up with a solution.

Also, the ads can be very stimulating, whether it's the funny, clever, artistic ads, or the serious ads, or the classified ads. Each ad indicates a problem that someone has a solution to. All of this is good stimulus for your mind.

Think Like a Successful Person

Everyone has motivation. The only issue is finding something to excite you and expose your motivation. Typically, those things that excite you will somehow make you feel good about yourself. All our lives we are driven to find or exercise ways to make us feel good about ourselves. If what is made available to you in your present environment or situation does not accomplish that goal, seek it out. Just because others think a "museum" should be important to you doesn't mean that you are wrong or bad for not finding it interesting. Seek out a "museum" that genuinely interests you and you'll find motivation in abundance.

RESOURCES

"Who ya
gonna call?"

Resources

One of the hardest challenges on the road to success is knowing where to start. On top of that, there are all sorts of unknowns that you fear you won't be able to understand or deal with. The good news, however, is that you will not have to blaze a new trail all by yourself. This is a road that many have traveled before you and there are many resources to share information, wisdom, and experiences. Whatever your endeavor, you can find lots of documentation, lots of people you can ask, people to lend or give you money, and organizations whose sole intent is to help people like you to succeed.

It's hard to envision building wealth given your present situation, isn't it? If you're like most, you're wondering how you can get a buck or two more per hour. Making millions probably seems beyond the scope of your reality. But that's where you need to look, beyond the scope of your present reality and what you think is presently possible. Assume that you can and will get there. Now you just have to find the proper vehicle.

It's not as if there's a special secret that wealthy people know about and they're not sharing. There are millions of opportunities to build wealth, right before your very eyes. You just need to recognize them and learn how to exploit the opportunities.

Where to Find Opportunities

Whether you're looking to make millions or just find a more rewarding career, whether you're looking to branch off on your own or just move up in your current company, I have only one recommendation for you—solve problems!

Problems abound everywhere! Every problem is an opportunity to build wealth, move up, start up, or to find life's satisfaction. People will pay money, sometimes vast sums of money, to have problems solved. The problems are not just those of big industry, the economy, the environment, or international affairs. The problems are in your home, your car, and your place of work.

Since you are a human and able to think, you have unlimited capacity to solve a wide range of problems. These problems need not be in nuclear physics or building a better mouse trap, they can be about how you think a remote control should really work, or a new way to wear blue jeans. Combine what you like to do with solving a problem, any problem, and this is where you will find your fortune. Problems fall into these key categories:

Harm Avoidance

This can be anything where there is a threat to safety and security, both real and imagined: burglar alarms, smoke detectors, ozone-safe products, tax protection, financial protection, physical protection, and health protection. Conceive of some way to help people avoid harm, pain, or difficulties, and you will have something tangible or intangible that will sell.

Convenience

People are always looking for ways to make their lives easier. It doesn't have to be the elimination of back-breaking work, just look at remote controls, or the multi-purpose remote controls. You don't need to invent something totally new, just think of how you would like to improve something you currently use—anything! Anything that makes something simpler to use, even by a few seconds or a couple of button pushes.

Find ways to save time, especially lots of time. The more time you can save someone the more money people will pay for it. Time is money!

Save manual labor and you'll make lots of money too. Manual labor is very expensive and saving it can help others to save lots of money.

Escape

No matter how many motivational books are sold, people will still want to escape from their realities. People want something different, new experiences, something to tell their friends about. Find a way to temporarily satisfy this unquenchable thirst for escapism with new and different ways to entertain them people and you'll make money.

Social Elevation

There are a great many things that are of *little* or *absolutely no practical value*, yet they help people to differentiate themselves.

Most clothing, jewelry, ornaments of all sorts, decorations, stickers, hats, toys, gimmicks, and stuffed cats to affix on car windows with suction cups fall into this category. Again, these have little or no practical value, but we buy them for a very special reason. Take, for example, most major athletic apparel manufacturers. They don't just sell apparel, they sell image! It's the image more than the quality that gets them three to five times more money than competitors.

People buy things to feel just a little bit better about themselves.

People buy things to elevate themselves just a little bit. We want to show that we are different, special, and unique, but not by too much. We want things that look cute, cool, funny, witty, wicked, impressive, or expensive. We want things that reflect what we feel about ourselves.

However, all things that we buy fall within our self-perceptions. We won't buy things that are below our self-perception, or too far above our self-perception. We want things that add to, emphasize, or affirm our self-perception, and we want them on a continuous, never-ending, and ever-changing basis.

What is considered elevating is subjective, that is, what elevates one person may not be elevating to another. For example, a black, slashed and torn tee shirt may elevate a heavy-metal fan, but be considered something of a downgrade for a yuppie. Conversely, a smart, cinnamon colored polo shirt with burgundy piping may be just smashing for a yuppie, but generate a great deal of criticism from heavy-metal fans. Things that accentuate an image that people want to project will sell very well, even when there's no practical value at all.

While you are a genuinely unique individual, you have tastes and ideas about what is elevating within your social circles that are common to many other people in your social circles. What you think you like, many others will like too. As long as it makes people feel a little bit cooler, cuter, more masculine, more feminine, or in some way helps them to emphasize their self-perception, people will buy it.

Assistance and Support

Some problems are merely the need for assistance. For example, employers need employees to work the line, sweep the floors, coordinate projects, sell their products, or motivate people. They can't do it all themselves, so they have a problem. They solve the problem by hiring people, maybe even you.

Some problems are the need for support, such as moral or intellectual support. Getting ahead at the office, or nearly anywhere, can be achieved easily by finding out who needs help, support, and information.

Find someone in a position of power, no matter how high or low, and help them in some way, and you'll be helping them solve their problems. It might be as simple as listening to their ideas, telling them what you know, telling them what others are saying, your observations, gut feel, anything. People need information to help them make decisions. Moving up is not all about intensive labor and producing the most widgets, it's all about helping others achieve their goals. If you can help others achieve their goals, they will help you achieve your goals.

In summary

What should be most exciting about all of this is that there is unlimited opportunity for you to solve problems. When one problem is solved, two more are created. Once put into practice, every solution can use some improvement. There are more and more problems being created every day, and some old ones that haven't yet been addressed. Absolutely everything can be improved in some way, even those things that happen to be in your favorite area of interests. People will pay big bucks to solve problems, whether they're real or imagined.

Information to Protect You

The first thing you should do in pursuing your goals is beware! Do whatever you can to get on the Internet and go to the web site for the Federal Trade Commission (FTC) **www.ftc.gov.** It has excellent articles on the many get-rich-quick scams that prey on people who wish to make a new life for themselves. This site can literally help to keep you from losing your shirt!

If you've become the victim of a get-rich-quick scam, the FTC has instructions on how to file complaints and possibly seek remedies. I personally lost $5,000 to a seemingly reputable, nationally famous, magazine-sponsored Internet web page development company that made many promises on the goldmine that is the Internet, but delivered on few, if any. Had I read one of these publications, I could have saved that $5,000 educational experience. The sharks are out there, so beware!

If you can't make it to the Internet, you can call the FTC *toll free* at 877-FTC-HELP (or 1-877-382-4357) and they will send you pamphlets on consumer issues. Ask for the names below and they'll gladly send them to you.

- Now Consumers Can Tell It to the FTC—Toll-Free Alert
- Investments: $100K a year? Mmmmm . . . Brief
- Don't Get Burned . . . by a Pyramid Scheme Campaign
- Get-Rich-Quick and Self-Employment Schemes Campaign
- So You've Got a Great Idea? Brief
- Infomercials
- Medical Billing Business Opportunity Schemes
- 'Net Based Business Opportunities: Are Some Flop-portunities?
- 'Net Based Business Opportunities: Beware of Flop-portunities Alert
- Dirty Dozen: 12 Scams Most Likely To Arrive Via Bulk Email Alert
- International Lottery Scams Alert
- Website Woes: Avoiding Web Service Scams Alert
- Answering the Knock of a Business 'Opp' Alert
- Could Biz Opp Offers Be Out for Your Coffers?
- Franchise & Business Opportunities
- The Gifting Club "Gotcha"
- Online Investment Opportunities: 'Net Profit or 'Net Gloss? Alert
- The Bottom Line About Multilevel Marketing Plans
- Border-Line Scams Are the Real Thing Alert
- Avoiding Office Supply Scams
- How to Avoid Losing Your Money to Investment Frauds Alert
- If You've Got "The Look" . . . Look Out! Avoiding Modeling Scams
- Spotting Sweet-Sounding Promises of Fraudulent Invention Promotion Firms Alert

- Multilevel Marketing Plans
- The Seminar Pitch: A Real Curve Ball
- Thinking of Buying a Business Opportunity?
- Wealth Building Scams
- Work-at-Home Schemes
- "Free" and "Low-Cost" PC Offers. Go Figure. Alert
- Catch the Bandit in Your Mailbox Campaign

There are many more, but if you ask for "Best Sellers" the FTC will send a catalog of all their titles.

Launching Your Ideas

The first place to go when trying to launch your idea is the school of hard knocks. That's right, the school of hard knocks! You will learn more in one pass at trying to launch an idea than you would in four years of college. This exercise will teach you volumes, and you will be tightly focused on your favorite subjects, so you should find it incredibly exciting.

Take one of your ideas, one that you think is genuinely worth something. Go through the paces of what it takes to market this idea. It can be a product idea or a business idea.

You may need to find out about patents, copyrights, trademarks, etc., whether it's establishing your own or finding if your idea infringes upon the protections of others. If it's a business idea, you may have to get a part-time job in the same or similar business to learn as much as you can and what your competition is all about.

Product ideas

Have an invention or a new product? There are many companies out there that cater to people in your shoes. But beware, there are also companies that will take advantage of you. There are many books in the library or bookstore that will describe things you can do to market your invention or product. On the Internet you can find several resources. Below are a few websites you might try.

www.ftc.gov/bcp/conline/pubs/services/invent.htm
This is the Federal Trade Commission again. This one is a MUST. It's put out by the government and makes you fully aware of the fraud

that can be perpetrated on enthusiastic inventors. Many invention promotion firms who advertise on the radio may offer a free brochure, but will charge you an arm and a leg for doing patent work or market research for you.

www.inventionconvention.com

This is the National Congress of Inventor Organizations. Look for "Inventors Help" which will point you to many articles that can protect you from scams, protect your ideas, and teach you what you need to know about bringing your invention to market. It will teach you about beginning steps to copyrights, trademarks, patents, disclosure and non-disclosure agreements, marketability, patentability, and finding a good patent attorney.

www.about.com/education/inventors

About.com specializes in being an informative resource for many topics. I recommend it highly for when you begin to explore your topics of interest.

Taking Your Idea to Business

Take product ideas to people in the particular business for which your product is best suited. Ask them how you can present them with an idea. They will probably have rules for idea submissions. They may even ask you to sign a *disclosure* form which is a legal document releasing them from penalty if they steal your idea. How about that? It may be just the risk you have to take to give yourself the education you will need to promote future ideas.

At this point you have two alternatives.

One is you can follow their rules and submit your idea in the manner they describe. No matter what, you will still need to sign the disclosure agreement. If you don't, someone may open your envelope, see that it lacks a disclosure agreement and *freak out*. They don't want to risk being sued. They'll treat it like it has a contagious virus, put it back into an envelope, send it back to you, and ask you to sign the disclosure agreement.

The other option you have is to break their rules and go straight to the top. You have something very important working for you in any organization, called politics. As I mentioned in a previous chapter, people are constantly battling one another inside an organization. It may seem like they're all of one mind and one spirit, but they are battling. They're trying to get promotions, special recognition, stock options, more money, what have you. If they see an idea, feel it is brilliant, they will potentially see it as a mechanism to help them compete with their peers. At the same time you're trying to solve a problem for people like you, you can also solve a problem for some company bigwig who is wondering, "How can I get the Golden Pig-shoe award at this year's annual kickoff?" Ushering in a brilliant idea like yours may be just the ticket they need.

The key people to submit your ideas to are the vice presidents of marketing and sales. These are typically the hungriest and most aggressive people in a company and can see the marketing and sales potential in your idea. The president is too often consumed with keeping the board off his or her back and meeting company goals and direction. Call the company and ask who fills each VP spot. If long distance charges are an issue, consider how much you spend on beer or other frivolous wants, and just make the call anyway.

Put together a package to each of them and send it off. Don't forget to include a signed copy of the disclosure form for everyone to whom you send your package. They don't want to get canned because they got all excited over an idea without proper legal protection.

Keep a record of everything you do. Get a 99¢ notebook and write down what you do on each day that you do something. Write down what you're sending, to whom, as well as make copies of anything you send them (if you can). If you have drawings or detailed descriptions of your idea, keep the originals.

Again, you may lose control of the idea, but don't spend too much time and energy worrying about whether a company will steal it. Most companies are on the up-and-up and won't steal your idea anyway. If they do, consider it your tuition money in the school of hard knocks. You'll always come up with new ideas later and you'll begin to get a feel for the business. You can use your documentation as evidence to the next company that you have great ideas.

Present your ideas as clearly as you possibly can. If you must handwrite letters, so be it, but make them as neat as possible. If you cannot afford a graphic artist and must do drawings yourself, that's fine too. Multi-billion dollar deals have been launched based on plans scribbled on a cocktail napkin. You don't have to impress people with expensive preparation; impress them with the idea and its benefits as clearly as you can.

Above all, make absolutely certain that the benefit of your idea is clearly spelled out. Don't leave it up to people to understand a product you think is the coolest if they don't live in your circles. Make it unmistakable and compelling. Give everyone to whom you present your idea the reasons why someone would want your product.

Selling Your Ideas On Your Own

If you want to launch a product yourself, that is, without some big company doing it, you'll likely need some capital. Prepare a business plan, do some research, and apply for loans or seek investors. Writing business plans and seeking investment capital is spelled out in many "how-to" books at your library or bookstore.

You may need to build a prototype, or the original run of products to sell. You may consider patents and copyrights, so read up on what it takes to get them.

Identify people who would buy your product and ask them what they think of the idea. *Don't worry about them stealing your idea.* Very few people have enough ambition to pursue their own ideas, so they'll be even less motivated to pursue yours.

If you want retailers to carry your product, go to their stores and ask the people who work there, specifically managers, what they think of the product. Ask if they think it would sell, and how much people might pay for it. Take a notebook along and write down things people tell you as well as names, dates, and stores you visit. Use the things that your target buyers say as evidence when you need to persuade others to invest in your ideas. Through this investigative work you may discover that someone has already had an idea like yours. Or, it will expose you to other ideas that are similar to your own and help you gauge the merit of your idea and ways you can improve yours.

On-the-Job Ideas

Bringing ideas to those at the top is not exclusively for products outside your current employment. If you spot a problem that you know how to solve within your organization, write out the problem, what the (potential) costs are, how you would solve it, and what the benefits are. Find aggressive people within your organization who want the Golden Pig-shoe award, and present it to them.

Executives at big companies often become detached from the people lower in the organization. However, they like to be viewed as "in touch" with those on the front line. You can help them solve that problem too.

Don't feel bad about bypassing your immediate supervisor if it has nothing to do with his or her role or area of responsibility. Bringing all your brilliant ideas to your immediate supervisor runs the risk of having them squelched through criticism or being forbidden to spend more time on them. If you do have a supervisor who is trying to keep you under his or her thumb, *you might want to consider getting out from under it.*

Again, document things, make copies, save the originals, and keep a logbook. Even if others take all the credit, most people will know that it was your idea and you'll have proof that you have brilliant ideas.

New Business Ideas

Have an idea for a new kind of business? Get a job in the same or similar market. Find out all you can about the business, what it takes, what the customers are like, what kinds of problems are to be expected. Wear as many hats as you possibly can. Deal with as many problems as you possibly can. Look for additional things to improve. Try things out to see how they work, what works well, and what flops. Visit your competitors, find how they do things differently. Most any business will have trade journals that you can browse through to find out what problems others in the industry face. You will see who is advertising what, and what pricing practices are like. Talk to the customers! Find out what they like and don't like about the place you're working.

By doing these things you will be gaining an education far more valuable and far more specific than you can in college—and you're getting paid for your education! You may even move up in the ranks of the business which you're investigating. You will gain practical experience that will help you to launch the business or to raise the necessary capital.

Capture Your Brilliance

You possess brilliance and creativity just like everyone else in this world. It is part of your nature as a human being to solve problems, big and small, important or seemingly unimportant. You may, however, be in the habit of letting your brilliance escape with the wind.

Brilliant ideas are fleeting. They come and go in a moment. You may ponder them for a while, but may forget them, just as you forget dreams. Even if you tell yourself to remember an idea, it may become fuzzy upon recall or you may forget to recall it at all.

Spend 49¢ on a small pocket, spiral notebook, those little bitty things that seem almost too useless to have a purpose. Carry that and a pen or pencil around in your pocket for a day. Anytime you have an idea, no matter how insignificant it might seem, capture it with a few quick words. Of course, the more words you put down, the better. Try to express a complete thought. Many times I have jotted down only two or three words only to lose the context and surrounding ideas, making the words meaningless.

Your brilliance is not aware of any clocks and cannot be scheduled. You may decide to set aside an hour each evening for your creative work, but your creativity knows no clock. Ideas are stimulated by conditions and situations in which you encounter problems. Ideas might come to you while driving in a car past a particular road sign. Ideas might come while you're at a fast food restaurant. Move away from the environment which stimulated the idea and it may be lost. You might not be able to rekindle it later when your schedule permits time to sit and think.

Capture the ideas you have, as completely as possible. Then during your scheduled "creative time," transpose those ideas from your 49¢ notepad into a very expensive, ultra-deluxe, 99¢ spiral notebook. Date it, and write up as much as you can recall about the situation in which the idea occurred. Write down anything and everything, regardless of the value that you may feel it has at the time. Later, when you're rich and famous, these ideas can be easily applied and generate even more income.

What's most important about capturing your ideas now rather than later when you're rich and famous, is you're solving problems and concerns of the, shall we say, common person, that is, others just like you. Once you're rich and famous, you'll lose touch with the problems and concerns of the common person and may not be able to recall them. Writing down your thoughts and ideas now may yield fortunes down the road.

The ideas and thoughts don't necessarily have to be product ideas either. They can be simply thoughts and observations about life. Everything in your brain can yield something. What will make you different from all the other people who also have continuous streams of brilliant thoughts is that you're taking them seriously, taking notes, taking action, and solving problems with them.

As Jimmy Calano and Jeff Salzman of CareerTrack say in their audio tape series, *CareerTracking, 26 Success Shortcuts to the Top*, "It's inspiration, not hard work, that makes things happen."

Resources

I would feel negligent if I did not point you in a few directions to discover further opportunities and resources to help you.

The Small Business Administration (SBA)

This government agency can help with practical advice, guidance, and potential funding for your projects. They can provide you with government-produced pamphlets and literature on nearly every topic, from the basics of how to run a business to some extremely specific topics that may be exactly what you are getting into. Most all of this is free of charge. The SBA can also guide you to government-sponsored training programs in your field of interest or classes to help you launch your business. Once you have a project or business in mind, give them a call, they're in your Yellow Pages.

SCORE

This is an organization of retired business people who volunteer their time and expertise to help out people who are starting up a business. They can lend their practical experience, advice, and possibly contacts. You can reach SCORE through the Small Business Administration.

About.com

This website is a great resource for finding out nearly anything that you will need to know regarding business, entrepreneurial or otherwise. It has articles that inform you on a wide variety of topics by industry experts. It also has links or references to other sites and resources, including where and how to find investment capital.

Magazines

There are several magazines that cater to entrepreneurs. They feature articles on how other entrepreneurs made it big. You'll be able to glean insights and ideas from the practical advice columns as well. They have lots of ads featuring home-based businesses you can start with small to quite large investments. Many new magazines cater specifically to home-based businesses.

Franchises

Franchises are businesses that you buy, almost like a kit, or a "business in a box." Many fast food places, card shops, mail box shops are franchises. There's an individual who owns and runs the business (the franchisee), but that person must follow guidelines and rules laid out by the company who created and packaged the business (the franchisor). The franchisee must pay an initial sum to buy into the franchise, between a few thousand to over a hundred thousand dollars, depending on the franchise. The franchisee, in exchange, gets a business that has a proven formula and national recognition. The franchisor will offer assistance and business consulting to make certain it runs smoothly. It's a great way for someone to get into a business that's almost certainly going to make money. However, unless you have the start-up capital, they may be too expensive.

You might consider going to work part-time for one in which you're interested. If you're going to sink a bunch of money into a franchise, the fewer the surprises the better. This will let you know what's really involved, lets you hear the owner's real perspectives as a franchisee, and give you the practical experience you will use to launch your own. The experience you gain can also be cited when applying for a business loan for your start-up capital or when influencing an investor.

National Business Incubation Association

A "business incubator" is a place where you can start up your business on a shoestring budget. Government, educational, and sometimes private organizations make available facilities and office space, typing, copying, management advice, and sometimes financial assistance. There are over 800 such incubators across the country, so chances are there's one in a metropolitan area near you. Check out the National Business Incubation Association on the web at **www.nbia.org** or call them at 740-593-4331 to find out about resources available to you.

How-to Books

There are "how-to" books on nearly every topic. Some topics have many dozens of books written about them. Go to the library and check their computer files under the categories in which you're interested. Ask the reference librarian if you're not finding what you're looking for.

The "how-to" books can range from how to do something in which you're specifically interested, to the "how to's" of launching a business, a product idea, and invention, writing a business plan, and getting investors. There is not a business problem that cannot be solved.

Clubs and Associations

Very often people will get together in clubs and associations focused on a specific industry or interest. Look in your yellow pages under "associations" or "clubs" and you may find there are a lot of people who share your interests. Call them.

You'll also find a book at the library called *Encyclopedia of Associations* which will tell you everything you need to know to get in touch with them. They'll generally welcome potential members with open arms, invite you to the next meeting, and so on. This would be a great way for you to network and get to know more about the field and people who can help you.

Internet Websites

There are millions of 'em. But a few that you may find useful are listed below. If you don't have a computer and/or Internet connection, nearly every public library has one that you can use for free.

Search engines and ISP home pages

Search engines scour new websites all the time catching key words and phrases within the titles and content. You can search for words and topics of your interest in a random search of the millions of web pages out there. The upside is a maximum search of all potentially related sites. The downside is you may wind up with a good deal of garbage that does not help you. Most search engines and Internet Service Providers (ISPs) have their own home page with categorized references to other web pages and resources. For example, if you want to look for a job online, there are thousands of references to job search engines, lists, and libraries. Wading through all of this can be tedious, but you'll get much further ahead than if you don't do it at all or wait around for something less tedious to come along.

Some popular search engines are:

- www.about.com (highly recommended)
- www.lycos.com
- www.metacrawler.com (searches all the other web sites for a one-stop-shopping, comprehensive search)
- www.webcrawler.com
- www.altavista.com
- www.google.com
- www.goto.com
- www.ask.com—A real language search engine that lets you phrase a question, like, "What kind of businesses can I get into if I'm really good at drawing cartoons?"

Investment capital websites

If you have a great idea, a good business plan, and a good team to carry out the business plan, there are people out there who are anxious to invest in your company to make it fly. They may be interested in investing anywhere from $200,000 to $10,000,000 (or more) if you can lay it out logically for them. Buy or borrow a few books on writing business plans. The few months it takes to write up a business plan could win you a huge investment and the opportunity to run your own company. But do your homework, figure out the details, and have your business plan ready before you go knocking on doors looking for a couple million dollars.

The Angel Capital Electronic Network	www.ace-net.sr.unh.edu
The Capital Network	www.thecapitalnetwork.com
Enviromental Capital Network	www.bizserve.com/ecn
Investor's Circle	www.icircle.org
Private Investors Network	www.mava.org/pin.html
Technology Capital Network	www.tcnmit.org

And, while you're browsing the bookshelves at the library or bookstore you will probably notice there are lots of books on raising investment capital as well. These will give you the full details on what investors look for, so read them. This section of my book is simply intended to let you know that there are millions, if not billions of dollars out there in the hands of investors who are anxious to invest it.

There is a "class" of investors called "angel investors" who invest in smaller companies. These investors are typically people who've made a few million from their own entrepreneurial efforts and want to "give back" by helping other entrepreneurs. The Small Business Administration estimates that there are 250,000 angel investors in the United States with more than $20 billion invested in small companies. Usually angel investors will get together to pool amounts, say, $50,000 each, to supply the capital needed by an entrepreneur.

Then there are "venture capitalists," who usually invest $2 million or more in a start-up or ongoing business. Anything less and they're not typically interested.

As an investor friend of mine who owns several buildings in downtown Seattle said to me, "I don't look for someone with a lot of fancy packaging. I want to find someone who has a good idea and is passionate about it. That's someone who's going to make me money on my investment."

Hmmm . . . someone with a good idea and a lot of passion . . . does that sound like you? If so, there are people out there who will be excited to talk to you.

Non-Entrepreneurial

Okay, so you're not an entrepreneur. That's quite okay. No one ever said you have to start and run a business. But let's say you just want to get into a particular line of work where you think you'll be able to utilize your strengths and talents best. Here are a few things you can do to exercise your passions besides launching a business.

Talk to Those in the Business

The absolutely best resource for finding out about the line of work that interests you is to talk to someone already doing it. Ninety percent of the over 5.5 million businesses in the U.S. have 20 or fewer employees. They should be very approachable and will likely welcome someone who's truly interested in the business. They may even hire you, as enthusiasm is a rare and very valuable commodity. Give it a try! It won't kill you!

Non-Profit Organizations

Let's say that you want to "give back" to the community or to the world through a charitable, non-profit organization. There are references on the web, again, I suggest **www.about.com**, which can direct you to everything you need to know to start and fund one. There are more than 54,000 foundations established in the U.S. whose sole purpose is to give (that's right, *give*) money to non-profit organizations and/or research projects. The Council on Foundations (**www.cof.org**) reports that in a 1998 foundations gave away $16 billion, and they do this every year!

Apprenticeships

As an apprentice you work in a particular field under the watchful eye of a craftsman. You learn every aspect of a craft and its associated business until you are ready to "leave the nest." Interestingly, this was a large part of the practical, if informal, education of people for centuries, and is still largely at work in countries around the world, such as Germany. According to the U.S. government, which regulates apprenticeship programs, there are 825 apprenticeship occupations. You can check the blue pages of the phone book for State Apprenticeship Council. There are also regional offices of the Bureau of Apprenticeships and Training, the phone numbers of which are listed below.

Denver	303-844-4791
San Francisco	415-975-4007
Atlanta	404-562-2335
Chicago	312-353-7205
Boston	617-565-2288
Kansas City	816-426-3856
New York	212-337-2313
Philadelphia	215-596-6417
Dallas	214-767-4993
Seattle	206-553-5286

Think Like a Successful Person

Opportunities to build wealth and/or exercise your strengths and passions are everywhere and never-ending. There are two essential things to keep in mind when seeking opportunities. One, solve problems, big or small, real or imagined, and you will make money, potentially lots of it. Two, *do only what you love.* You can craft whatever job you want in the world, you don't have to be strapped down to filling other people's jobs. Doing what you love will make work into play, you will excel, move up, and potentially make a fortune in the process.

Success Stories that Prove You Can!

Since publishing my first edition a few years ago, I have run into many, many people who had surprising reactions.

Some of them held very tightly to the conventional wisdom that success is not possible without a formal education. They felt the very suggestion of my book was preposterous, or that I was offering an "easy way out," kind of like selling snake oil.

Despite this skepticism, I've heard the stories of countless people who were successful despite their lack of a college degree. Unfortunately, almost all of them felt they needed to keep that fact a secret, out of a sense of shame or embarrassment.

I did many radio interviews to discuss my book and the topic in general. Callers to these talk shows would share with me (and the listening audience) how they turned parental threats into good fortune. One such caller told me, "My father said I'd be flipping burgers, and I did. I found that I liked cooking, and I liked it so much, today I'm an executive chef for a five-star restaurant."

Another caller shared, "I was told a thousand times that I would be a ditch digger. Maybe it was just drilled into me so much that it came true. Now I own the company that does all the contracting work digging ditches for the state highway department."

These callers were very proud of their accomplishments, of turning negative and degrading threats into something very positive for their lives. And, not only was their success positive for their own lives, but it often had an impact on the lives of others with new jobs and income. At least once, it even meant saving lives.

This was the story told by Donna, who found herself divorced at 35 with three sons to support. With no formal education, and no experience beyond being a mother, she learned to sell. She wound up excelling in sales, starting companies, and creating innovative products. After much success, she went to work for a small rescue organization that dispatched doctors, nurses, and volunteer help to areas stricken by war, famine, disease, and disaster. Her knack for sales helped the non-profit organization raise over $79 million. So many people are alive today because Donna believed, tried, and succeeded, rather than wallowing in self-doubt and self-pity.

There are so many stories like Donna's that I have put them

together in a separate book called *Success Stories Without A College Degree*. My hope is that these real-life stories prove to you that it can be done, that you will see yourself in the people, and that you will conclude, "If they can do it, I can do it too." Hopefully, you will not only be inspired by their stories, but will find ideas and clues to use in crafting your own story.

I've included two here so you can see what I mean. The selection was difficult because so many of the stories are so compelling, some so unbelievable, you might think I was making them up. But fact is often stranger than fiction, and it is also more inspiring than fiction.

As I've mentioned before, these stories are real and the people depicted are real. I've taken no creative liberties, and have often used words their very own words as written or told to me. I have, however, changed their names to protect their privacy.

Eddy

"I remember my boss telling me with very clear disdain, 'I am really sorry that I hired you!'" Eddy reflects on his first job in the computer business as a telemarketer for a software company. "I had only been on the job two weeks, and already he's trying to fire me. He hadn't even given me a chance!" It's true, Eddy didn't have any computer knowledge or tele-sales experience, but he sensed that it was a personal issue, rather than a performance issue.

"You just don't have the intelligence to be selling at all, let alone trying to sell a very technical database product to people who are ten times smarter than you," the company president told him. "You've got two weeks to make your sales goal, or you're out of here."

One might have thought that Eddy would tell his boss and the president to take this $8.00-an-hour job and do you know what with it. But more was at stake for Eddy, much more. He wasn't about to let this yuppie, preppy, self-important, college-educated jerk of a boss, or this inconsiderate president who failed to live up to his leadership role, intimidate him out of a job.

Eddy had survived much more than that. He grew up poor, on the south side of Boston, a street-fighter by necessity and defiant of authority. "I didn't exactly idolize Jeff Spicoli (of *Fast Times at Ridgemont High)*," Eddy admits. "But I did live a radical life just like that character, bleach blonde, long hair, the whole bit. Thanks to my very dysfunctional family life I took the common rebellious path that many young people do when growing up in abusive and poor environments."

Eddy wasn't going to take the humiliation from his new boss and be robbed of his dignity. He was going to show them. Not only was he determined to survive, but he set his goals on being the best tele-sales person in the company's history.

His first step was to learn the best selling features of the software product, what made it so great and would motivate people to buy it, then hammer away at selling just those features. Next, he set up his personal guidelines: 1) Maximize calling time by taking both East and West coast territories, and call from 6 a.m. to 6 p.m. 2) Do time-consuming paperwork after hours. 3) Don't participate in the idle chit-chat others would easily slip into that wasted time. 4) Don't take "No" for an answer; keep looking for the selling feature that would turn those "no" customers to "yes."

Eddy worked miracles. He brought in thousands of orders from territories that had been proclaimed "dead" by previous sales people. He was merciless in breaking company records: most consecutive months of surpassing quotas; highest revenue in any one year; highest revenue in any one month at 400% of quota; and all-time highest-producing rep in the company's history.

By the time he left the company after two and a half years, Eddy had gone from $8.00-an-hour to over $80,000 a year. So much for not having the "intelligence" to sell anything at all.

But it didn't stop there.

Eddy went on to another company, a small consulting firm that sold software products to its clients. As the sole sales rep, he brought in so much revenue that a major international accounting firm acquired the company to build its consulting and software products division. A year and a half later, and now earning around $150,000 a year, Eddy was sought after by companies in the "big leagues."

Eddy accepted a position as the Senior Sales Executive for another software company to handle a regional office of just two people. The territory? Just a small patch of land called Alaska, Idaho, Oregon, Montana, and Washington. The previous sales rep had brought in a total of $550,000 in revenue the year before, which was not too bad, but not close to the $1.2 million per year quota.

The regional manager, having low expectations, told him, "In your first four months, we don't expect much because you're just getting your feet wet. Besides, it's the end of the year and it's tough to get people to spend money. If you can bring in $500,000, it will be a miracle." Eddy, quite used to performing miracles, brought in $800,000 in four months.

He continued to work with the major corporations of the area, bringing in $250,000, $350,000, and $500,000 deals at a time. In just two years he brought in $7.5 million dollars.

His polished style, expensive suits, frequent scuba diving vacations around the world, and Porsche Carerra belie his defiant, rough-and-tumble upbringing. To this day Eddy shocks people when he tells them of his youth. It just seems unbelievable. In just six years, he went from an $8.00-an-hour job to earning over $300,000 a year in an industry where he had no experience whatsoever.

In identifying the source of his determination, Eddy points to events after a motorcycle accident he had in his early twenties. He had suffered broken ribs, facial lacerations, a crushed jaw, and internal injuries.

"During my nine and a half months of rehab from my accident, I learned that there are two kinds of people. There are those who let any mishap become a convenient excuse for giving up, comforting themselves with self-pity and depression. Then there are those who are determined to never let setbacks and injuries much worse than mine hold them back from leading productive, happy, and fruitful lives. I decided to be with the latter group."

Kathleen

"I'm very glad that I was able to make amends with my parents before they died," Kathleen begins at the end of her story, "but I led a very tough life in a very strict disciplinary home. I escorted both parents to Heaven's gate with great love and respect. They were just a dysfunctional pair carrying their baggage way too long and taking it out on their children. I just would hate to dishonor them at this late stage of the game as it serves no purpose."

A military brat, the daughter of an Army Sergeant Major, Kathleen didn't stay in one place very long, having been in 13 schools before finally settling in Olympia, Washington, in ninth grade.

At 17 she finished high school early, only to wind up married six months later, a move toward freedom so many young women mistakenly make. But it seemed the right thing at the time. Her young husband had wicked good looks, and a wicked temperament to match. After six years, she managed to escape that situation as well, but with much less sense of security this time.

At 23, with a difficult marriage behind her and three young daughters, she found herself a single mom looking for work with no formal education. To make matters worse, during her entire life she had been told she would never amount to anything, by both her parents and her ex-husband as well.

Kathleen's first job was at a jewelry store, and she recalls favorably the people there who helped her get started.

At 24 she heard about a sales position at a local hotel in Olympia. She applied and got the job, with the duty of keeping the rooms booked. But without any hotel experience, her odds of succeeding were low. She convinced the general manager to let her train herself. She outlined a course through which she would learn about the business.

Over eight weeks, she served in every department of the hotel, from front desk, to housekeeping, to maintenance, the kitchen, catering, and office work. So thorough was the training, and so impressed was the general manager, that Kathleen's curriculum was made official and all department heads had to go through the course she had devised.

Soon, her supervisor left and the job was offered to Kathleen. Then the catering manager's job opened up, and she jumped at the chance for double duty. The general manager was reluctant because such a thing had never been done. Kathleen convinced him to let her try by offering to do the job WITHOUT a pay raise, but WITH an increase in the gratuity percentage traditionally given to the catering manager, from 3% to 4.5%.

Kathleen worked her fanny off. With the help of two full-time baby sitters, she managed to work two shifts and still spend time with her three daughters. She religiously shared breakfast with them, sent them off to school, then spent every evening with them for dinner and before bed. Then she was off to work again until 1 or 2 a.m.

Service became her middle name and the gratuity percentage made the job lucrative.

Her hard work, knowledge, and attitude paid off when, at the age of 26, she was approached to open a new Sheraton hotel in Olympia as the general manager. At first she turned it down, believing she wasn't up to the task. But a few months later after a second offer, she accepted. She's very glad she did.

Her new boss, a European man with a heavy accent, taught her a lot, opened many doors for her, and introduced her around to the "big shots" in the hotel chain's headquarters. In the mid-seventies in the heat of the women's movement, she at first met resistance from the "good old boys" network. However, Kathleen learned quickly not to force her way in, but to work with them. Resistance faded, barriers dropped, and she gained much respect. She found that often the "good old boys" were more fearful than territorial, and that when she allayed their fears, they became welcoming and respectful.

At 28, she interviewed to take charge of a dilapidated hotel recently acquired by the hotel chain and independent investor/owners. After three interviews by a panel of ten men, she was turned down because she was a woman. Kathleen wasn't about to take that answer after all the interviews and all that she'd accomplished. She urged them to call the references she'd given. If they rejected her after that, she would accept their decision, but NOT because they didn't want a woman. They called the references, were convinced, and hired her.

The dilapidated hotel was a huge challenge. It was run-down, infested with drug dealers and prostitutes, and had a seedy reputation. In less than two years, Kathleen led the turnaround of the hotel with solid systems to account for moneys, foods, liquors, and other assets. The cost-cutting, efficiencies, and profit margins were so record-breaking that when they were quoted to peers in the industry, no one believed them.

At 31, Kathleen took her talents into a new phase by opening up a hotel management consulting company. What she did for the run-down hotel she did for twelve others, even buying her own.

At 40, she sold all the management contracts, ready to retire, convinced that she would be forever a single mom. But her plans were pleasantly changed when she started dating and later married a man she had known since age 28. Yes, that's right, one of the men from the interview panel twelve years prior.

Now she travels the world and is friends with many corporate executives, who she finds to be wonderful and warm people.

"I cannot tell you how much I enjoy my life now. How at times I thought I should, could, or would throw in the towel from sheer exhaustion. I just want others to know that whether it is a domestic violence issue and/or lack of confidence, it all can be overcome. At the darkest point in my life I did not think that I would end up living the life I live today. It wasn't until I opened my eyes and my heart that my life was filled with splendid friends, loving, respectful, successful daughters, a husband I adore and who adores me. There is hope for every woman out there. Just focus and keep your eyes and heart open to opportunity."

Kathleen passes along this insight, "If you were to see a room full of all the food you would ever eat in your lifetime, you'd be overwhelmed and disbelieving that it could be done. But when you take life one bite at a time, anything is possible."

Think Like a Successful Person

When you rely upon the experiences and impressions of your own life, it may seem difficult to believe that you could possibly accomplish anything of great significance. However, when you learn of the many, many people who have overcome incredible obstacles in their lives, and accomplished amazing things that have touched the lives of many, it should help to convince you.

The people in these stories all agree on one thing. If someone had told them ten or twenty years prior what was to become of their lives, they would have thought it impossible, even crazy. For them, the future was as much a mystery as your future likely seems to you.

Even if you can't exactly believe in yourself because of your past or because those around you won't, don't let it stop you. At the very least, believe that it can be done. Without question, it has been done by others just like you, and who sometimes came from more humble beginnings than you.

With the undeniable knowledge that it can be done to galvanize you, try.

If you try and fail, learn from it and try again.

You will soon find that you are learning a great deal, building confidence, and discovering new strengths. But it all begins with trying.

If they can do it, you can too!

Godspeed—Parting Words

All that I relate to you comes from my own mistakes, failures, pain, rejection, disappointments, sometimes gut wrenching agony; from times of being flat broke, aimless, hopeless, and questioning my own existence. What I have to teach comes, not from living a charmed life full of advantages, but from struggling, learning to survive, recover, overcome, and thrive despite all the bad.

Many of the books I've read have helped me through this. But were it not for that first book that turned the light on for me (*Your Child's Self-Esteem*) I never would have pursued the paths that I have. I would have continued to believe that I was born a bad example of a human being and that there was no escaping such a fate. Yet that one book let me know that I'm not such a bad person after all. And it was because of that glimmer of hope that I read voraciously. That book did me a huge favor and it's my turn to pass that along to you.

This is not meant to be a be-all, end-all book on success. It is meant to be a book that you would pick up and read when you might have otherwise picked up none. It is meant to be a book that gives you some clarity when the world around you offers only confusion and struggle. It is meant to be the first of many books, books that you choose in accordance with your individual likes, strengths, and talents.

You can learn, you can succeed, the opportunities exist and the information to help you pursue it is all there waiting for you. This book was meant to help you see it and believe that it is possible for you.

And so it is that I hope I've accomplished my most important goal in writing this book, to turn the light of hope on for you.

When the student is ready to hear a message, a teacher is presented. This book wound up in your hands for a reason. Apparently you were ready.

Selected Quotes

- There are many roads to success; a college degree is but one of them.

- Success comes from the heart, not from a diploma.

- Without a specific direction, everyone, even college grads, will find themselves in lifelong careers into which they've fallen rather than chosen.

- Live a life of your own design, not someone else's.

- The more passion you pour into a job, the more life you will get out of it.

- The only thing stopping you from pursuing your dreams and passions is you.

- Success is the complete satisfaction with who you are, what you're doing, and where you're going in life.

- Everyone has faults, from the President of the United States to your parents. It's okay for you to have faults too.

- You can blame your past or succeed despite it. But it is you who must live with the consequences.

- You have both the ability and freedom to craft yourself into what ever person you wish to be.

- Hurtful words come from a troubled soul. The louder the shout, the more the self-doubt.

- Live a life of your own design, not someone else's.

- People often make you feel bad to make themselves feel good.

- People who judge you are seeking to elevate themselves at your expense.

- The negative feelings we have of ourselves are shaped by the unqualified and unsubstantiated opinions of others.

- Don't let troubled people ruin your life.

- Forgive those who have hurt you, not for their sake, but for your own.

- Your life is a story. Write it deliberately, not passively.

- Discard what others have created of you and craft a "you" that you genuinely like.

- Think and act like the character you create and that is who you will become.

- Interpret events, not in accordance with events of the past, but always in your favor.

- The only difference between those who achieve great things and those who achieve little or nothing is what they think.

- Humans have the unique ability to elevate themselves within a social order through perception, rather than through brute strength or beauty.

- Each major advance in human history has come from an individual rising up out of obscurity. The next one could be you!

- Your strengths count, even if they don't show up on the SAT.

- Guide your life, not by your limitations and faults, but by your strengths and passions.

- Without a goal, opportunities will slip by unnoticed. With a goal, opportunities will be plucked out of the morass.

- Your mind will continue to work on solving the problem of reaching your goal until you tell it to stop.

- Even an elephant can be eaten one bite at a time.

- There will be lots of people in your life who will gladly put you down. Don't be one of them!

- Negative labels limit and weaken us. Positive labels enable us to grow stronger.

- "I can't" is really a cloak for the phrase, "I choose not to."

- Don't become a slave to "shoulds" at the expense of your goals.

- Just outside your comfort zone is where you will find growth and opportunity.

- By asking others for our direction, we begin to live the life they construct for us, rather than a life we construct for ourselves.

- Being defeated by an excuse, no matter how good it sounds, still means that you are defeated.

- I have met my oppressor and my oppressor is me!
- Would you rather fight, win, and enjoy the victory, or quit and have only blame as your prize?
- Don't expect old friends to accept your new ideas. Seek new friends who share your beliefs and attitudes.
- Don't let pressure from friends hold you back.
- To achieve something incredible, surround yourself with those who believe incredible things are achievable.
- Anyone who tells you that you can't has a hidden motive.
- Don't become a victim of someone else's past. Avoid negative people.
- Love is a degree of attraction to someone or something based on how it makes you feel about yourself.
- Attraction is envisioning how the close association with someone or some thing highly valued by society will elevate our own status.
- Hate is a degree of repulsion toward someone or something based on how it makes you feel about yourself.
- Anger is the frustration you feel when things don't go your way, no matter how hard you try.
- Conquer self-doubt and you will succeed at everything!
- Believing I can enables me. Believing I can't disables me.

Look for these other books from Achievement Dynamics in 2001.

Success Stories Without A College Degree (by John Murphy)

Getting a Job Without a College Degree (by John Murphy)

Common Things, Uncommon Ways – Proven techniques to grow any business through your employees (by Sunny Kobe Cook)

Inspire others with YOUR story!

If you or someone you know has an inspiring story of success despite the lack of a college degree, contribute it at our web site. Your story may touch the lives of hundreds, or even thousands.

Visit our web site!

Achievement Dynamics maintains a web site with many up-to-date resources to help you in your career. Our "Resources" page has links to cool jobs, free personality testing, job hunting advice, government resources for small businesses, ways to market inventions, raise capital, and more. Visit or contact us at:

http://www.thisismychance.com

Television program

Achievement Dynamics is putting together a television talk show to help people learn how they can improve their lives and achieve great things. Check our web site for the latest developments.

Job opportunities

Want to accomplish something fantastic in your career? Achievement Dynamics is taking applications online for many ground floor opportunities, from staff writers, researchers, sales, administrative, and TV production positions. No college degree required, just ambition, attitude, and a desire to accomplish.